ECONOMICS AND FINANCIAL STUDIES FOR ENGINEERS

ECONOMICS AND FINANCIAL STUDIES FOR ENGINEERS

D. J. LEECH
Department of Management Science
University College of Swansea

ELLIS HORWOOD LIMITED
Publishers · Chichester

Halsted Press: a division of
JOHN WILEY & SONS
New York · Brisbane · Chichester · Toronto

First published in 1982 by

ELLIS HORWOOD LIMITED

Market Cross House, Cooper Street, Chichester, West Sussex, PO19 1EB, England

The publisher's colophon is reproduced from James Gillison's drawing of the ancient Market Cross, Chichester.

Distributors:

Australia, New Zealand, South-east Asia:
Jacaranda-Wiley Ltd., Jacaranda Press,
JOHN WILEY & SONS INC.,
G.P.O. Box 859, Brisbane, Queensland 40001, Australia

Canada:
JOHN WILEY & SONS CANADA LIMITED
22 Worcester Road, Rexdale, Ontario, Canada.

Europe, Africa:
JOHN WILEY & SONS LIMITED
Baffins Lane, Chichester, West Sussex, England.

North and South America and the rest of the world:
Halsted Press: a division of
JOHN WILEY & SONS
605 Third Avenue, New York, N.Y. 10016, U.S.A.

© 1982 D. J. Leech/Ellis Horwood Ltd.

British Library Cataloguing in Publication Data
Leech, D. J.
Economics and financial studies for engineers.
1. Corporations – Finance
I. Title
658.1'5'02462   HG4026

Library of Congress Card No. 82-16250

ISBN 0-85312-484-1 (Ellis Horwood Ltd. – Library Edn.)
ISBN 0-85312-521-X (Ellis Horwood Ltd. – Student Edn.)
ISBN 0-470-27351-8 (Halsted Press – Library Edn.)
ISBN 0-470-27352-6 (Halsted Press – Student Edn.)

Typeset in Press Roman by Ellis Horwood Ltd.
Printed in Great Britain by Butler and Tanner, Frome, Somerset.

Table of Contents

Author's Preface

This text was written to provide lecture material and exercises for about thirty teaching hours for students who are studying the

TEC/U79/615 Unit of the Technician Education Council
UNIT TITLE: Economic and financial studies
UNIT LEVEL: IV
UNIT VALUE: Half design length 30 HOURS

The Technician Education Council's Programme Committee, A5, list the objectives of the topic area as:

A. COMPANY ECONOMICS

1. Understands the basic economic concepts relevant to a company.
    1.1 Examines demand behaviour, indifference curves, demand curves.
    1.2 Analyses supply behaviour in terms of: fixed costs, variable costs, revenue, contribution, profit maximisation, marginal revenue.
    1.3 Describes the constraints imposed by resource availability and opportunity costs.
    1.4 Makes calculations involving 1.2 and 1.3.
    1.5 Analyses case studies.

B. ESTIMATING AND TENDERING

2. Understands the use of estimating and tendering.
    2.1 Explains the relationship between estimating and work measurements.
    2.2 Explains the production of costing standards from estimated and measured times.
    2.3 Explains the effect on tenders of cost standards, labour performance, and plant performance.
    2.4 Identifies other factors involved in tendering price, delivery, quality, reliability.

C. PROJECT DECISIONS

3. Understands the techniques used to evaluate projects.

   3.1 Describes the concepts of cash flow across a company boundary.
   3.2 Discusses the time value of money.
   3.3 Explains the meaning of rate of return on investment.
   3.4 Makes present and future worth calculations.
   3.5 Uses the following techniques to compare the value of different projects:

   (a) discounted cash flow
   (b) rate of return
   (c) pay-back period.

In laying out the text I have reversed the order of these objectives so that objective C is largely covered by Part I (Chapters 1-11), objective B is largely covered by Part II (Chapters 12-19), and objective A is largely covered by Part III (Chapters 20-23). The reasoning behind this is that most engineering apprentices will find it easier to cope with the straightforward mathematics of discounted cash flow than the rather more abstract ideas of supply and demand, elasticity, etc. I hope, therefore, that I am working from ideas which are close to the student's experience to those which he will find less so.

It can also be argued that the ideas of Parts I and II are directly applicable in a company, whereas Part III introduces some of the classic ideas of the economist which may offer useful concepts but do not provide tools which are of immediate use in decision making.

It is intended that the objectives will be met by

(a) examples and exercises offered in the text to be presented and extended by the teacher. Some of the examples are quantitative and some quali-tative;
(b) discussions generated by the teacher around the examples;
(c) numerical examples worked by the student and submitted to the teacher for assessment. Many exercises are worked in the text. Those not worked in the text have specimen solutions, answers, or hints at the end of the chapter;
(d) essays by the student which discuss the unquantified parts of each topic. These essays are intended to provide material for classroom debate and for assessment.

It is believed that much of the book can be used in courses other than that of TEC/U79/615, A5 level IV.

Possible applications would be at first year undergraduate engineering level, some BEC courses, and some management courses.

Although the book has been written for the student with no knowledge of calculus, alternative calculus discussions of marginal costs and maximum profit have been given as footnotes.

It has generally been assumed that the student has a pocket electronic calulator on which he is able to evaluate such expressions as $(1 + i)^n$ where i and n are known.

Logarithms can be used if the student knows that $\log (1+i)^n = n \log (1+i)$.

Because many students and teachers will have access to a computer, an appendix to Part I gives a number of BASIC programs which have been used in the calculations of present values and rates of return of cash flow streams. These programs are interactive, and examples of their use are also provided.

Part I
DISCOUNTED CASH FLOW

1

Cash flows

1.1 CASH FLOWS

When a person or a company buys a machine or invests in a project the first payment is usually only the first of many. Normally, an investment is made in the hope of making money so that the project becomes a stream of payments and receipts. Buying a car usually involves making a first payment for the car and then a stream of daily payments for petrol, perhaps six-monthly payments for servicing, annual payments for tax, insurance, AA or RAC membership, MOT tests and random payments for repairs. When a company buys a numerically controlled machine tool, it must consider its initial purchase, its installation, its periodical servicing, repairing it if it fails, paying for the power it consumes, paying the operator, and reaping a financial benefit from the goods the machine produces. Many of these payments and receipts will occur over the life of the machine.

Example 1.1
Charlie Brown buys a car on 1st January 1981

He immediately pays   £4000   for the car
           80   for a year's insurance
           20   for membership of a motoring club
           50   for a year's licence

therefore the total payments
made on 1/1/81   = £4150

During the first year of ownership, Charlie Brown pays
         £ 80   for two services
         520   for petrol

For simplicity we will assume
that these payments are made
at the end of the first year of
ownership on 1/1/82

together with   150   for insurance, motoring club
                                                        subscription, and licence
                                                 _____

therefore the total payment
made on 1/1/82   = £750
                                  _____

During the second year of ownership, Charlie Brown pays

                                    £100   for servicing
                                      50   for repair
                                     520   for petrol
                                     150   for insurance, motoring club
                                            subscription, and licence
                                     _____

therefore the total payment
made on 1/1/83   = £820
                                  _____

During the third year of ownership, Charlie Brown pays

                                    £100   for servicing
                                     100   for repairs
                                     520   for petrol
                                     150   for insurance, motoring club
                                            subscription, and licence
                                     _____

therefore the total payment
made on 1/1/84   = £870
                                  _____

During the fourth year of ownership, Charlie Brown pays

                                    £100   for servicing
                                     150   for repairs
                                     520   for petrol
                                     150   for insurance, motoring club
                                            subscription, and licence
                                     _____

therefore the total payment
made on 1/1/85   = £920
                                  _____

During the fifth year of ownership, Charlie Brown pays

£100	for servicing
200	for repairs
520	for petrol
150	for insurance, motoring club subscription, and licence

therefore the total payment
made on 1/1/86　　　　　　　　　= £970

At the end of the fifth year
he sells the car for　　　　　　£800
therefore the net payments
on 1/1/86　　　　　　　　　　= £170

Over the five years of owning the car, Charlie Brown has thus made the following net payments:

At the end of year 0	£4150
At the end of year 1	750
At the end of year 2	820
At the end of year 3	870
At the end of year 4	920
At the end of year 5	170

One way of picturing this series of payments is:

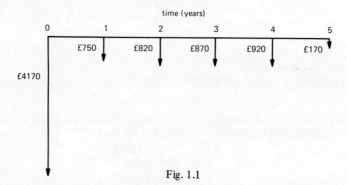

Fig. 1.1

The above example demonstrates that a piece of hardware involves the owner in not only one payment, to buy the hardware, but a series of payments made over its life.

The example has been simplified in order to make one or two major points, and it may be that those simplifications have taken away some realism.

Exercise 1.1
How justified were we in assuming that all costs incurred in a year were paid at the end of the year?
Not very justified. Some motorists do not pay cash for petrol but run up an account at the garage, but not many garage owners would be content with the bill being settled only once a year, at the end of the year. Some motorists use credit cards to pay for petrol, servicing, and repairs, but this means that costs incurred during a calendar month must be paid at the end of the month or they will attract interest. Perhaps the annual payments made by Charlie Brown should be increased to allow for the interest. Perhaps we should make Fig. 1.1 more realistic by showing payments made every month.

Were there any other costs, or even revenues which we should have included in the example?
Perhaps we should have included the cost of Charlie Brown's garage, although as it cost £1600 to build and lasts longer than the car it is not immediately clear how we should allow for it. In any case Charlie Brown bought his house with a garage attached before be bought the car. Charlie Brown does pay rates on the garage, so should we not include these in his costs? Should we ignore the cost of Charlie Brown's driving licence? What other costs can you think of, incurred by Charlie Brown because he owns a car? Season parking ticket? Is the cost of oil included in the cost of servicing? Is the cost of the MOT certificates included in the costs for years 3, 4 and 5?

Does Charlie Brown only pay out?
Is there no advantage in owning the car? Has he saved £100 a year on bus fares? Are some of the 10 000 miles a year travelled on his firm's business, for which he is reimbursed 16.4p a mile?

Have we allowed for inflation?
Provisionally we will ignore inflation. The subject will be discussed to some extent when the student is familiar with the time value of money.

Example 1.2
Steele-Butcher Ltd, the fabricators, buy a numerically controlled milling machine on 1 January 1981.

They immediately pay		£100 000	for the machine
		10 000	to install it
		2 000	for the associated programming equipment
and	£	1 000	to train an operator

Therefore the total cash flow
on 1/1/81   = −£113 000

During the first year of ownership, Steele-Butcher pay

£10 000	for wages for the operator
2 000	for wages for the man who produces the tapes (this man has other duties, and so only part of his cost results from owning the NC machine)
4 000	for material for the parts made on the machine
1 000	for labour involved in maintenance of the machine
3 000	for spare parts

therefore the total running
costs paid on 1/1/82   = £20 000

But during the first year of ownership, Steele-Butcher save

£50 000	because they no longer buy the components from an outside supplier

therefore the net cash flow
on 1/1/82   = £30 000   (i.e. £50 000 gain less £20 000 costs)

During the second year of ownership the net cash flow is increased because, the company having learnt to use the machine and having fitted it into the production control system, it now has a greater output, saving the company £70 000 in bought components while operating costs are unchanged at £20 000. Therefore the total cash flow
on 1/1/83   = £50 000   (£70 000 gain less £20 000 costs)

During the third year of ownership, the saving on bought out components remains at £70 000, but more maintenance is required as the machine ages so that costs have risen to £30 000.
Therefore the total cash flow
on 1/1/84   = £40 000   (£70 000 less £30 000 costs)

During the fourth, fifth, and sixth years the output continues to save the company £70 000 a year in bought out components, but repair and maintenance costs rise still further as the machine ages. Also, at the end of the sixth year of ownership, Steele-Butcher decide that they will invest in a more advanced replacement, and so they sell the machine for £20 000.
Therefore the total cash flow
on 1/1/85   = £30 000   (£70 000 gain less £40 000 costs),

the total cash flow
on 1/1/86   = £25 000   (£70 000 gain less £45 000 costs) and
the total cash flow
on 1/1/87   = £40 000   (£70 000 gain less £50 000 costs
                                              plus £20 000 salvage)

Notice that we have used the term **cash flow** to describe costs or revenues. Where the net payment was *by* the company we have regarded this as a cash flow *from* the company and have called it a *negative* cash flow. Where the payment was *to* the company we have regarded this as a cash flow *into* the company and have called it a *positive* cash flow.

The series of cash flows is called a **cash flow stream**, and so we may say that the purchase of the numerically controlled milling machine generates the following cash flow stream:

	£
Year 0	−113 000
Year 1	+ 30 000
Year 2	+ 50 000
Year 3	+ 40 000
Year 4	+ 30 000
Year 5	+ 25 000
Year 6	+ 40 000

Alternatively we may show the cash flow stream pictorially as in Fig. 1.2.

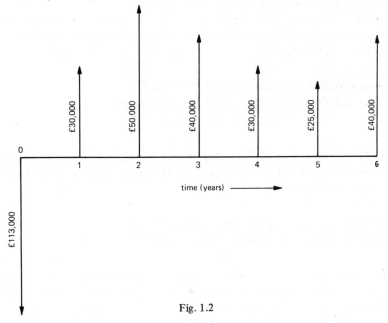

Fig. 1.2

The cash flow each year is made up of a number of contributing revenues and payments. We see that in the above example, there were, in the first year, negative cash flows for wages, a negative cash flow for raw materials, a negative cash flow for spare parts, and a positive cash flow from the sale of the parts made on the machine (revenue). All these added up to £30 000, the *net* cash flow.

Example 1.3

A company designs and builds a copying machine. In the first year, the machine is designed and the main cash flow is for the payment of the designers' wages.

The net cash flow in the first year is −£20 000.

In the second year, the prototype and early production machines are being built. The main contributions to this year's cash flow are wages for operatives, raw materials for the manufacture of the copying machines, tooling for the production line, salaries for test engineers, and salaries for salesmen.

The net cash flow in the second year is −£250 000.

In the third year much of the manufacturing facility is still being developed but some sales are made, and this offsets what would otherwise be a considerably larger cash outflow.

The net cash flow in the third year is −£100 000.

In the fourth year, sales increase and revenue more than offsets manufacturing costs, but setting up the servicing and spares network generates a considerable negative cash flow.

The net cash flow in the fourth year is +£50 000.

In the fifth, sixth, and seventh years, sales are near the expected market share for the product. Revenue from sales exceeds the costs of manufacturing and product support to give

a net cash flow in the fifth year of +£250 000
a net cash flow in the sixth year of +£300 000 and
a net cash flow in the seventh year of +£300 000

In the eighth and ninth years, sales are falling because of competition from more modern copiers, and at the end of the ninth year, manufacture and sale of the copying machine cease.

The net cash flow in the eighth year is +£150 000
The net cash flow in the ninth year is +£50 000

Diagrammatically, the cash flow stream from the project is shown in Fig. 1.3. Note the simplification which assumes that a cash flow during year n is actually paid or received at the end of year n.

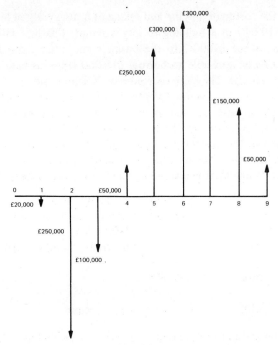

Fig. 1.3.

Example 1.4

Charlie Brown decided to set up a business of his own. He had worked for Steele-Butcher Ltd as a machinist and he thought that he could manage maintenance also. When Steele-Butcher sold off a numerically controlled milling machine Charlie Brown bought it, set it up in a workshop that he rented from a local development agency, overhauled it and looked for special machining work. Starting up in business cost Charlie Brown

£20 000	for the second hand NC mill
2 000	for parts to overhaul the machine
3 000	to transport the machine, set it up in the rented workshop, lay on appropriate power, and generally get the whole set-up into working order and
5 000	working capital; i.e. money that he had to have in hand to pay any bills which arrived before he earned enough money to pay them.
£30 000	

Through the fortunate buying and selling of houses early in his married life, Charlie had £10 000 in a building society account. Charlie's father, who had retired, agreed to put £5000 into the business and, after some discussion and consultation, Charlie was able to borrow £15 000 from his bank, guaranteeing the loan with his house. The bank charged him 20% interest.

During the year, Charlie did £35 000 worth of business but he had to pay the bank £3000 in interest charges and £2500 for raw materials and other expenses (such as rent, rates, electricity, and telephone bills).

As Charlie was the managing director and the only worker in the business, he agreed with his father that he could reasonably pay himself a salary of £10 000.

It looks as though Charlie lost money in the first year because he spent

	£30 000	setting up the business
	15 500	running the business (£10 000 salary, £3000 loan charges, £2500 for raw materials and other expenses)
total	£45 500	
while	£35 000 was the revenue.	

The first objection to this reasoning is that we have included £5000 working capital in the £30 000 that it took to set up the business. Now working capital is really a **float**. It enables the company to pay some of its bills before the customers all pay theirs. In theory, the £5000 should be intact at the end of trading, and so we would include it in the expenses only if it had been spent and not made up again. Consider running a shop for the day: in order to be able to give change, the shopkeeper will start the day with a float of coppers, silver, and notes of small denomination, but at the end of the day that float should be exactly in value what the shopkeeper started with.

A second objection is that the machinery may not be expected to pay for itself in the first year of its operation. In this case, Charlie Brown guesses that, provided he maintains his plant well, it has a life of 5 years. Even at the end of 5 years, the plant will probably be operable but its maintenance cost will be increasing, its breakdown will be more frequent, and more modern, cheaper to run, equipment will be available. It is therefore a matter of some judgement, to decide how long capital equipment should be allowed to pay for itself. The amount that the machine must be expected to pay for itself in any year is called **depreciation**. Note that the concept of depreciation is not necessarily related to the price that could be got for the machinery if it were to be sold.

In this case, then, Charlie Brown decides that the machinery must pay for itself in 5 years, an equal amount in each year. Since the machinery cost £25 000 (£20 000 plus £5000 to repair and install), this means that it would be depreciated by £5000 per year.

If we look at Charlie's balance sheet we could derive Table 1.1 to show his performance over the first year.

Table 1.1

| | At beginning of year 1 | Operations during year 1 | | | | | At end of year 1 |
		I	II	III	IV	V	
Assets Cash	5 000		−3 000	−2 500	+35 000	−10 000	24 500
Plant	25 000	−5 000					20 000
Inventory	−	+5 000	+3 000	+2 500	−20 500	+10 000	−
Liabilities Equity	15 000			+14 500			29 500
Debt	15 000						15 000

The column headed 'At beginning of year 1' shows the state of the company at the beginning of its operation.

There was

	£5000	cash in hand (the working capital)
	£25 000	the value of the plant
and	£ 0	the value of the inventory because no goods for sale had yet been made.

The company had liabilities to the extent of

| | £15 000 | equity (i.e. the money that the owners had invested) |
| and | £15 000 | debt (i.e. the money owed to the bank). |

Note that the total of Assets and Liabilities must be zero. This means that the total of the money that is owed to creditors (debt) and to the owners (equity) must exactly equal what the company possesses in cash, plant and inventory.

The column headed I indicates that the plant was reduced in value by £5000 during the year. This does not mean that the plant could be sold for £20 000; it means that, at the end of the year, the plant has repaid one fifth of its original cost.

This £5000 of depreciation must be paid for by the goods which are sold, and so £5000 must be added to the cost of the goods available for sale, i.e. £5000 must be added to the cost of the inventory.

Column II indicates that 20% interest had to be paid on the £15 000 that the company owed the bank. When this interest was paid, the cash in the company's account was reduced by 20% of £15 000 = £3000.

This £3000 is added to the cost of the inventory because, in the end, the only way in which the money can be earned is from sales.

Column III indicates that £2500 was spent for raw materials and other running expenses (other than labour). This sum was paid out of cash and then had to be added to the cost of the inventory.

Column IV indicates that £35 000 was received (into cash) by selling the goods produced. As all the goods were sold, the value of the inventory was reduced to zero. This gives an apparent imbalance − £35 000 received for goods which cost £20 500 to make. The difference is the profit on the sales − £14 500 which is added to the equity. That is, the value of the owner's stake in the company has been increased.

Column V indicates that £10 000 was paid in salaries (from cash) and had to be added to the cost of the inventory.

The column headed 'At end of year 1' shows, by adding across the rows:

- The cash increased from £5000 to £24 500 during the year;
- the value of the plant was reduced from £25 000 to £20 000 during the year;
- the initial and final inventories were both zero. The goods cost

£5000	towards the cost of plant,
£3000	in interest charges,
£2500	in raw materials and other running costs and
£10 000	in labour

totalling £20 500

This value of goods was withdrawn from the inventory when the goods were sold.

- the value of equity was increased by £14 500 (the profit on sales) from £15 000 to £29 500; the value of the debt remained unchanged at £15 000.

This seems to have been a very successful year for Charlie Brown's company, with the owner's share of the company increasing from £15 000 to £29 500. Probably, however, Charlie Brown would want to pay off some of the loan. Also, both Charlie and his father will feel that they have a right to some return on their original investment − after all the bank earned 20% on their loan while taking no risk, and something more than 20% might be a reasonable dividend for the owners.

Note that Charlie Brown's company has paid no tax despite the profit that it appears to have made. Tax will, to some extent, be discussed later, but in this example no tax is paid because at the time of writing, the government allows the whole of the cost of capital equipment to be written off in one year, for tax purposes. This means that for calculating tax, column I in Table 1.1 would show £20 000 written off the value of the machinery and £20 000 added to the cost of the inventory. The cost of inventory would then be £35 500, which exceeds the revenue. For tax purposes, then, no profit will have been made.

Exercise 1.2

(i) A company invests in plant with the object of making goods for sale. What payments and revenues might contribute to the cash flow in any year of operation?

Answers should include:
buying the plant,
installing the plant,
commissioning the plant (i.e. making sure that it works as intended),
rent,
rates,
taxes,
wages to operators,
wages to support staff,
the cost of raw materials,
the costs of repair and maintenance,
the costs of down time (i.e. the cost of owning a machine which is not producing while it is being repaired or waiting for repair),
the cost of storing goods made,
the cost of repairing goods sold but still under warranty,
interest on debts,
dividends to shareholders,
taxes,
revenue from the sales of goods made,
revenue from the sale of spares,
money received from the sale of plant.

(ii) Why does it cost money to store goods after they have been made and before they are sold?

There is rent for the space used,
the cost of materials handling (e.g. fork lift trucks),
the cost of recording what is in stock,
but most of all there is interest on the value of the stock held. If £100's worth of goods are held then either that £100 has been borrowed at, say, 20% interest or, if not borrowed, could have been invested.

(iii) Give an example of how the down time of a machine can create a cost.

Imagine a chemical plant making phosphoric acid and intended to run continuously for 24 hours a day. If a pump breaks down, the whole plant will stop. There will be lost production, payment of wages to idle operatives, the cost of the capital tied up in plant that is not working (if a plant costing £1m were bought with money borrowed at 20%, the cost would be £200 000/year or about £200 a shift).

(iv) If you buy a new car, how much will it cost to buy and how much will it cost you over its whole life?

The price of a car is easy to find in newspaper advertisements. The number of miles travelled per year will vary from one owner to another, but about 10 000 miles is typical.

The miles per gallon of petrol, per gallon of oil, per service, per breakdown, etc. are all variable, but consensus views should not be difficut to reach in a class.

Cost of repairs (£10/hour for labour) will depend on the seriousness of breakdowns.

Membership of the AA or RAC may be thought necessary.
Insurance is necessary.
Tax is necessary.
Is a garage desirable?
How long would the car last and would it be sold or scrapped?

(v) Pick a small business and describe the costs that you would be involved in, in starting the business and running it.

Where would the money come from?
Where would the money go?

You could
buy and run a pub,
set up a car repair service,
make and sell jig-saw puzzles of the *Sun* page three,
set up a decorating business,
grow vegetables for sale from door to door, etc.
Whatever business you choose you will have to buy equipment,
pay wages (if only to yourself),
maintain equipment,
pay taxes (unless you fail to make a profit).

(vi) A lathe costs £10 000, the operator is paid £6000 a year, maintenance costs £400 in the first year, £600 in the second year, £600 in the third year, £800 in the fourth year, and £1000 in the fifth year. After 5 years the lathe is sold for £1000. Raw material costs are £2000 a year, and the goods made on the lathe are sold for £12 000 a year. The contribution that the lathe must make to rent, rates, power, and other costs is assessed at £500 a year.

Draw a diagram of the cash flow stream which results from owning the lathe.

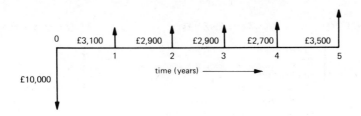

(vii) What do we mean by the depreciation of a capital asset? Illustrate your answers with such examples as

> *a private house,*
> *the motor car,*
> *an injection moulder in a factory which makes plastic goods for the consumer,*
> *the Severn Bridge.*

At least the following points should be brought into any discussion:

the actual decline in the value of the asset, i.e. what it could be bought and sold for,

the fact that it might be good policy to replace a perfectly sound machine by a more modern one that is capable of greater or cheaper production,

the fact that a perfectly sound machine may produce goods that are no longer required,

the period over which a machine is capable of earning money to pay for itself (depreciation form this point of view may be quite unrelated to the resale value of the machine),

the cost of maintenance may suggest that it is good policy to buy a new machine (note that the cost of maintenance may be related to the machine's wearing out but could also derive from the lack of spares support, the lack of maintenance expertise).

1.2 A NOTE ON TEROTECHNOLOGY

Terotechnology provides us with a useful discipline for considering the cash flows associated with a project.

Terotechnology is defined as 'a combination of management, financial, engineering, and other practices applied to physical assets in pursuit of economic life cycle costs.'

In *Life Cycle Costing in the Management of Assets, A Practical Guide*, published by Her Majesty's Stationery Office, London, in 1977, a list of cost elements is offered in the following form:

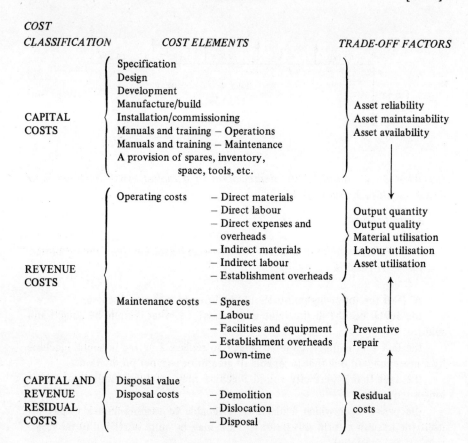

COST
CLASSIFICATION   COST ELEMENTS   TRADE-OFF FACTORS

CAPITAL COSTS
- Specification
- Design
- Development
- Manufacture/build
- Installation/commissioning — Asset reliability, Asset maintainability, Asset availability
- Manuals and training — Operations
- Manuals and training — Maintenance
- A provision of spares, inventory, space, tools, etc.

REVENUE COSTS

Operating costs
- Direct materials
- Direct labour
- Direct expenses and overheads
- Indirect materials
- Indirect labour
- Establishment overheads

Output quantity
Output quality
Material utilisation
Labour utilisation
Asset utilisation

Maintenance costs
- Spares
- Labour
- Facilities and equipment
- Establishment overheads
- Down-time

Preventive repair

CAPITAL AND REVENUE RESIDUAL COSTS
- Disposal value
- Disposal costs
  - Demolition
  - Dislocation
  - Disposal

Residual costs

It is not the purpose of this book to discuss, in detail, each of these cost elements and their interactions. Many of the names of the elements are self explanatory, however, and the list can provide a useful check list against which we can forecast the costs associated with a project involving capital investment.

Exercise 1.3
Attempt to relate the listed elements to the examples of projects described in this chapter.

2

Borrowing money

Example 2.1

Arnold wanted to buy a motorbike costing £500, and his mother lent him the money at an interest rate of 10% on the understanding that the money was paid back in 5 years.

At the end of year 0 (or the beginning of year 1)

Arnold received	£500	

At the end of year 1

Arnold owed his mother	£500	
plus 10% interest	50	
totalling	£550	
He paid his mother	£150	so that he
then owed his mother	£400	

At the end of year 2

Arnold owed his mother	£400	
plus 10% interest	40	
totalling	£440	
He paid his mother	£140	so that he
then owed his mother	£300	

At the end of year 3

Arnold owed his mother	£300	
plus 10% interest	30	
totalling	£330	
He paid his mother	£130	so that he
then owed his mother	£200	

At the end of year 4

Arnold owed his mother	£200
plus 10% interest	20
totalling	£220
He paid his mother	£120 so that he
then owed his mother	£100

At the end of year 5

Arnold owed his mother	£100
plus 10% interest	10
totalling	£110
He paid his mother	£110 so that the
debt was then cleared.	

Diagrammatically, the cash flow stream of this debt and its repayment was:

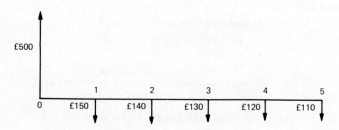

Note that Arnold borrowed £500 and paid back £650.

Example 2.2

Betram also borrowed £500 at 10% interest from his mother to buy a motorbike, but his method of repaying the loan was different.

At the end of year 0, Bertram received	£500	
At the end of year 1, Bertram paid	£50	interest only
so that he still owed	£500	
At the end of year 2, Bertram paid	£50	interest only
so that he still owed	£500	
At the end of year 3, Bertram paid	£50	interest only
so that he still owed	£500	

At the end of year 4, Bertram paid   £50   interest only
   so that he still owed   £500

At the end of year 5, Bertram paid   £50   interest *and*
                                                   £500   to clear the debt.

Diagrammatically, the cash flow stream of Bertram's debt and its repayment was:

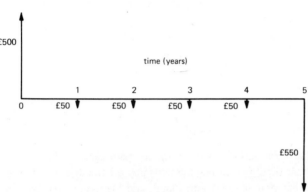

Note that Bertram borrowed £500 and paid back £750.

Example 2.3

Claud, who borrowed £500 at 10% interest, used a different repayment pattern and his cash flow stream was:

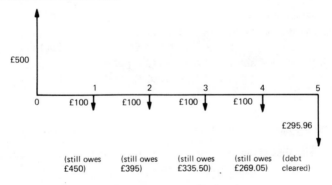

Note that Claud borrowed £500 and paid back £695.96.

Exercise 2.1

Work out year by year how much of Claud's payment is interest and how much is repayment of the original debt.

At the end of year 1, Claud has borrowed £500 for one year. He thus owes £50 interest. Since he pays £100, and £50 of this is interest, he reduces his debt by

£50 to £450. At the end of year 2, Claud has owed £450 for a year, and he thus owes £45 interest. Since he pays £100, and £45 of this is interest, he reduces his debt by £55 etc.

Example 2.4

Desmond, who also borrowed £500 at 10% interest used yet another repayment pattern and his cash flow stream was:

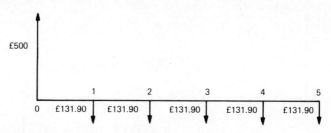

Note that Desmond borrowed £500 and paid back £695.50.

Check that these five equal payments pay off the debt in 5 years.

We see that Arnold, Bertram, Claud, and Desmond each borrowed £500 at 10% interest and repaid the money over 5 years, yet each paid back different amounts in each year and each paid back a different total amount.

Consider borrowing the sum p at interest i and repaying the whole debt, including interest, after n years.

Initially the amount owed is   £p

After one year, the amount owed is £p plus

interest £ip $= £p(1+i)$

After two years, the amount owed is £$p(1+i)$ plus

interest £$ip(1+i)$ $= £p(1+i)^2$

_____

And after n years the amount owed $= £p(1+i)^n$

We see then that if we borrow p at interest i and repay the debt after n years with the single payment, f,

$$f = p(1+i)^n \quad .$$

Alternatively we may argue that a payment of f at the end of year n, will repay a debt of $= f/(1+i)^n = p$ when p was borrowed at the end of year 0 at an interest rate of i.

Consider a debt of £p, borrowed at the end of year 0, at interest i and repaid by a series of payments f_1 at the end of year 1, f_2 at the end of year 2; . . . , and f_n at the end of year n. The debt is completely cleared after the nth payment.

The first payment, f_1 will repay $\dfrac{f_1}{(1+i)}$;

The second payment, f_2 will repay $\dfrac{f_2}{(1+i)^2}$;

The third payment, f_3 will repay $\dfrac{f_2}{(1+i)^3}$

The nth payment, f_n, will repay $\dfrac{f_n}{(1+i)^n}$,

The n payments completely paid back the debt p so that

$$p = \frac{f_1}{1+i} + \frac{f_2}{(1+i)^2} + \frac{f_3}{(1+i)^3} + \ldots\ldots + \frac{f_n}{(1+i)^n} \ .$$

Let us check this formula, using Arnold's and Bertram's repayment plans.
In each case $i = 10\%$ and $n = 5$.
In Arnold's case $f_1 = 150, f_2 = 140, f_3 = 130, f_4 = 120,$ and $f_5 = 110,$

$$\text{and} \quad p = \frac{150}{1.1} + \frac{140}{(1.1)^2} + \frac{130}{(1.1)^3} + \frac{120}{(1.1)^4} + \frac{110}{(1.1)^5}$$

$$\text{therefore} \quad p = 136.364 + 115.702 + 97.671 + 81.962 + 68.301$$

$$= \underline{500} \ .$$

$$\text{In Bertram's case } p = \frac{50}{1.1} + \frac{50}{(1.1)^2} + \frac{50}{(1.1)^3} + \frac{50}{(1.1)^4} + \frac{550}{(1.1)^5}$$

$$= 500$$

Exercise 2.2
Check that Claud's and Desmond's repayment plans really do repay debts of £500.

In the formula $p = \dfrac{f}{(1+i)^n}$ (i)

we usually call p the present value of
f, the future value.

and $\qquad \dfrac{p}{f} = \dfrac{1}{(1+i)^n}$ is called the present value factor
for a future single payment . $\qquad\qquad$ (ii)

When we calculated the value of the debt that Arnold's and Bertram's cash flow streams repaid we were calculating the total present value of each of the repayments made. In each case, the sum of these present values was the value of the debt that had been repaid.

It is convenient to rewrite equation (ii) in the form

$$\left(\frac{p}{f}\right)_n^i = \frac{1}{(1+i)^n}$$

Thus $\left(\dfrac{p}{f}\right)_5^{0.20}$ gives the present value factor when $i = .20 = 20\%$ and $n = 5$ years

$\left(\dfrac{p}{f}\right)_{20}^{0.15}$ gives the present value factor when $i = 0.15 = 15\%$ and $n = 20$ years

$$\left(\frac{p}{f}\right)_5^{0.20} = \frac{1}{(1+0.20)^5} = \frac{1}{(1.2)^5} = 0.4019$$

$$\left(\frac{p}{f}\right)_{20}^{0.15} = \frac{1}{(1+0.15)^{20}} = \frac{1}{(1.15)^{20}} = 0.0611$$

Exercise 2.3
What is the present value of a payment of £1000 in 5 years' time if the interest rate is 20%?

$$p = \frac{f}{(1+i)^n} = \frac{f}{(1+0.20)^5} = f \times \left(\frac{p}{f}\right)_5^{0.20} = 1000 \times 0.4019 = £401.90$$

Exercise 2.4

$$Calculate \left(\frac{p}{f}\right)_{10}^{0.10} \ ; \ \left(\frac{p}{f}\right)_{20}^{0.05} \ ; \ \left(\frac{p}{f}\right)_{15}^{0.12} \ ; \ \left(\frac{p}{f}\right)_{4}^{0.25}$$

$$\left(\frac{p}{f}\right)_{12}^{0.16} \ ; \ \left(\frac{p}{f}\right)_{5}^{0.5} \ ; \ \left(\frac{p}{f}\right)_{10}^{0.025} \ ; \ \left(\frac{p}{f}\right)_{20}^{0.15}$$

See answers in Appendix 1.

Exercise 2.5

(i) Calculate the present values of the following future sums:

£20 paid in 10 years' time with an interest of 10%;	[£7.71
£100 paid in 20 years' time with an interest of 5%;	[£37.69
£100 paid in 15 years' time with an interest of 12%;	[£18.27
£1000 paid in 4 years' time with an interest of 25%;	[£409.60
£25 000 paid in 12 years' time with an interest of 16%;	[£4211.57

(ii) If you borrow £20 and intend to pay it back in 10 years' time with an interest of 10% a year, what will be the future single payment that clears the debt?

$$p = f \frac{1}{(1+i)^n} \qquad\qquad = f \frac{1}{(1.1)^{10}}$$

therefore $\quad p = f \times \left(\dfrac{p}{f}\right)_{10}^{0.1} \qquad\qquad = f \, (0.3855)$

therefore $\quad f = £20/\left(\dfrac{p}{f}\right)_{10}^{0.1} \qquad\qquad = £51.88$.

Exercise 2.6

(i) If you borrow £100 at 5% and pay the debt back in one future payment after 20 years, what will be the payment that clears the debt?   [£265.33

(ii) If you borrows £100 at 12% and pay back the debt in one future payment after 15 years, what will be the payment that clears the debt?   [£547.36

We often have to calculate the present value of a future cash flow. We could, of course, calculate the appropriate present value factor every time we need it, but it is simpler to use tables from which we can read present value factors that have already been calculated.

Appendix 1 is a table of present value factors for commonly used interest rates.

Exercise 2.7

Use the figures of Appendix 1 to calculate the present value of the cash flow stream shown in Fig. 1.2. Assume an interest rate of 15%.

The cash flow stream, present value factors, and present values may be tabulated as follows.

	Cash flow	Present-value factor	Present value
End of year 0	−£113 000	1	−£113 000
End of year 1	30 000	$\left(\dfrac{p}{f}\right)^{0.15}_1 = 0.8696$	$30\,000 \times \left(\dfrac{p}{f}\right)^{0.15}_1 = 26\,088$
End of year 2	50 000	0.7561	37 805
End of year 3	40 000	0.6575	26 300
End of year 4	30 000	0.5718	17 154
End of year 5	25 000	0.4972	12 430
End of year 6	40 000	0.4323	17 292
Net present value			24 069

Notice that we have calculated that at 15% interest, the present value of the cash flow stream that was generated by Steele-Butcher's purchase of the NC mill is £24 069.

If we consider the cash flows generated by the machine at the ends of years 1, 2, 3, 4, 5, and 6 we can calculate their net present value to be

£113 000 + £24 069 = £137 069

In other words, the cash flows generated by the machine's earning power would have paid back an initial debt of £137 069, borrowed at 15%.

But if the whole project had been financed by money borrowed at 15%, Steele-Butcher needed to borrow only £113 000 to get the project started.

The net present value of the project (£24 069) thus represents an amount of money by which the project enriches the owners of Steele-Butcher.

We have regarded the net present value of a cash flow stream as the debt that the cash flow stream would repay.

We now see that we can regard the net present value of the cash flow stream generated by a project as a measure of how profitable that project is to the owners of the company.

Exercise 2.8

Use the tables of Appendix 1 to find the net present value of the cash flow stream of Fig. 1.3. Assume an interest rate of 18%. [£134 168]

If the company had financed the project wholly by borrowing money at 18%, what is the significance of the net present value that you have calculated?

A particular cash flow stream is that in which all cash flows are equal.

An obvious case is where a debt is repaid by equal annual payments. This frequently happens during the repayment of a mortagage. A numerical example was Example 2.4, earlier in the chapter.

Consider the following cash flow stream:

$$a, a, a, \underbrace{- - - - - - , \, a}_{n \text{ terms}}$$

Often we use the symbol a when we wish to denote one of a number of equal annual payments.

The present value of this cash flow stream is

$$p = \frac{a}{1+i} + \frac{a}{(1+i)^2} + \frac{a}{(1+i)^4} + \frac{a}{(1+i)^4} + \ldots \frac{a}{(1+i)^{n-1}} + \frac{a}{(1+i)^n} \qquad \text{(i)}$$

Now multiply both sides of this equation by $1/1+i$ to obtain

$$\frac{p}{1+i} = \frac{a}{(1+i)^2} + \frac{a}{(1+i)^3} + \frac{a}{(1+i)^4} + \frac{a}{(1+i)^5} \ldots + \frac{a}{(1+i)^n} + \frac{a}{(1+i)^{n+1}} \qquad \text{(ii)}$$

Subtract equation (ii) from equation (i) and we obtain

$$p - \frac{p}{1+i} = \frac{a}{1+i} - \frac{a}{(1+i)^{n+1}} \qquad \text{(iii)}$$

or $\quad p \left(1 - \dfrac{1}{1+i}\right) = a \left(\dfrac{1}{1+i} - \dfrac{1}{(1+i)^{n+1}}\right)$

That is, $\quad p \cdot \dfrac{i}{1+i} = \dfrac{a}{1+i} \left(1 - \dfrac{1}{(1+i)^n}\right)$

That is, $\quad \dfrac{p}{a} = \dfrac{1}{i} \left(\dfrac{(1+i)^n - 1}{(1+i)^n}\right)$

$\dfrac{p}{a}$ is called the **present value factor** for an annuity.

Sometimes we write the present value factor in the form $\left(\dfrac{p}{a}\right)^i_n$ in order to show the interest rate and the number of payments.

Exercise 2.9

What sum of money has been borrowed at 10% interest if the debt is repaid by five annual payments of £131.90?

$$p = \frac{a}{i}\left(\frac{(1+i)^n - 1}{(1+i)^n}\right)$$

$$= \frac{£131.90}{0.1}\left(\frac{(1.1)^5 - 1}{(1.1)^5}\right)$$

$$= \frac{£131.90}{0.1}\left(\frac{1.6105 - 1}{1.6105}\right)$$

$$= £131.90 \times \frac{0.6105}{0.16105}$$

$$= £131.90 \times 3.7908$$

$$= £500 \quad.$$

It is, of course, much more common to want to know how a known debt can be repaid. In other words, given p find a.

But if $\dfrac{p}{a} = \dfrac{1}{i}\left(\dfrac{(1+i)^n - 1}{(1+i)^n}\right)$

then $\quad \dfrac{a}{p} = \dfrac{i(1+i)^n}{(1+i)^n - 1}\quad.$

In the above example we calculated

$$\left(\frac{p}{a}\right)^{0.1}_{5} = 3.7908$$

therefore $\left(\dfrac{a}{p}\right)^{0.1}_{5} = 1 / \left(\dfrac{p}{a}\right)^{0.1}_{5} = 1/3.7908$

If we now ask how a debt of £500 at 10% interest may be repaid in five annual payments we have

$$\frac{a}{p} = \frac{1}{3.7908}\quad \text{where } p = £500 \text{ and } a \text{ is to be determined.}$$

Therefore $a = \dfrac{£500}{3.7908} = £131.90$.

Exercise 2.10

A man buys a house for £30 000. To do this he takes out a mortage for £30 000 at 15% to be repaid in 25 equal, annual payments. What is the annual payment?

$$\frac{a}{p} = \frac{i(1+i)^n}{(1+i)^n - 1}$$

$$= \frac{0.15(1.15)^{25}}{(1.15)^{25} - 1}$$

$$= 0.1547$$

Therefore $a = p \times (0.1547)$

$$= £30\ 000 \times (0.1547)$$

$$= £4641$$

Note that the man actually pays £116 025 for his £30 000 house.

If we use formulae the present value factor for annuities is even more difficult to calculate than the present value factor for future single payments. Because it is used frequently in industry, tables of values are available so that we do not need to use the formula for every calculation.

Appendix 2 is a table of present value factors for annuities that has been calculated for commonly used interest rates.

Exercise 2.11

A company needs to buy a grinding machine and two alternatives are available.
Alternative A costs £10 000, will last six years, and cost £4000 a year to run. The major part of these annual costs are for maintenance.
Alternative B costs £15 000, will also last six years, but because it has been designed to reduce maintenance, the running cost will be £3000.
If the interest is 16%, which is the better machine to buy?

The better machine will be the one for which the present value of costs is lower.

The cash flow streams of costs are shown in the following table:

	A	B
End of year 0	− 10 000	− 15 000
End of year 1	− 4 000	− 3 000
End of year 2	− 4 000	− 3 000
End of year 3	− 4 000	− 3 000
End of year 4	− 4 000	− 3 000
End of year 5	− 4 000	− 3 000
End of year 6	− 4 000	− 3 000

We see that in each case the annual cash flow is constant, and so we may use the present value factor for an annuity.

Using Appendix 2 we see that $\left(\dfrac{p}{a}\right)_6^{0.16} = 3.685$

The net present value of the cost of A $= -£10\ 000 - (3.685 \times £4000)$
$$= -£24\ 740$$
The net present value of the cost of B $= -£15\ 000 - (3.685 \times £3000)$
$$= -£26\ 052$$

We see that, over whole life, B is more expensive than A.

This may be a surprising result because if we do not take account of interest rates,

A costs £10 000 + (6 × £4000) = £34 000
while B costs £15 000 + (6 × £3000) = £33 000

The student may ask why he should choose the project with the lower net present value cost rather than the one with the lower actual cost.

The reasoning is this. If the interest rate is 16%, the company could place £24 740 into a deposit account which earns an interest of 16%[†]. In effect, the company is lending £24 740 and may withdraw immediately £10 000 to pay for grinder A and £4 000 at the ends of years 1,2,3,4,5, and 6 to pay for running the machine; at the end of the sixth year the bank will have paid back all of the original £24 740.

Had the company wished to use the same method to pay for the whole of the life cycle costs of machine B, it would have had to deposit £26 052.

We have, so far, concentrated on finding present values or constant annual payments. Sometimes, however, it is useful to find future values.

[†]This is not strictly true. The fact that you can borrow at 16% does not necessarily imply that you can lend at 16%. This assumption will generally be made in this book.

Suppose a man saves £a per year for n years at $i\%$ interest; how much could be withdrawn at the end of the nth year?

The cash flow stream is:

$$\underbrace{a, a, a, ------, a;}_{n \text{ payments}}$$ the first payment being made at the end of year 1.

The first deposit will be worth $a(1+i)^{n-1}$ at the end of the nth year
The second deposit will be worth $a(1+i)^{n-2}$ at the end of the nth year

_ _

_ _

The $(n-1)$th deposit will be worth $a(1+i)$ at the end of the nth year
and the nth deposit will be worth a at the end of the nth year

The net future worth of all the deposites will be

$$f = a[1+(1+i) + (1+i)^2 + \ldots\ldots\ldots(1+i)^{n-1}]$$

or $$\frac{f}{a} \equiv \left(\frac{f}{a}\right)^i_n$$

$$= 1 + (1+i) + (1+i)^2 + \ldots\ldots\ldots(1+i)^{n-1}\ldots \qquad (i)$$

If we multiply both sides of this equation by $(1+i)$ we obtain

$$(1+i)\left(\frac{f}{a}\right) = (1+i) + (1+i)^2 + \ldots\ldots\ldots\ldots(1+i)^{n-1} + (1+i)^n \quad . \quad (ii)$$

If we subtract equation (i) from equation (ii) we obtain

$$i \times \left(\frac{f}{a}\right) = (1+i)^n - 1$$

or $$\left(\frac{f}{a}\right) = \frac{(1+i)^n - 1}{i} \equiv \left(\frac{f}{a}\right)^i_n$$

We do not often use this formula because we can see that

$$\frac{f}{a} = \frac{p}{a} \cdot \frac{f}{p}, \text{ and from our formulae for } \frac{p}{a} \text{ and } \frac{f}{p}$$

$$\frac{f}{a} = \frac{1}{i}\left(\frac{(1+i)^n - 1}{(1+i)^n}\right)(1+i)^n$$

$$= \frac{(1+i)^n - 1}{i}, \text{ as we would expect.}$$

As we have tables for p/a and p/f we usually find future values using those tables rather than by using the formula.

Exercise 2.12
A man pays £100 a year for 20 years into an insurance policy which pays 6% interest. How much can he withdraw at the end of 20 years?

We wish to find the future net value of 20 equal payments of £100 at an interest rate of 6%.
that is, find f, given a, i, and n when

$$f = \frac{(1+i)^n - 1}{i} \cdot a$$

$$= \frac{(1.06)^{20} - 1}{0.06} \times 100$$

$$= £3\,679 \quad .$$

Alternatively

$$\frac{f}{a} = \left(\frac{p}{a}\right)_n^i \div \left(\frac{p}{f}\right)_n^i \quad \text{and we may find the expressions on the right-hand side in Appendices 1 and 2.}$$

that is, $f = (11.470) \div (0.312) \times 100$

$$= £3\,673$$

The slight difference in these two answers results from using tables of three-figure accuracy.

It is sometimes useful to know the annual equal cash flows that are equivalent to any given cash flow stream. One case is where we wish to compare two competing projects which have different lives.

Example 2.5
A company needs to buy a special-purpose machine of which two versions are available. Machine A costs £20 000 and is expected to last 10 years. Machine B costs £15 000 and is expected to last 6 years. If interest rates are 14%, which machine is the better buy?

Consider machine A. At 14% interest rate, its cost of £20 000, spread over 10 years, has the equivalent annual cost of

$$£20\,000 \div \left(\frac{p}{a}\right)_{10}^{0.14}$$

$$= £20\,000 \div 5.216 = £3834 \quad .$$

Consider machine B. At 14% interest rate, its cost of £15 000, spread over 6 years, has the equivalent annual cost of

$$£15\ 000 \div \left(\frac{p}{a}\right)_6^{0.14}$$

$$= £15\ 000 \div 3.889 = £3857$$

In fact, on an annual cost basis, machine A is slightly cheaper.

Exercise 2.13
What is the situation in Example 2.5 if the interest rate is 16%?

Consider machine A. Its equivalent annual cost is

$$£20\ 000 \div 4.833 = £4138$$

Consider machine B. Its equivalent annual cost is

$$£15\ 000 \div 3.685 = £4070\ \ .$$

At this slightly higher interest rate, machine B is slightly cheaper.

The above example shows how it is sometimes convenient to think of the purchase price of a machine in terms of the money that the machine must earn every year in order to pay for itself. Of course, the machine must earn much more than just enough to pay for itself; it must earn enough to pay for the raw materials it uses, the power it uses, the cost of its maintenance, a profit for its owners, the wages of its operatives, and more besides. The part of its earnings which pays for its initial cost is, nevertheless, a significant contribution.

Exercise 2.14
A car costs £5 000 to buy and £1 000 a year to run. The car is expected to last 8 years, after which it will have no resale value. The owner travels 10 000 miles a year. If interest rates are 10%, how much does each mile of motoring cost?

At 10% interest rate, the 8 equal annual payments that are equivalent to a present value of £5 000 are

$$£5\ 000 \div \left(\frac{p}{a}\right)_8^{0.1}$$

$$= £5\ 000 \div 5.335$$
$$= £937$$

Effectively, then, the cost of running the car is £937 + £1000 = £1937.

The cost per mile is therefore $\dfrac{£1937}{10\ 000}$

$$= 19.37\text{p per mile}$$

(Notice that this is considerably more than the cost per mile if we ignore interest charges.)

Summarising Chapter 2:

We have learned how to calculate the present value of any cash flow stream and we may do this using the formulae

$$\left(\frac{p}{f}\right)^i_n = \frac{1}{(1+i)^n}$$

and $$\left(\frac{p}{a}\right)^i_n = \frac{1}{i}\left[\frac{(1+i)^n - 1}{(1+i)^n}\right]$$

or by using the tables of Appendix 1 and Appendix 2. We can calculate the stream of equal cash flows (a) equivalent to any given stream of cash flows. We can also calculate the future value of any stream of cash flows.

Assuming that a project is financed with borrowed money, if the present value of the cash flows generated by the project is positive, then that project will more than pay back the money that was borrowed, and net present value of the cash flows generated by the project is a measure of the amount of money that may be withdrawn from the project after all debts are paid. This amount for withdrawal may be used to finance other projects or may be paid as dividends to the shareholders of the company.

Exercise 2.15
What is the present value of the following cash flow streams?

(i)   *End of year 0;* −£10 000
     End of year 1; + £2 000   *Assume the life of the project is 5 years*
     End of year 2; + £3 000   *and the interest rate is 12%*
     End of year 3; + £4 000
     End of year 4; + £3 000
     End of year 5; + £1 000   [−£500

(ii)   *End of year 0;* −£250 000
     Equal cash flows of + £50 000 *for 10 years*
     Assume the life of the project is 10 years and the interest rate is 15%

                                                               [£950

(iii) *You are the production director of a company. You have been offered an electron beam welder at a purchase cost of £20 000. You believe that after maintenance costs and operating costs have been taken into account the new machine will be such an advance over your present method of welding diaphragms that you will save £4 000 a year, regularly over the life of the machine. You also believe that the new machine will last 7 years and that you will be able to salvage £2 000 of scrap parts from it at the end of its life. Your finance director tells you that he can borrow the necessary £20 000 at an interest rate of 16%.*

Should you buy the electron beam welder?

[No. Net present value is −£3 136

(iv) *You buy a house for £30 000. You pay a deposit of £5 000, and the remainder is paid through a mortgage over 25 years. At an annual interest rate of 15%, what will be your annual payments?*

[£3867.76

(v) *The interest payments on a mortgage are eligible for tax relief. If, with the data of question (iv), you believe that tax relief effectively reduces your mortgage interests to 10%, what will be your effective annual payments?*

[£2754.21

(vi) *You need a grinding machine which costs £10 000, and you can borrow the money at 12% to buy it.*

You will need to spend £1000 a year servicing and repairing the machine.

The machine will last 5 years, and at the end ot its life it can be sold for £1000.

An alternative policy is to rent a grinding machine. The rent for the machine is £4000 a year, and this covers the cost of maintenance, which is done by the supplier. Is it better to buy or rent?

The effective annual cost of the purchase price of £10 000 is £2774; the effective annual gain from the sale of the time-expired machine is £157. Together with the maintenance cost of £1000 a year, the effective annual cost of owning the machine is £3617, which is cheaper than renting.

(vii) *A proud grandfather pays £100 a year into a savings account so that his grandson may withdraw a lump sum when he goes to college at the age of 18. The first payment of £100 is made on the grandson's first birthday; the last payment and the withdrawal are made together on the grandson's 18th birthday. How much does the grandson withdraw if the interest is 8%?*

[£3749

(viii) *What are the present values and annual equivalent payments of the following cash flow streams? Assume an interest rate of 14%*

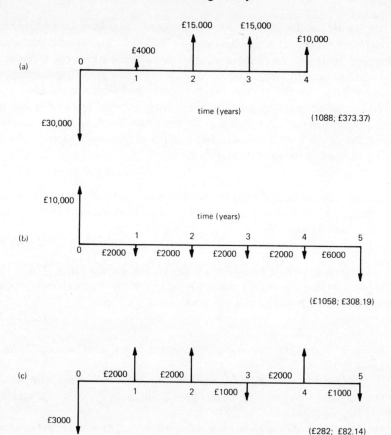

(ix) You undertake to design, build, and deliver a special-purpose machine tool. You estimate that the work will take you 3 years and cost you £20 000 a year for labour and raw materials. When the machine is delivered at the end of 3 years you will be paid £90 000 for it.

Unfortunately the work goes slower than you had hoped, and although you spend only £15 000 a year on labour and materials, the work takes 4 years. Although the customer is annoyed by the late delivery, he nevertheless pays £90 000 for the machine (but a year later than you originally intended).

If the cost of capital is 16%, how much do you lose, in present value terms, by your inability to deliver on time?

The originally intended cash flow stream was −£20 000, −£20 000, + £70 000 with a present value of £12 770; the actual cash flow stream was −£15 000, −£15 000, −£15 000, + £75 000 with a present value of £7710).

(x) You embark on a project which involves an initial investment of £10 000, an annual running cost of £1000, and a project life of 5 years. As a result of this expenditure you make 1000 items a year which you are able to sell for £4 each. When you commit yourself to the project you believe that capital will cost 12%, but there is an immediate change in the bank rate and capital, in fact, costs 16%. What does the change in interest rates do to the profitability of the project?

(In present value terms it turns a profit of £815 into a loss of £178).

3

Discounting more than once a year

In Chapter 2 we discussed loan repayment as though the interest is always calculated every year. There are many cases where this is not so, however. Consider the case of the credit card; companies such as Access, Barclaycard, or Mastercharge usually calculate interest every month. Banks sometimes calculate interest every month; building societies often calculate interest every 6 months. Quarterly, daily, or even continuous calculation of interest is sometimes used.

A typical interest rate on a credit card has been 1½% per month. You might think that 1½% per month is the same as 18% per year, but you would be wrong.

Suppose you borrow £100 at 1½% interest per month and repay at the end of the year.

> At the end of 1 month you owe £100 × 1.015
> At the end of 2 months you owe £100 × 1.015^2
> At the end of 3 months you owe £100 × 1.015^3
>
> At the end of 12 months you must repay £100 × $(1.015)^{12}$
> $= £100 × (1.1956)$.

This means that 1½% interest per month is the equivalent of 19.56% per year.

Usually there is no problem in calculating interest more frequently than once a year, and we may use the tables of Appendices 1 and 2 provided only that present value factors are given for sufficiently low interest rates and for sufficiently large numbers of years.

Exercise 3.1
What is the amount owed at the end of 2 years if £100 is borrowed at an interest of 2% per month?

The interest calculated for 24 months at 2% per month will be exactly the same as that calculated for 24 years at 2% per year so that, using the table of Appendix 1 and reading the present value factor of 0.622 against 24 years at 2%, we obtain the future value of £100 after 24 months

$$= £100 \div \left(\frac{p}{f}\right)^{2\%}_{24}$$

$$= £100 \div 622$$

$$= \underline{£160.77}$$

Exercise 3.2
Arnold buys a car for £3 000. He pays £500 down and agrees to pay the remainder in monthly instalments over 3 years at an interest calculated at 1½% per month. What are his monthly instalments?

$$\left(\frac{p}{a}\right)^{1\frac{1}{2}\%}_{36} = 27.66 \text{ from Appendix 2}$$

therefore   if $p = £3000 - £500 = £2500$
$a = £2500 \div 27.66 = £90.38$.

Exercise 3.3
If a building society wishes to use an effective annual interest rate of 15% but calculate interest every 6 months, what interest rate must be used in the calculations?

Let the 6-monthly interest rate be i. If an amount £P is borrowed, after 6 months the amount owed will be £$P(1+i)$, and after 12 months the amount owed will be £$P(1+i)^2$.

If the effective interest is 15% per year

$$£P(1+i)^2 = £P(1.15)$$
so that $$(1+i)^2 = 1.15$$
that is $$1+i = (1.15)^{\frac{1}{2}}$$
$$i = (1.15)^{\frac{1}{2}} - 1$$
$$= 0.0724$$
$$= 7.24\% \ .$$

One special case of discounting more often than once a year is where the discounting is continuous.
Consider first where

the number of discounting periods per year $= m$
the interest every discounting period $= i$
the effective annual interest rate $= i_{\text{eff}}$

then £$P(1+i)^m = P(1+i_{\text{eff}})$.

Define the nominal annual interest rate $\qquad = i_{nom}$

where $i_{nom} \qquad = i \times m$

$$(1+i)^m \qquad = (1+i_{eff})$$

therefore $\qquad \left(1+\dfrac{i_{nom}}{m}\right)^m \qquad = 1+i_{eff}$

therefore $\qquad i_{eff} \qquad = \left(1+\dfrac{i_{nom}}{m}\right)^m - 1 \qquad$ (i)

or $\qquad i_{nom} \qquad = (1+i_{eff})^{1/m} - 1 \quad .$ (ii)

Consider the expression $(1 + i_{nom}/m)^m$ found in equation (i). If we wish to discount continuously, the number of discounting periods in a year becomes infinite, or we need to find

$$\mathop{Lt}_{m\to\infty} \left(1+\dfrac{i_{nom}}{m}\right)^m$$

That is the limiting value of $\left(1+\dfrac{i_{nom}}{m}\right)^m$ as m increases to infinity.

But one definition of the quantity e^x is

$$e^x = \mathop{Lt}_{m\to\infty}(1+\dfrac{x}{m})^m \text{ where e is the base of natural logarithms.}$$

Therefore when discounting is continuous

$$i_{eff} = e^{i_{nom}} - 1 \quad .$$

If the period of the loan is t years, and we are discounting m times a year at an interest of i per period, we have

the future value $= f = p(1+i)^{tm}$

$$= p\left(1+\dfrac{i_{nom}}{m}\right)^{tm} \quad ;$$

and if the discounting is continuous, that is, in the limit as $m\to\infty$,

$$f = p \exp(ti_{nom}) \quad \text{where } p = \text{present value.}$$

Although continuous discounting is only occasionally used in practice, the formula $f = p \exp(ti_{nom})$ is a useful approximation in some calculations even when the discounting is not continuous.

Compare (p/f) calculated from $f = p \exp(ti_{nom})$ with the values read from the table:

(i)	$i = 10\% = 0.1; \quad n = 10$	[0.3679; 0.386
(ii)	$i = 15\% = 0.15; n = 5$	[0.4724; 0.497
(iii)	$i = 4\% = 0.04; n = 20$	[0.4493; 0.456
(iv)	$i = 20\% = 0.20; n = 5$	[0.3679; 0.402
(v)	$i = 6\% = 0.06; n = 5$	[0.7408; 0.747

The above example shows that the results of using continuous discounting calculations when the discounting is not continuous are approximate, and as one would expect, the approximation is greater for the higher interest rate at shorter periods. The approximation may well be acceptable in some cases, paritcularly where the interest rate is not given in the tables.

Consider a credit card debt for three years at 1½% per month. The true p factor is 0.5851, but if continuous discounting were assumed we would calculate p to be 0.5827. This may not be good enough for the actual calculation of repayment (it would be 24p out in £100), but it would be good enough for many comparisons.

It may be argued that there is not often much difficulty in calculating $(p/f) = 1/(1+i)^n$ for values of i and n that are not in the tables, and generally we would be forced to use the continuous discounting formula only when discounting really is continuous or when we are making comparisons between projects that have fractional or probabilistic lives. These topics are beyond the requirements of the present course, but the student needs to know the formula for continuous discounting if he is to cope with later, more theoretical considerations.

The approximation of continuous discounting may be more valuable when we wish to find equivalent annual payments. We know that

$$\frac{p}{a} = \frac{1}{i}\left(\frac{(1+i)^n - 1}{(1+i)^n}\right),$$

and if we convert this to continuous discounting we obtain

$$\frac{p}{a} = \frac{1}{i_{nom}}\left(\frac{\exp(ni_{nom}) - 1}{\exp(ni_{nom})}\right) . \qquad \text{(This assumes that payment is continuous too)}$$

Consider a mortgage for £25 000 at a nominal 16% per year, discounted quarterly for 25 years. What is the annual repayment?

From the formula

$$\frac{p}{a} = \frac{1}{i} \left(\frac{(1+i)^n - 1}{(1+i)^n} \right)$$

$$a = \frac{£25\ 000 \times 0.04 \times (1.04)^{100}}{(1.04)^{100} - 1}$$

therefore $a = £1020.2$ per period,

that is annual payments

$$= £4080.8$$

If we calculate on an annual basis (16% a year for 25 years) we obtain, from tables

$$\frac{p}{a} = 6.097$$

therefore $a = £25\ 000 \div 6.097$

$$= £4100.4 \text{ per year.}$$

If we calculate on a continuous discounting basis we have

$$\frac{p}{a} = \frac{1}{0.16} \left(\frac{e^{(0.16)\ (25)} - 1}{e^{(0.16)\ (25)}} \right)$$

$$= 6.1355,$$

therefore $a = £25\ 000/6.1355$

$$= £4074.6 \text{ (Payments must be sufficiently frequent to be regarded as continuous)}$$

We see that the continuous discounting calculation is here slightly more accurate than annual discounting would be. In this case, we were able to use tables for annual discounting, and the inaccuracy obtained might have been acceptable for a first approximation.

Consider, however, the calculation of a mortgage that is discounted quarterly for a fractional period of time. Suppose, for example, the mortgage is for £25 000 at a nominal 16% per annum, discounted quarterly, for 21 years 9 months. The tables fail us for annual discounting. For quarterly discounting we have

87 periods, and only very extensive tables cover such a time. We could use the formula to obtain

$$\frac{p}{a} = \frac{1}{0.04} \left(\frac{(1.04)^{87} - 1}{(1.04)^{87}} \right)$$

$$= 24.1758 \text{ (the accurate value)},$$

giving a payment of £1034.1 a quarter; or we could approximate by continuous discounting to obtain

$$\frac{p}{a} = \frac{1}{0.16} \frac{e^{(0.16)\,(21.75)} - 1}{e^{(0.16)\,(21.75)}}$$

$$= \frac{1}{0.16} \frac{31.4597}{32.4597}$$

$$= 6.0575 \ ,$$

giving a payment of £4127.1 a year or £1031.8 a quarter.

Using continuous discounting would yield an underpayment of 77p a month.

Exercise 3.4

(i) A moneylender charges 3% interest per month. What is the effective annual interest?   [42.58%

If Bertram borrows £100 from the moneylender and repays it in 12 equal monthly installments, starting one month after he borrowed the money, what are the monthly payments?   [£10.05

(ii) Claud bought a car on hire-purchase. He paid £500 down and £79.30 a month for 2 years. At monthly discounting and a nominal annual interest of 24%, how much did Claud pay for the car?   [£2000

(iii) Desmond takes out a 25 year mortgage for £30 000. He may pay in annual payments with annual discounting at 15% or in monthly payments with monthly discounting at 1¼%. Which is better for Desmond and by how much a year?

[Annual discounting: annual payment = £3867.6
[Monthly discounting: monthly payment = £320.21 = £3842.5/year

(iv) Use a nominal annual rate of interest of 12% and calculate the effective annual rate if discounting is
   (a) six-monthly, (b) quarterly, (c) monthly, (d) continuous
                                                [12.36%, 12.55%, 12.68%, 12.75%

(v) You expect a payment of £100 in 5 years' time. What is the present value of this payment if discounting is continuous and at a nominal annual rate of 10%?
[£60.65

(vi) You borrow £100 at a nominal annual rate of 12%. Discounting is continuous. You intend to repay over 10 years by regular equal payments. What are your annual repayments if (a) made once a year, and (b) made sufficiently frequently to be regarded as continuous?   [£18.25, £17.172

4

Rate of return

In Chapter 2 we saw that if you borrow money to invest in a project, the cash flow stream generated by that project must have a positive (or, at least, non-negative) present value. But what if you do not borrow the money? What if you have the money already and wish to invest it in a project?

What if you have money and are prepared to lend it? It is likely that you would want to lend the money at the best rate of interest that you could get. This means that we must be able to calculate the interest that we will get.

Example 4.1
Arnold bought a vacuum cleaner on hire purchase. The advertised price of the cleaner was £50. Arnold paid £20 down and the rest in 9 equal monthly payments of £3.68. What interest was Arnold charged?

Effectively, Arnold borrowed £30 which he repaid in 9 equal, monthly cash flows of £3.68.

The cash flow as it relates to this loan was

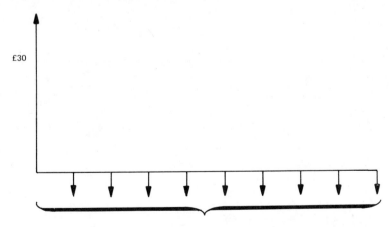

9 equal cash flows of £3.68

We see that,

$$\left(\frac{p}{a}\right)^i_9 = \frac{30}{3.68} = 8.1522$$

Look at the entries in the table of Appendix 2 for

n = 9 and we find

$$\left(\frac{p}{a}\right)^i_9 = 8.162 \text{ where } i = 2\%$$

This is as near the actual value as we can find, and we can say, with acceptable accuracy, that Arnold is paying 2% per month.

As we have seen in Chapter 2, 2% calculated every month is equivalent to

$$(1.02)^{12} - 1 = 26.8\% \text{ per year.}$$

Example 4.2
Basil bought a motor car on hire purchase. The advertised price of the car was £2000. Basil paid £500 down and the rest in 36 equal monthly instalments of £54.17. What was the rate of interest?

If we look at the cash flow stream as it relates to the loan, we have

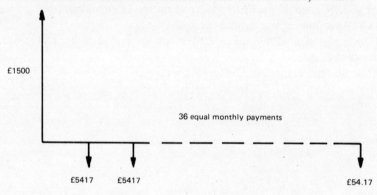

£1500

36 equal monthly payments

£5417   £5417   £54.17

The monthly instalments repay the loan so we have a cash flow stream in which

$$p = £1500, \ a = -£54.17, \ n = 36$$

and i is to be found.

Therefore $\left(\dfrac{p}{a}\right)^i_{36} = \dfrac{1500}{54.17} = 27.69$.

Unfortunately the tables of Appendix 2 do not quote present value factors for 36 periods, and we will need to use the formula to calculate the required value of i.

that is   find i when

$$27.69. = \frac{(1+i)^{36} - 1}{i(1+i)^{36}} \, .$$

This is not an equation which can be solved analytically, and we have to solve it by trial and error.

Suppose $i = 1\%$ per month $= 0.01$

$$\left(\frac{p}{a}\right)^{0.01}_{36} = \frac{(1.01)^{36} - 1}{(0.01)(1.01)^{36}} = 30.10 \text{ which is higher than the}$$
$$\text{required value of } 27.69.$$

Suppose $i = 2\%$ per month $= 0.02$

$$\left(\frac{p}{a}\right)^{0.02}_{36} = \frac{(1.02)^{36} - 1}{(0.02)(1.02)^{36}} = 25.48 \text{ which is lower than the}$$
$$\text{required value of } 27.69.$$

We obviously have an interest rate which lies between 0.01 and 0.02. Try $i = 0.015$, then

$$\left(\frac{p}{a}\right)^{0.015}_{36} = \frac{(1.015)^{36} - 1}{(0.015)(1.015)^{36}} = 27.66 \text{ which is an acceptable}$$
$$\text{approximation to the}$$
$$\text{required figure.}$$

Sometimes when a company wishes to raise money to invest in a project, it will sell debentures. Anyone who buys a debenture will receive an agreed interest every year for an agreed number of years. At the end of its life, the debenture will be bought back by the company, usually at the price for which it was sold. There is, of course, nothing to stop a debenture being bought and sold before it matures and the company buys it back.

Example 4.3
Claud buys a £1000 debenture at the end of 1980. The debenture pays £100 interest at the end of every year until 1990 (inclusive). At the end of 1990 the company which issued the debenture buys it back for £1000. Had Claud paid £1000 (its face value) for the debenture, the interest would have been 10%. In fact, at the end of 1980, Claud was able to buy the debenture for £750. What interest was Claud receiving?

The cash flow stream, as seen by Claud, is

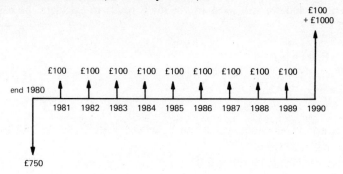

Therefore $750 = (100)\left(\dfrac{p}{a}\right)^{i}_{10 \text{ years}} + (1000)\left(\dfrac{p}{f}\right)^{i}_{10 \text{ years}}$ 4.3(i)

where i has yet to be found.

This is quite a difficult equation to solve for i, and we can either resort to to trial and error or solve it by graphical means.

If we make a first guess at possible values of i, we can see that $i > 10\%$ because an investment of £1000 at 10% would have yielded an interest of £100 a year until the final repayment. Claud has obviously done better than this because he has obtained these payments for an investment of only £750. Nevertheless, it is constructive to consider values of i which start $i = 0$.

If we rewrite equation 4.3(i) as

$$PV = -750 + 100\left(\dfrac{p}{a}\right)^{i}_{10} + 10000\left(\dfrac{p}{f}\right)^{i}_{10}$$ 4.2(ii)

we are looking for the value of i when $PV = 0$.

If $i = 0$
$PV = -750 + 100(10) + 1000(1)$
$\quad = 1250$.

If $i = 5\%$
$PV = -750 + 100(7.722) + 1000(0.614)$
$\quad = 636$.

If $i = 10\%$
$PV = -750 + 100(6.145) + 1000(0.386)$
$\quad = 251$.

If $i = 15\%$
$PV = -750 + 100(5.019) + 1000(0.247)$
$= -1.1$.

If $i = 20\%$
$PV = -750 + 100(4.193) + 1000(0.162)$
$= -169$.

We see from these calculations that, to an acceptable accuracy, the value of i which gives a present value of zero is 15%.

It is worth plotting PV against i, and Fig. 4.1 shows this curve.

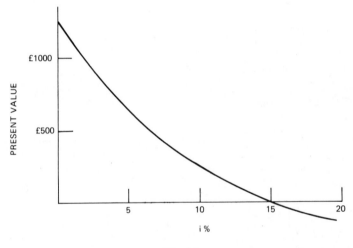

Fig. 4.1

The shape of the curve is typical in that, with most projects, if we plot a curve of present value against interest rate, we find that present value is high and positive for $i = 0$ and decreases as i increases. This does not happen in every case, however, and some notable exceptions will be discussed later.

Sometimes, people who lend money do not quote the true interest rate.

Example 4.4
Desmond bought a motor car on hire purchase. The advertised price of the car was £2000 and Desmond was able to pay £500 down. Desmond went to his bank manager to ask if he could borrow the remaining £1500, and he was given a 'personal loan' over 2 years at '10% interest'. However, the way the bank manager calculated the repayments was as follows:

amount borrowed	£1500
10% interest for 2 years	300
Bank's charge for arranging the loan	20
Total	£1820
Monthly payment	= £1820 ÷ 24
	= £75.83 .

What interest rate was Desmond really paying?
From Desmond's point of view, the cash flow stream is

+£1500 at the end of month 0

and   −£75.83 at the ends of months 1 to 24.

We therefore have

$$0 = 1500 - (75.83)\left(\frac{p}{a}\right)_{24}^{i}$$

where i is the monthly interest rate.
That is,

$$\left(\frac{p}{a}\right)_{24}^{i} = \frac{1500}{75.83} = 19.78$$

Tables show us that $\left(\frac{p}{a}\right)_{24}^{2\%} = 18.91$

and $\left(\frac{p}{a}\right)_{24}^{1.5\%} = 20.03$

Obviously, the interest that Desmond is being charged is nearer 1.5%/month than 2.0%/month.

We can obtain a nearer approximation to the required answer by interpolating between the two values we already have.

If we were to plot $\left(\frac{p}{a}\right)_{24}^{i}$ against i we would have

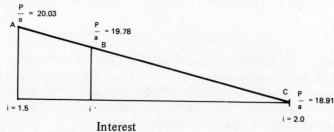

Interest

If we assume ABC is a straight line, then

$$\frac{19.78 - 18.91}{20.03 - 19.78} = \frac{2.0 - i}{i - 1.5}$$

or

$$\frac{0.87}{0.25} = \frac{2.0 - i}{i - 1.5}$$

that is $\quad 0.87i - 1.305 = 0.5 - 0.25i$

that is

$$i = \frac{1.805}{1.12} = 1.612 \ .$$

ABC is not really a straight line, and so it is as well to check our calculation:

$$\left(\frac{p}{a}\right)_{24}^{1.612} = \frac{(1.01612)^{24} - 1}{(0.01612)(1.01612)^{24}}$$

$$= 19.77 \ .$$

Clearly $i = 1.612\%$/month is of more than sufficient accuracy.

Of course, 1.612% per month is nominally

$$1.612 \times 12 = 19.344\% \text{ per year and actually}$$

$$(1.01612)^{12} - 1 = 21.155\% \text{ per year.}$$

Either of these estimates of the annual interest rate is far from the bank manager's 10%. The reason for the difference, of course, is that the bank manager calculates the interest on a personal loan as though Desmond owes £1500 for 2 years. In fact as Desmond makes monthly payments, the amount he owes reduces from month to month.

When we invest in a project, we are not actually lending money to a borrower, but we can consider that we are lending money to the project.

Example 4.5

Suppose Edward buys a taxi and operates a taxi service. He buys a car which he uses as a taxi, for £10 000, new.

The car costs £3000 a year to run and maintain. It lasts five years, and at the end of that time it is sold for £750. The driver costs £8000 a year, and the takings are £14 000 a year.

What is the rate of return of Edward's project?

The cash flow stream is

	Car (£)	Running costs (£)	Wages (£)	Income (£)	Net cash flow
Year 0	−10 000				−10 000
1		−3 000	−8 000	14 000	+ 3 000
2		−3 000	−8 000	14 000	+ 3 000
3		−3 000	−8 000	14 000	+ 3 000
4		−3 000	−8 000	14 000	+ 3 000
5	+ 750	−3 000	−8 000	14 000	+ 3 750

Although Edward is investing in a project, so far as the money is concerned, the result is the same as if he lent £10 000 and was repaid £3000, £3000, £3000, £3000 and £3750 in years, 1, 2, 3, 4, and 5.

Just as when money is being lent, we need to find the value of i for which the *NPV* of the cash flow stream is zero. That is, determine i for which

$$-10\,000 + 3000 \left(\frac{p}{a}\right)^i_5 + 750 \left(\frac{p}{f}\right)^i_5 = 0 \quad .$$

Try $i = 20\%$

$$-10\,000 + 3000\,(2.991) + 750(0.402) = -725.5$$

Try $i = 16\%$

$$-10\,000 + 3000(3.274) + 750(0.476) = 179 \quad .$$

Clearly i lies between 16% and 20%
Try $i = 18\%$

$$-10\,000 + 3000(3.127) + 750(0.437) = -291$$

i lies between 16% and 18% .

By linear interpolation we have

$$i = 16\% + \frac{179}{179 + 291} \times 2\%$$

$$= \underline{16.76\%}$$

Exercise 4.1

Frederick & Co. are considering investment in a new machine. They estimate that the cost of the machine is £10 000, the costs of operating and maintaining the machine will be £1000, £1000, £2000, £1000 and £1000 in years 1, 2, 3, 4, and 5 of its use. The reason for the high cost in the third year is that it will then require an expensive overhaul. The project with which the machine is associated

Economics and Financial Studies for Engineers   61

will come to an end after 5 years, and the machine will then be sold for an estimated salvage of £1500.

The income from the project will be £2500, £5000, £7000, £4000 and £2500 in the 5 years. Note that the income increases as the project gets under way, but it later reduces because of competition.

What is the rate of return which derives from investment in the machine?

The cash flow is:

	Buying and selling the machine	Running costs	Income	Net cash flow
End year 0	−£10 000			£10 000
1		−£1000	£2500	1 500
2		− 1000	5000	4 000
3		− 2000	7000	5 000
4		− 1000	4000	3 000
5	+ 1 500	− 1000	2500	3 000

We can estimate the rate of return by trial and error in which we find the discount rate for which the *NPV* is zero.

	Net cash flow	$\left(\dfrac{p}{f}\right)$ at 20%	PV	$\left(\dfrac{p}{f}\right)$ at 18%	PV
End year 0	−10 000	1	−10 000	1	−10 000
1	1500	0.833	1 250	0.847	1 271
2	4 000	0.694	2 776	0.718	2 872
3	5 000	0.579	2 895	0.609	3 045
4	3 000	0.482	1 446	0.516	1 548
5	3 000	0.402	1 206	0.437	1 311
			−427		47

By interpolating between these two *NPV*s we see that the rate of return is $i = 18.2\%$.

One of the expenses that we have in any project is working capital. If we buy a machine with the intention of making products to sell, if we buy a shop and run it for a living, if we build a power station and sell electricity, sink a coal mine and sell coal, we are involved in many contributions to cash flow. Among these are the costs of labour, of raw material, of capital equipment, of rates, of taxes, of insurance, of buildings, of canteens, of superannuation for employees. On the positive side, there are incomes from the sale of the products, returns from investments, grants from government agencies, and other sources of money. Usually it is not reasonable to expect cash flows to occur in such a sequence that payments can be made out of funds earlier received. Wages will have to be paid and raw materials paid for before goods are sold. Because of this there must be injections of working capital from time to time. This working capital must all be withdrawn at or before the end of the project.

Example 4.6

George & Co. are setting up a subsidiary. The expected life of the plant is 6 years. The total cost of the plant is £380 000 with £280 000 spent at the beginning of the first year, £90 000 spent at the beginning of the second year, and £10 000 spent at the beginning of the third year. The running costs are £579 000; £1 112 000; £1 274 000; £1 112 000; £810 000; and £469 000 in the 6 years of the project.

The sales revenues are £600 000; £1 300 000; £1 500 000; £1 300 000; £1 000 000; and £500 000 in each of the 6 years of the project. Because of the need to pay costs before income is received, there must be injections of working capital. At the start of the project £10 000 is set aside for wages, stock, and petty cash. A further £155 000 must be injected at the end of year 1; £187 000 at the end of year 2; £51 000 at the end of year 3. This working capital is reduced at the ends of years 4, 5, and 6 by £51 000; £82 000; and £270 000. The final amount of £270 000 assumes that all stocks are used up and all customer and supplier accounts are settled.

Note that the sum of these changes in working capital is zero over the life of the project.

What is the rate of return of the project?

	Plant	Working capital	Running costs	Sales revenue	Net cash flow
End year 0	−280	− 10			−290
1	− 90	−155	− 579	+ 600	−224
2	− 10	−187	−1112	+1300	− 9
3	0	− 51	−1274	+1500	175
4	0	+ 51	−1112	+1300	239
5	0	+ 82	− 810	+1000	272
6	+ 50	+270	− 469	+ 500	351

Finding the net present value of these cash flows at different rates of interest we have

	Cash flow	$\left(\dfrac{p}{f}\right)$ at 16%	PV	$\left(\dfrac{p}{f}\right)$ at 20%	PV
End year 0	−290	1	−290	1	−290
1	−224	0.862	−193	0.833	−187
2	− 9	0.743	− 7	0.694	− 6
3	+175	0.641	+112	0.579	+101
4	+239	0.552	+132	0.482	+115
5	+272	0.476	+129	0.402	+109
6	+351	0.418	+147	0.335	+118
			30		−39

We see that the rate of interest for which the net present value of project is zero will be between 16% and 20% (slightly below 18%).

Exercise 4.2
Calculate the rates of return of the projects with the following cash flow streams:
See Table on next page.

Exercise 4.3
A company buys a lathe for £1000, expecting to make net profits before major overhaul expenses of £450, £400, £350, and £300 at the ends of the 1st, 2nd, 3rd, and 4th years of operation. A major overhaul at the end of the 2nd year is expected to cost £200. At the end of the 4th year, the lathe is expected to have a salvage value of £250.
    What would be the rate of return of the project?   [19%

Exercise 4.4
(i) A B Co. buy a mill for £7000. It is expected to have a useful life of 4 years at the end of which it will be traded in for an expected scrap value of £900. During its life the mill is expected to generate a cash flow at the end of each year as follows:

year 1	year 2	year 3	year 4
£700	£1 500	£4 200	£1 200

Estimate the rate of return of the project.   [7%

(ii) The company may make a once-off maintenance payment of £1000, payable at the time of purchase. Although this will not alter the cash flow stream it will result in a higher resale price for the mill at the end of year 4. If the increased price is £2 300, determine the internal rate of return and hence deduce whether the maintenance contract is worthwhile.   [7.3%

Exercise 4.5
Some answers to exercises have been given to the nearest quarter of a percent; other answers have been given to different accuracies. How accurate would the engineer expect to be when assessing whether a project is worthwile?

Year	(i)	(ii)	(iii)	(iv)	(v)	(vi)	(vii)	(viii)	(ix)	(x)
0	−40 000	−8 000	−1 000	−70 000	−15 000	−4 000	−15 000	−2 000	−6 000	−500
1	−40 000	3 500	− 800	−40 000	−10 000	5 820	4 900	949	2 000	300
2	10 000	2 600	500	20 000	− 5 000	−3 000	5 700	525	2 200	300
3	12 000	2 100	500	22 000	10 000	924	6 200	1 836	3 100	250
4	20 000	2 000	600	50 000	12 000	772	6 700	282	5 000	220
5	30 000	2 000	600	60 000	15 000	375	7 100	421	5 700	200
6	40 000	1 500	700	75 000	12 000	359	7 500	477	5 200	186
7	32 000	1 000	700	8 000	10 000	1 600	8 100	468	3 400	200
8	42 000	600	800	100 000	8 000	1 280	6 400	588	3 000	188
9	28 000	600	800	65 000	6 000	616	4 600	326	2 000	180
10	14 000	600	700	42 000	—	1 640	5 500	147	1 500	133
Ans.	(20.75%)	(24.25%)	(25.5%)	(31.25%)	(20.5%)	(32.5%)	(38%)	(38.5%)	(48.75%)	(52.5%)

5

Depreciation, writing down allowance and taxation

When a man buys a motor car he probably expects it to last 9 or 10 years. He may sell it after one year in which case it will have a salvage value and he will be able to calculate how much the car has cost him over one year. He may sell the car after 2, 3, or more years, and in every case it is possible to calculate how much the car has cost.

Example 5.1

Alan buys a car for £5000 and sells it after one year for £4000. If we consider only the money involved in buying and selling then we see, simply, that the car has cost Alan £1000 for a year. We could be more precise and argue that the *PV* of the cost of the car, calculated at the beginning of the year of ownership, is (£'s)

$$-5000 + 4000/(1 + i),$$

and if Alan's overdraft costs 17%, the *PV* for his year of ownership, calculated at the beginning of the year is

$$-5000 + 4000/(1.17)$$
$$= -£1581 \quad .$$

If Alan sells the car after 2 years for £3000 we could oversimplify and say that the car has cost £2000 over 2 years, or £1000/year. But this would ignore the time value of money and the *PV* of the cost of the car, calculated at the beginning of Alan's ownership is (£'s)

$$-5000 + 3000/(1.17)^2$$
$$= -£2808 \quad .$$

We cannot compare directly a *PV* of £1581 for one year of ownership with a *PV* of £2808 for 2 years of ownership, and we need to ask the question, 'How much per year has the car cost?' The easiest way of answering the question is to calculate the cost of the car as equal amounts per year.

Owning the car for one year has a cost with a present value of

£1581

which is equivalent to a payment of

$$£(1581)(1.17) = £1850$$

at the end of year 1.

Owning the car for 2 years has a cost with a present value of

£2808 which is

equivalent to payments of

$$2808 \times (a/p)_2^{17\%} = £1771$$

at the ends of year 1 and year 2 of ownership.

Alan may decide to keep the car until he can sell it only for scrap. Say that he keeps it for 10 years and then sells it for £100 for spare parts. The cash flow stream is

$$- £5000, 0, 0, 0, 0, 0, 0, 0, 0, 0, + £100 \quad .$$

The equivalent annual cost is

$$\left(- 5000 + 100/(p/f)_{10}^{17\%} \right) \times (a/p)_{10}^{17\%}$$
$$= - £1073 \quad .$$

The policy of keeping the car for 10 years is equivalent to paying £1073 at the end of each of those years. Note that in these comparisons we are looking only at the cost of buying the car when it is new and selling it when the owner wishes to. The owner will, of course, be committed to many other costs of ownership – fuel, maintenance, insurance, licence, etc.

Alan buys a new car and expects it to last for several years, or if he keeps it for only one year assumes that the cost for the year will not be the whole purchase price of the car. In the same way, if a company buys a machine with which they will make goods for sale, they will not necessarily expect that machine to pay for itself in a year.

Example 5.2
A company buys a rolling machine, on which they intend to make expansion joints. The machine costs £20 000 and lasts for 10 years, after which its scrap value is £1000 and during each year of its life, the machine makes components which sell for £10 000. The costs of labour, material, maintenance, and indirect costs involved in making the components is £6000 a year. In addition to the annual costs, the machine must, of course, pay for itself. One way of allowing for this is to spread the cost of the machine equally over the years of ownership.

Assume that the discount rate is 12% and calculate the profit each year (ignore the effect of tax).

The present value of the cost of the machine is (£'s)

$$20\ 000 - 1000/(1.12)^{10}$$

$$= £19\ 678 \quad .$$

The equivalent annual cost of the machine is (£'s)

$$19\ 678 \times (a/p)_{10}^{12\%}$$

$$= £3483 \quad .$$

On a yearly basis, then, we can argue that our revenue is £10 000 and our costs are:

direct operating costs	£6000
cost of machine	£3483
	£9483

The surplus of income over expenditure is thus £517 a year. This may seem a small figure for so expensive a project, but as long as there is a surplus, however small, the project is acceptable because the surplus implies that all bills have been paid, and all workmen have been paid; and because we have used discounted cash flow calculations, all those who lent or invested money in the project will get their money back with interest.

In the above examples, we have argued that a machine will not necessarily be expected to pay for itself in the first year of its life. Before the use of discounted cash flow methods, the concept of **depreciation** was used to deal with this situation.

Depreciation looks at the value of a capital asset from two points of view:

(i) in calculating the annual profit and loss account, only a portion of the capital asset is required to be paid for in any one year, and

(ii) in listing the values of the assets of a company each year it must be recognised that as a machine grows older it will decline in value.

The concept of depreciation is still used and is still useful. In many countries, depreciation policy is used in determining the corporation tax to be paid. In some cases, depreciation reflects a genuine estimate of what the asset could be sold for, but in many cases the machine could not be sold for anything but scrap value.

An asset declines in value for many reasons. It may wear out, new technology may produce a machine that can do the job quicker, better, and cheaper, fashion or new technology may reduce the sales for the products made by the machine, competitors may force the owner of the machine out of business, etc.

The fact that a machine will not be sold during its useful life and the many unpredictable reasons for its reduction in value mean that whatever depreciation programme is assumed will be fiction.

A commonly used programme is straight-line depreciation. In this, we simply draw a straight line from the new value of the machine to its salvage at the end of its useful life.

Example 5.3

A machine is bought for £20 000 and is expected to last 10 years with a salvage value of £1000 at the end of its life. Draw the depreciation curve and determine the machine's value at the end of each year of its life. How much will the machine cost, each year?

If we draw a straight line from £20 000 at time zero to £1000 at 10 years, we obtain the graph of Fig. 5.1.

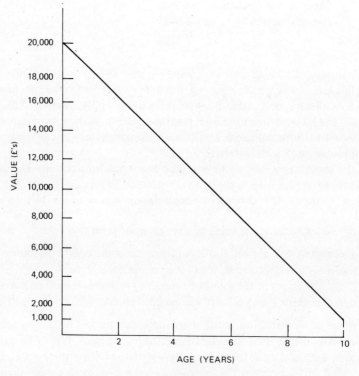

Fig. 5.1

From this graph we may read the value at the end of each year. Alternatively we can see that the value of the machine declines by £(20 000 − 1000) = £19 000 over the 10 years, that is by £1900 per year. The value of the machine at the end of years 1, 2, 3, 4 etc. would be £18 100, £16 200, £14 300, £12 400, etc.

We could use a formula to find the depreciation per year in the straight line method.

$$D = \frac{C - S}{N}$$ where C = initial cost
S = salvage value
N = life

Exercise 5.1

Find the value at the end of each year when a machine is depreciated by the straight-line method, in the following cases:

(i)   Initial cost   = £10 000
         Salvage value = £ 2000
         Life   = 8 years   (Depreciation/year = £1000)

(ii)   Initial cost   = £1M
         Salvage value = 0
         Life   = 25 years   (Depreciation/year = £40 000)

(iii)   Initial cost   = £1M
         Cost of clearing site at
         end of life   = 0.1M
                   life   = 33 years   (£33 333)

(iv)   Initial cost   = £5000
         Resale value   = £ 500
         Life   = 5 years   (£900)

(v)   Initial cost   = £11 000
         Salvage cost   = £   300
         Life   = 4 years   (£2 675)

Sometimes it is thought to be more realistic if we assume that the value of an asset falls faster in the early part of its life. This may well be the case with a car if we consider it from the point of view of re-sale value. A new car which costs £5000 may re-sell at only £4000 at the end of its first year of life, £3500 at the end of its second, and £3100 at the end of its third. After 6 or 7 years, the value of the car may change only very slowly with age. Of course, the resale value of anything depends on many factors. A trade recession may depress the selling price, a reputation for unreliability may depress the price, scarcity value may enhance the price.

One way of defining values which fall more rapidly early in the life of an asset is to assume that the asset declines in value by a fixed proportion each year.

Example 5.4

A machine is bought for £10 000 and declines in value each year by a quarter of its value at the beginning of the year. How does it depreciate year by year?

Value at the beginning of year 1	$= £10\ 000$
Decline in value during year 1	
$= (0.25) \times 10\ 000$	$= £\ \ 2\ 500$
Value at the beginning of year 2	$7\ 500$
Decline in value during year 2	
$= (0.25) \times 7\ 500$	$=\ \ \ \ 1\ 875$
Value at the beginning of year 3	$5\ 625$
Decline in value during year 3	
$= (0.25) \times 5\ 625$	$=\ \ \ 1\ 406.25$
Value at the beginning of year 4	$4\ 218.75$

etc.

What we have said is that if the value at the end of year 0 is $v(0)$ and the value at the end of year n is $v(n)$, then the decline in value during year n is $kv(n-1)$.

The value at the end of year n is

$$v(n-1) - kv(n-1) = (1-k)v(n-1)\ .$$

We thus have
$$v(1) = (1-k)v(0)$$
$$v(2) = (1-k)v(1) = (1-k)^2 v(0)$$
$$\cdot$$
$$\cdot$$
$$\cdot$$
$$v(n) = \qquad\qquad (1-k)^n v(0)\ .$$

Example 5.5

A machine that is bought for £100 000 declines by a fifth of its value each year. How much is it worth after 6 years?

$v(0)$	$=$	$£100\ 000$
k	$=$	0.2
$1-k$	$=$	0.8
$v(6)$	$=$	$(0.8)^6 (100\ 000)$
	$=$	$£26\ 214.4$

If $\quad v(n) \qquad = (1-k)^n v(0)$

then $\quad \log v(n) \quad = n \log (1-k) + \log v(0)$

and if we plot $\log v(n)$ versus n, we obtain a straight line.

Example 5.6

Repeat example 5.5 by plotting a graph of log $v(n)$ versus n.

   We can use the solution of Example 5.5.

   When $n = 0$, $v(0) = £100\,000$ and log $v(0) = 5.0$
   When $n = 6$, $v(6) = £26\,214.4$ and log $v(6) = 4.4185$

   Fig. 5.2 shows the graph that we obtain.

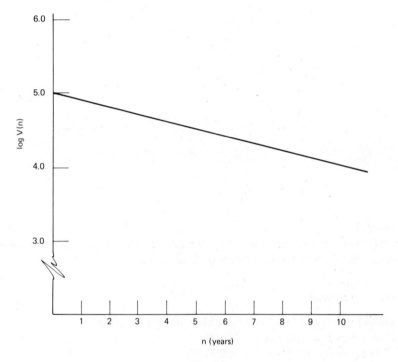

Fig. 5.2

It is clear that reading the log of the required value against any particular value of n is not a particularly quick method of obtaining an answer.

   However, if we use graph paper with a vertical scale that is logarithmic and a horizontal scale that is linear, we can read values directly.

   If we repeat example 5.6 using such log-linear paper, we obtain the graph of Fig. 5.3.

   With Fig. 5.3 we may clearly read the value of the asset directly off the vertical scale for any given value of n.

   The decline in value, when calculated in this way (a constant fraction each year), may be called exponential.

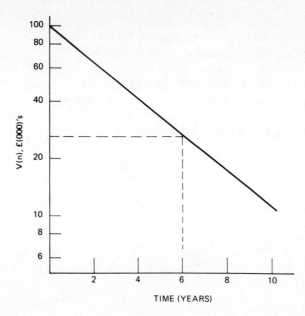

Fig. 5.3

Exercise 5.2

An asset is worth £10 000 when new and £2000 when it is disposed of after 10 years. What is its value year by year if its depreciation is

 (i)   linear?
 (ii) exponential?

(i)   Initial value = £10 000; final value after 10 years = £2000
      Change in value in 10 years = £8000
      Change in value per year   = £8000/10
                                  = £800

The value of the asset is thus

£10 000; £9 200; £8 400; £7 600; £6 800; £6 000; £5 200; £4 400; £3 600; £2 800; and £2 000 respectively at the ends of years 0, 1, 2 . . . 10.

(ii) $v(0) = £10\ 000$
       $v(10) = £\ 2\ 000$ $= (1-k)^{10} \times 10\ 000$
       therefore $\log 2\ 000$ $= 10 \log(1-k) + \log 10\ 000$
       therefore 3.3010 $= 10 \log(1-k) + 4$
       therefore $\log(1-k)$ $= -0.06989$
       therefore $1-k$ $=\ \ \ 0.8513$

therefore k =   0.1486

$v(0)$ = £10 000

$v(1)$ = £ 8 513

$v(2)$ = £ 8 513 × 0.8513 = £7248

$v(3)$ = £ 7 248 × 0.8513 = £6170

$v(4)$ =   £5253

$v(5)$ =   £4472

$v(6)$ =   £3807

$v(7)$ =   £3241

$v(8)$ =   £2759

$v(9)$ =   £2349

$v(10)$ =   £2000

Observe the different ways the asset declines in value according to the assumptions made.

Note too that we could have readily solved Exercise 5.2 (ii) using log-linear graph paper. This solution is shown on Fig. 5.4.

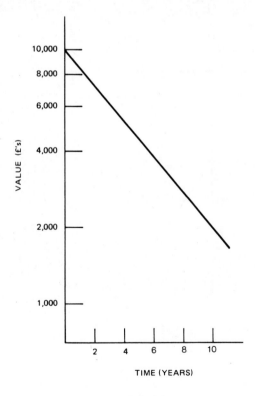

Fig. 5.4

Exercise 5.3

Find asset values, year by year, in the following cases of exponential depreciation:

	Value new	Value after *n* years	*n*
(i)	£5000	£1000	4
(ii)	£2M	£1M	25
(iii)	£30 000	£3000	10
(iv)	£1000	£100	3
(v)	£10 000	£1500	5

Solutions are shown on Figs. 5.5 (i), (ii), (iii), (iv) & (v).

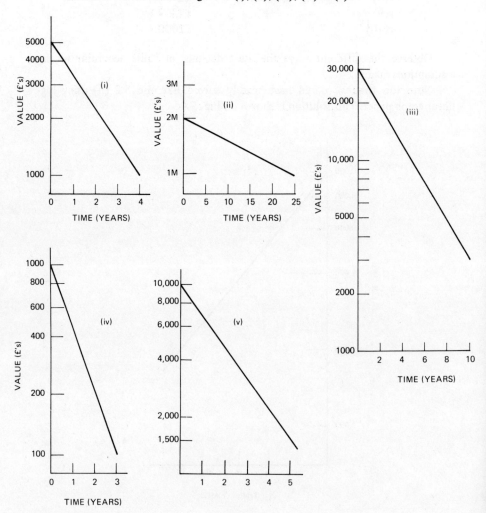

Fig. 5.5

How one depreciates capital equipment is not often important because the valuation is rarely put to the test. It is necessary to state the value of the assets of a company, every year, in the balance sheet and the depreciated value of an asset will be quoted because it is the best estimate of the value when the balance sheet is written. With this information, the owners of the company (usually the shareholders) have some idea of the value of what they own. Only if an asset is sold is the estimate of its depreciated value put to the test.

It is sometimes suggested that depreciation is really the setting aside of sums of money during each year in the life of an asset so that at the end of the asset's life, enough money will have been accumulated to replace it. Because of this, methods of depreciating that are described in textbooks often determine ways of putting annual amounts into a sinking fund so that, **with interest**, the amount in the sinking fund will enable an asset to be replaced at the end of its life. This idea of sinking fund as a sort of savings account which is intended for the replacement of an asset is unnecessarily complicated. The calculations, from cash flow streams, of the net present value or the rate of return of a project take full account of the payment for the asset when determining whether a project is worthwhile.

In some countries (for example, in the USA) the year's depreciation of an asset is an allowed expense for taxation purposes. When depreciation is allowable for tax purposes, the method of calculating it is specified by the taxing authority (in the USA, three or four methods are approved; one is linear depreciation, but others give greater amounts of depreciation during the earlier years of the life of an asset).

In Britain, depreciation is not associated with taxation. For the purposes of taxation a 'writing-down' allowance is used, and this 'writing down' allowance is prescribed by Parliament in the Finance Act, each year. At the time of writing, the writing down allowance on most plant is 100% in the first year of its life. Most buildings are written down by 4% in each of 25 years of life. These figures should not be accepted as universally applicable because they will no doubt change from year to year as new Finance Acts change procedures. They also vary from place to place because some areas are designated for special development. As an example, at the time of writing, some areas in Britain are designated 'Enterprise Zones', and in an Enterprise Zone, the writing down allowance for a building is one quarter of its cost in each of the first 4 years of its life.

Example 5.7
Consider the cash flow stream generated by the purchase of an asset during the first year of its life, when tax is taken into account. Corporation tax, at present, is 52% of profits. Writing down allowance on the asset is 100% in the first year of its life.

A machine costs £10 000, it makes products which are sold for £4000 a year, the running expenses (labour costs, raw material costs, maintenance, etc.)

are £1000 a year, and the project lasts for 10 years, with no salvage at the end. The assumed discount rate is 12%.

At the beginning of the project (at the end of year 0) the company spends £10 000 to buy the machine.

During the first year (computed at the end of year 1) the company has a revenue of £4000 and expenses of £1000. Tax would normally be paid on the £3000 profit, but the writing down allowance for the purchase of the machine is £10 000. For tax purposes, then, the profit is assumed to be

$$£4000 - £1000 - £10\ 000 = -£7000$$

The tax paid on this loss will be

$$-(0.52) \times £7000 = -£3640 \ .$$

The cash flow computed at the end of year 1 will therefore be

$$£4000 - £1000 + £3640 = £6640 \ .$$

This calculation hides some complication by assuming that there is such a thing as negative tax in implying that the government pays the company instead of the company paying the government. The real situation is more complicated than this. What we have calculated is really a tax reduction and not a negative tax; but if, as is often the case, the project we are discussing is only one of many which the company has undertaken, it is probable that the company is making enough profit from other projects for the negative tax to be a genuine reduction in the amount that the company would otherwise pay. If this is not the case — if the company would not otherwise pay sufficient tax in the year to take advantage of the tax reduction — then that reduction may be held over until use may be made of it.

This does, of course, require further calculation because taking advantage of tax reduction in later years will change the present value of that reduction. Generally we will ignore these complications and assume that a company can take immediate advantage of any tax reduction.

A further complication arises because tax is not paid immediately at the end of the year in which the company makes the profit that is taxed. Tax is paid about a year after this (not less than eight months after). This again alters the timing of the cash flows so that our calculations are approximate.

Still more complication is introduced when the company pays a dividend since it becomes liable for immediate payment of Advanced Corporation Tax (based on the income tax that shareholders might be expected to pay). This does not increase the company's costs, but again it alters the timings of the cash flows and, once again, our calculations must be assumed to be approximate.

Example 5.8
Complete Example 5.7 (assuming that immediate advantage may be taken of tax allowances).

Year 0	Cash flows	= − £10 000 (cost of machine)
Year 1	Revenue	= 4 000
	Tax allowable expenses	= 1 000 (running costs)
		plus 10 000 (writing down allowance)
	Profit for tax purposes	= − 7 000
	Tax	= − 3 640

Net cash flow for the year is

Revenue − Running costs − Tax = 6 640 .

Note that the writing down allowance is not a cash flow because it is merely a book transaction and no money changes hands.

Year 2	Revenue	= 4 000
	Running costs	= 1 000
	Profit before tax	= 3 000
	Tax	= 1 560
	Net cash flow	= 1 440

Note that once the value of the assets have been completely written down they cannot again be claimed as an expense.

Years 3–10 will be as for year 2, so that the cash flow stream will be

year	£
0	− 10 000
1	6 640
2	1 440
3	1 440
4	1 440
5	1 440
6	1 440
7	1 440
8	1 440
9	1 440
10	1 440

The student may verify that, at 12%, the Present Value of this cash flow stream is £2 779.

Exercise 5.4
What is the rate of return of the cash flow stream in Example 5.8?

The student may verify that this is about 21.5%.

Notice that we have now broken new ground. What we have calculated in Exercise 5.4 is the rate of return of the project AFTER TAX.

This, of course, is what ultimately interests the investor.

Exercise 5.5

A company invests £100 000 in a machine with which it makes products which sell for £90 000 a year. The annual running costs are £30 000 a year. The life of the project is 4 years and at the end of that time the plant sells for enough money to pay for its clearance. The company also allocates £100 000 working capital to the project and maintains this as an approximately constant figure until the entire amount is withdrawn at the end of the project.

Derive the after tax cash flow stream and calculate its rate of return when corporation tax is at the rate of 50%, and the writing down allowance on plant is 100%.

The cash flow stream is

$$- £200\ 000; + £80\ 000; + £30\ 000; + £30\ 000; + £130\ 000$$

The rate of return is about 11.85%. ✓   → $NPV = 0$

Exercise 5.6

A company invests in a project which involves buying plant for £20 000 and erecting a building in which to house the plant for £30 000. Goods are sold for £40 000 a year and annual operating costs are £30 000 a year.

Tax is paid at the rate of 50%.
The plant may be written down in 1 year and the building in 4 years.
The project lasts 10 years and there is no salvage.
What is the cash flow stream and what rate of return does it yield?

The cash flow stream is

$$- £50\ 000; £18\ 750; £8\ 750; £8\ 750; £8\ 750;$$
$$£5\ 000; £5\ 000; £5\ 000; £5\ 000; £5\ 000; £5\ 000.$$

The rate of return is about 11%.

Exercise 5.7

In the following examples assume that corporation tax is 50% and plant can be written down in one year.

Calculate, in each case the after tax cash flow stream and the after tax rate of return.

	(i)	Plant costs	£20 000
		Annual revenue is	£ 8 000
		Annual running cost is	£ 3 000
		Life is	5 years
		Salvage is	zero

Cash flows are: − £20 000; £12 500; £2 500; £2 500;
                      £2 500; £2 500 ✓
Rate of return = 5.8% .✓

(ii)   *Plant costs*   £200 000
        Annual revenue   £100 000
        Annual running cost   £ 60 000
        Life   10 years

There is no salvage, but a major overhaul costs £50 000 at the end of year 5.

The cash flows are   − £200 000 in year 0
                              120 000 in year 1
                               45 000 in year 5 ~~←~~ − 5000
                               20 000 in all other years to year 10

The rate of return = 15%

*Possibly 45 k in yr 6 if refurb.
cost written down (but
already offset against
profit in year 5)*

(iii)   *Plant costs*   £25 000
        Annual revenue   £10 000
        Annual running cost   £ 5 000
        Life   8 years
        Salvage   £ 5 000

Here, the salvage at the end of 8 years will be treated as profit which will be taxed at the normal corporation tax rate.

The cash flows are (£000's):

$$-25; 15; 2.5; 2.5; 2.5; 2.5; 2.5; 2.5; 5.0$$

The rate of return = 11.25%

$$-25$$
$$+ 15/1.1125$$
$$+ 2.5/1.1125^2$$
$$\vdots$$
$$+ 5/1.1125^8$$
$$\rightarrow .053$$

(iv)   *Plant costs*   £100
        Annual revenue   £ 80
        Annual running cost   £ 40
        (All costs in thousands of pounds)
        Life   10 years

In addition we have to erect a building to house the plant. The building is written down (for tax purposes) by one tenth of its value each year.

        Building costs   £50

The cash flows are (£000's)

$$-150; 72.5; 22.5; 22.5; 22.5; 22.5; 22.5; 22.5;$$
$$22.5; 22.5; 22.5$$

The rate of return = 16.5%.

(v)   Plant costs   £100
       Annual revenue   £ 80
       Annual running cost   £ 40
       Life   10 years
       Building costs   £ 50
       Resale value of plant   0
       Resale value of building   £ 35

The building is written down by 4% of its value every year. Any excess of resale value over written down value at the end of year 10 is treated as taxable income. — *but not other revenue from sale of building.*
                              written down

Cash flow stream is (£'s)

$$-150; 71; 21; 21; 21; 21; 21; 21; 21; 21; 53.5 \quad \checkmark$$

Rate of return = 16.50%   ✓

Note that the cash flow for year 10 is obtained by:

Revenue from sale of products	= 80	
Revenue from sale of building	= 35	
		115
Written down value of building	= 30	
Write down allowance for year	= 2	
Operating costs	= 40	
		72
Taxable income	=	43
Tax	=	21.5
Net cash flow	=	53.5 ✓

(= Revenue from sale of goods +
Revenue from sale of building —
operating costs   —
tax   )

6

Cost of capital

If Charlie Brown is in business on his own account and has borrowed the necessary capital, he knows that he is interested in any project which has a positive present value at the discount rate at which he has borrowed the money. Charlie Brown is also more concerned with after tax cash flows.

The interest that Charlie pays on borrowed money is an expense which is allowed for the purposes of calculating tax.

Example 6.1
Charlie Brown borrows £1000 from the bank to help him run his business. He agrees with the bank manager that he will repay the full amount after five years and he will pay interest of 20% every year.

Charlie's cash flow stream, so far as the bank is concerned, is therefore:

$$+ £1000, - £200, - £200, - £200, - £200, - £1200 .$$

Before he raised this loan, Charlie was working with a revenue of £15 000 and running expenses of £5000 a year, before tax. Tax is at 52%. How much does the loan cost, in effect?

At the end of year 0 Charlie will have increased his capital by £1000, but this will not affect his tax.

At the end of year 1 Charlie's cash flow will be

       £15 000 revenue
  − £ 5 000 running costs
  − £   200 interest on debt

His taxable profit will therefore be £9800
His tax will be £5095
His profit after tax will be £4704

Before Charlie borrowed the money his cash flows were

	£15 000	revenue
	5 000	running costs
His profit before tax was	10 000	
His tax was	5 200	
His profit after tax was	4 800	

His profit has therefore been reduced by £96 although he is paying the bank £200 in interest charges.

Effectively, when allowance is made for tax, the loan is costing Charlie £96 a year and not £200 a year.

Effectively, when money is borrowed and the interest is a tax allowable expense, the tax adjusted cost of the money is

$$i(1 - t) \text{ where } t \text{ is the tax rate, and}$$
$$i \text{ is the interest on the debt.}$$

Considering Example 6.1, the tax adjusted cost of the debt is

$$0.2 \times (1 - 0.52) = 0.096$$
$$= 9.6\%$$

Note that, if we are using the tax adjusted cost of debt as our discount rate we are interested only in after tax cash flows.

Exercise 6.1

(i) A bank loan is offered at 18%, the company pays tax at 52%, what is the tax adjusted cost of a loan? [8.64%

(ii) Before tax interest 17%; tax rate 50%. What is the tax adjusted cost of debt? [8.5%

(iii) Before tax interest 15%; tax rate 30%. What is the tax adjusted cost of debt? [10.5%

(iv) Before tax interest 30%; tax rate 42%. What is the tax adjusted cost of debt? [17.4%

(v) Before tax interest 10%; tax rate 40%. What is the tax adjusted cost of debt? [6.0%

Because the payment of tax is about a year after making the profit on which tax is calculated, the cash flows are displaced from the times shown in the above examples. The above tax adjusted costs of debt must therefore be regarded as approximate.

Example 6.2

Plant costs	£20 000
Annual revenue is	£ 8 000
Annual running cost is	£ 3 000
Life is	5 years
Tax is at	50%

Plant is written down in one year

The project is financed with debt capital at an interest rate of 8%.

What is the present value of the project?

The after tax cash flows are (£'s)

$- 20\,000; 12\,500; 2500; 2500; 2500; 2500$

The tax adjusted cost of capital is 4%.

The present value is

$$- 20\,000 + \frac{10\,000}{1.04} + 2500\,(p/a)_5^{4\%}$$

$$= - 20\,000 + 9615 + 11\,130 = £745 \ .$$

Note that this is the problem of Exercise 5.7 (i), and if there were no tax allowance on debt interest the project would lose money. Note also that it has been assumed that sufficient profit is made from other projects to allow full advantage to be taken of the tax reduction of £10 000 in year one.

In many ways, the idea of a firm in isolation from its owners is a fiction. Nevertheless it is frequently useful to regard the firm as having an existence in its own right. We then regard the firm as an entity which is run by professional managers who raise capital to invest in worthwhile projects. There are many ways of raising capital, but these ways fall into two main classes – debt and equity.

Debt is money that has been borrowed from banks, from debenture holders, or from other sources. The lenders of the money have no interest in the company and only in exceptional circumstances do they have a say in its running. The firm and its creditors enter into agreements by which, for any loan, the interest and the repayment programme is fixed. The agreed interest and agreed repayments must be made before the firm is considered to have made a profit and, in theory, creditors take little risk when they lend money to the firm because even if little profit is made, the creditors get their interest first.

Of course, if the firm becomes bankrupt the creditors are likely to lose some of their money, but even in this case, what money there is will be repaid to creditors before shareholders are considered at all.

As we have seen, interest on debt is treated as a legitimate expense and is allowable against tax.

Equity is the money put into the firm by its owners — normally the share-holders. The shareholders hope that the projects undertaken will be so profitable that the firm will be able to distribute dividends from the profits made. As we have seen, however, profits are taxable, and only after taxes have been paid will the shareholder receive dividends. Sometimes the after tax profits are not all distributed as dividends, and some portion of those profits is retained for further internal investment. Retaining profit instead of distributing it does raise the value of the company so that, in principle, the value of the owner's shares will be increased.

Unlike creditors, shareholders may have a voice in the running of the company (if only through the annual shareholders' meeting) but there are several different sorts of shareholder. Two major sorts of shares are preference shares and ordinary shares. Generally the preference shareholders receive a lower dividend (often a fixed dividend year after year) than ordinary shareholders but are paid first out of any profits. We thus have different levels of risk taken by the creditors, the preference shareholders, and the ordinary shareholders. Least risk is taken by the creditors, and most risk is taken by ordinary shareholders.

Example 6.3

XY Ltd estimate that during next year

their sales revenue will be	£5 000 000
their operating costs will be	3 000 000
and depreciation will be	200 000

although all plant has been written off for tax purposes. Tax is at 52%.

Capital has been raised through 5 000 000 ordinary shares

1 000 000, 6%, £1 preference shares

and a   £3 000 000 debt at 10%.

Usually the company distributes, as dividend, about 60% of its earnings per ordinary share.

Operating revenues	5 000 000
Operating costs	3 000 000
Interest on debt	300 000
Taxable income	1 700 000
Tax	884 000
Income after tax	816 000
Subtract depreciation (To avoid distributing capital as well as earnings)	200 000
	616 000

Dividends to preference shareholders	60 000
	556 000
60% to be distributed to ordinary shareholders	333 600
Retained earnings	222 400

Note that if the £333 600 is distributed to shareholders, they will receive approximately 7p per share.

If we adjust the distribution to be an exact 7% per share, we distribute £350 000, and the retained earnings are £206 000.

Note that because the depreciation was not a cash flow (but merely a book transaction), the amount available for investment in new projects has increased by £206 000 + £200 000 = £406 000.

Note also that the equity has increased by £206 000. This means that the value of what the shareholders own has increased by £206 000. This is because although the plant has reduced in value by £200 000, £406 000 is retained in the business. In theory, the value of the ordinary shares will go up because the ordinary shareholders now own more, but the reasons for share prices rising or falling are manifold.

One reason for a share being valued is that the buyer of a share will know what is a reasonable, competitive return for his investment. If a dividend is 7½p and the buyer of a share expects 12% on his investment he could argue that he will be willing to pay 7.5/0.12 = 62.5p for a £1 share.

The above example is intended to show how the creditor takes less risk than the shareholder, and the fixed dividend shareholder takes less risk than the ordinary shareholder. Also, it shows the way in which debt interest is subtracted before calculating tax and dividends are subtracted after paying tax.

Real accounts would be more complicated because they would show deferred tax (which arises because depreciation is not the write down for tax purposes), advance corporation tax (which avoids double taxation for the shareholder) and timing.

Because capital is usually a mixture of debt and equity, we need to calculate the weighted average cost of capital.

Example 6.4

A project requires a capital investment of £100. £40 is borrowed from the bank at 17%, and 60% is put in by shareholders who expect 12% return on investment. What is the average cost of the capital? Tax is at 50%.

The bank will require an interest payment each year of

$$£40 \times 0.17 = £6.8$$

but because this interest is tax allowable, the true cost to the company will be

$$6.8 \times (1 - 0.5) = £3.4$$

The shareholder will expect a return of £60 × 0.12 = £7.2.

The total (tax adjusted) sum paid each year for the £100 capital is therefore £10.6. If £100 of capital costs £10.6 a year, the average cost is 10.6%.

Generally, if we require £C of capital investment for a project which we raise through £D of debt and £E of equity

$$C = D + E \; .$$

If the interest on debt is I_D, the shareholder expects a return of I_E on his investment and the tax rate is T then

the tax adjusted cost of debt $= I_D(1 - T)D$
the cost of equity $= I_E.E$
the total cost of the capital $= I_D(1 - T)D + I_E.E$

the average cost of capital $= \dfrac{I_D(1 - T)D + I_E.E}{C}$ per pound

$$= \frac{I_D(1 - T)D + I_E(C - D)}{C}$$

$$= I_D(1 - T)\frac{D}{C} + I_E(1 - \frac{D}{C}) \; .$$

If we write $D/C = R_D$, called the debt ratio, then the average cost of capital

$$= I_D(1 - T)R_D + I_E(1 - R_D)$$

Exercise 6.2
Calculate the weighted, average tax adjusted cost of capital in the following cases.

	R_D	I_E	I_D	T	
(i)	0.4	0.15	0.075	0	[0.12
(ii)	0.0	0.12	0.06	0.6	[0.12
(iii)	0.625	0.16	0.08	0.6	[0.08
(iv)	0.25	0.12	0.08	0.5	[0.10
(v)	0.30	0.20	0.17	0.52	[0.16448

It is worth observing that there is an approximate limit to the debt ratio. If the debt ratio is large, the creditors are providing a large proportion of the capital and are therefore taking much of the risk. Creditors who observe that they will take a risk by lending money to a company will either increase their

* Assumes both debt + equity repaid at similar rates. - See Solns to Exerc. 6.4

interest rate or refuse to lend money. The value of the debt ratio will depend on the type of business that is being financed, but typically will be about a third or a half.

One way of looking at the manager's job, then, is that he is borrowing money on behalf of the projects he initiates. The cost of the money is the tax adjusted, weighted average cost of capital, and so the projects must show positive present values at a discount rate which is that cost of capital. To use this discount rate does, of course, assume that cash flows are calculated after tax.

Example 6.5

A company operates with a debt ratio of 30%. Interest on debt is 10% and shareholders expect a return of 15% on equity. Corporation tax is at the rate of 50%.

How desirable for the company is the following project?

Invest in plant costing £100 000 and which may be written down for tax in its 1st year.

Invest in buildings costing £60 000 which may be written down in 4 years.

The revenue from products is £60 000 in a year and annual operating costs (material, labour and other annual costs) are £40 000.

The project will last 10 years at the end of which the plant and buildings will not be salvaged.

At the end of year 0 the cash flow will be		
£100 000 + £60 000		= £160 000
At the end of year 1 the revenue will be	60 000	
Operating expenses will be	40 000	
Allowable write down will be 100 000		for plant
15 000		for buildings
therefore taxable income will be	− 95 000	
tax will be	− 47 500	
therefore cash flow after tax will be		67 500
In years 2, 3, and 4 the revenue will be	60 000	
Operating expenses will be 40 000		
Allowable write down will be 15 000		
taxable income will be	5 000	
tax will be	2 500	
therefore cash flow after tax will be		17 500
In years 5 to 10 revenue will be	60 000	
Operating expenses will be 40 000		
There will be no further write down		
so that taxable income will be	20 000	
tax will be	10 000	
therefore cash flow after tax will be		10 000

The cash flows will therefore be $-£160\,000$; £67 500; £17 500; £17 500; £17 500; £10 000; £10 000; £10 000; £10 000; £10 000 and £10 000 at ends of years 0 to 10 respectively.

The tax adjusted cost of capital is

$$(0.3)\,(0.10)\,(0.5) + (0.7)\,(0.15) = 0.015 + 0.105 = 0.12 \quad .$$

At this discount factor, the student may confirm that the after tax cash flows give a present value of $-£36\,074$. The project is not, therefore, worthwhile.

The student may also confirm that the project has a rate of return of slightly more than 3%.

Example 6.6

Repeat the calculations of Example 6.5 to determine the revenue required in every year if the project is to have a rate of return of 12%.

With the cash flows determined in Example 6.6, the present value at 12% was $-£36\,074$.

To give a present value of zero we have to have an additional $£R$ of revenue after tax, each year where

$$R \times (\text{p/a})^{0.12}_{10} = 36\,074$$

i.e. $R = 36\,074/5.65$
                  $= 6\,385 \quad .$

Since this is an after tax revenue, the before tax revenue must be £12 770.

Exercise 6.3

A company has raised capital, $\frac{2}{7}$ of which is debt at 12½% interest and $\frac{5}{7}$ of which is equity. Shareholders expect a return of 20% on their investment. Tax is at 52%.

A project involves investing in plant costing £250 000 (which may be written down in one year, or as soon as profits permit) and in buildings costing £100 000 (which will be written down at £4000 a year).

Revenue from sales of the products made is £114 000 a year, while annual running costs (for labour, materials, etc.) are £20 000 a year. Working capital is maintained approximately constant at £50 000 throughout the project.

The company has no other projects in hand.

The project will last 25 years at the end of which salvage prices will exactly pay for site clearance. Ignore the timing of tax payments (assume that they are paid when the profits which generate them are earned).

(i) How may the value of the plant be written down?

At end year 0, the cash flow will be	− £400 000
At end year 1, the revenue will be	£114 000
the cash costs will be	£ 20 000
so that the before tax cash flow will be	£ 94 000
We may write down, for buildings	4 000
leaving	90 000

Now if we write down the whole of the cost of the plant, we will not in fact be able to take advantage of the tax allowance because we would have a taxable project cash flow (loss) of

− £160 000

As negative tax is not paid to the company, but carried forward, there is no point in writing down the plant by more than £90 000, leaving a taxable profit of

0

Clearly, this situation will exist for the second year.

In the third year we will have a revenue of	£114 000
cash costs of	20 000
buildings' write down of	4 000
leaving	90 000

As our plant has already been written down to £70 000 (£250 000 − £90 000 − £90 000) we have a permissible plant write down of

70 000

leaving a taxable profit of	20 000
tax is	10 400
so that the cash flow after tax is	9 600
plus plant and building write down of	74 000
i.e.	83 600

When plant has been written down we have, in each year

Revenue	£114 000
cash costs	20 000
building write down	4 000
taxable profit	90 000
tax	46 800
profit after tax	43 200
(add write down)	4 000
Cash flow after tax	47 200

(ii) What are the after tax cash flows during the life of project?

end year 0	− £250 000	plant
	− £100 000	building
	− £ 50 000	working capital
	− £400 000	
end year 1	£ 94 000	
end year 2	94 000	
end year 3	83 600	
end year 4	47 200	
end year 5	47 200	
. . . .		
. . . .		
end year 25	47 200	
	+ 50 000	(working capital)
	97 200	

(iii) What is the tax adjusted, weighted average cost of capital?

$$\frac{2}{7} (0.125) (1 - 0.52) + \frac{5}{7} (0.2)$$

$$= \frac{1.12}{7} = 0.16$$

(iv) What is the present value of the project?
In thousands of pounds, PV

$$= -400 + 47.2 \,(p/a)_{25}^{0.16} + 50(p/f)_{25}^{0.16}$$

$$+ 36.4 \,(p/a)_{3}^{0.16} + 10.4(p/a)_{2}^{0.16}$$

$$= -400 + 47.2(6.097) + 50(0.024)$$
$$+ 36.4(2.246) + 10.4(1.605)$$

$$= -12.575$$

or − £12 575 .

(v) What rate of return does the cash flow stream give?
Clearly the rate of return is less than 16% (from *(iv)*).
What is the Present Value at 10% discount rate?

$$-400 + 47.2(p/a)_{25}^{0.1} + 50(p/f)_{25}^{0.1}$$
$$+ 36.4(p/a)_{3}^{0.1} + 10.4(p/a)_{2}^{0.1}$$
$$= -400 + 47.2(9.077) + 50(0.092)$$
$$+ 36.4(2.487) + 10.4(1.736)$$
$$= 141.616$$

What is the present value at 14% discount rate?

$$-400 + 47.2(6.873) + 50(0.038)$$
$$+ 36.4(2.322) + 10.4(1.647)$$
$$= 27.955$$

What is the present value at 15% discount rate?

$$-400 + 47.2(6.464) + 50(0.030)$$
$$+ 36.4(2.283) + 10.4(1.6.26)$$
$$= 6.612$$

To an acceptable accuracy, the rate of return is 15%.

(vi) *What rate of return will shareholders get if other factors are unaltered?*
The tax adjusted, weighted average cost of capital is 15%.

therefore $\dfrac{2}{7}(0.125)(0.48) + \dfrac{5}{7}(i_e) = 0.15$

therefore $0.12 + 5\,i_e$	$= 1.05$
i_e	$= 0.186$
	$= 18.6\%$

(instead of the 20% expected)

Exercise 6.4

A project involves investing in plant costing £1M and buildings costing £0.5M. It is also necessary to start with working capital of £0.8M. Working capital remains approximately constant throughout the life of the project and is withdrawn, entire, at the end. Plant may be written down in one year and buildings in four years. Tax is at 52%. The project lasts ten years at the end of which the salvage just pays for site clearance. Annual revenue exceeds annual running costs by £0.625M a year. A quarter of the capital is debt at an interest of 10%, and shareholders hope to get a return of 18.4% on their investment.

Will the shareholders get their hoped-for return?

[Just. The tax adjusted, weighted average cost of capital is 15% giving a present
value of £0.0411M.

A note on the effect of timing on the cost of debt

Suppose a company making a profit before tax of £5000 a year borrows £10 000 at 10% for 10 years. Suppose also that tax is at 50%.

We have assumed that, because the interest on debt is tax allowable, the true cost is $i_d(1 - t)$ which in this case would be $(0.1)(1 - 0.5) = 0.05 = 5\%$.

Suppose, however, that tax on profits is paid one year after the profits are earned. In this case the cash flows would be

At end year 0, £1000 will be added to the after tax cash flow (this is the loan principal)

At end year 1, −£100 will be added to the cash flow stream (this is the loan interest)

At end year 2, −£100 will be added to the cash flow stream (loan interest) plus £50 (the tax reduction for year 1, paid in year 2)

. . . .

At end year 10, −£100 will be added to the cash flow stream (loan interest); −£1000 will be added (loan repayment); £50 will be added (tax reduction for year 9)

At end year 11, £50 will be added to the cash flow stream (tax reduction for year 10).

The cash flow stream generated by the loan will thus be (£'s)

$$+ 1000; -100; -50; -50; -50; -50; -50; -50; -50; -50; - 1050; + 50$$

At 5% interest, the present value of this cash flow is

$$1000 - 50(p/f)_1^{0.05} - 50(p/a)_{10}^{0.05} - 1000(p/f)_{10}^{0.05} + 50(p/f)_{11}^{0.05}$$

$$= 1000 - 50(0.952) - 50(7.722) - 1000(0.614) + 50(0.585)$$

$$= - 18.45$$

At 6% interest the present value of this cash flow is

$$1000 - 50(0.943) - 50(7.360) - 1000(0.558) + 50(0.527)$$

$$= 53.2$$

Linear interpolation between 5% and 6% gives an effective interest rate of 5.26%.

We see that our ignoring of the timing of tax payments has, in fact, introduced a slight error into our calculations.

7

Inflation

We have considered the values of projects in some cases by calculating their present values at what we believe to be the cost of capital and, in other cases, by determining their rates of return.

History shows that, if we are able to allow for the falling value of money, the growth in real purchasing power that has been provided by an investment is usually less than 5%. And yet we have considered discount rates of twenty or thirty per cent.

The reason for this is that for many years we have been living with inflation; that is, the value of money has been falling year by year. The use of high discount rates is an attempt to allow for the fall in the purchasing power of money.

Consider a time of inflation. At the end of year 0 we have £100 which will buy a shopping basket of mixed goods.

If we wish to buy those same goods at the end of year 1 we will require £$(100 + Y)$, and Y is the percentage rate of inflation.

Alternatively, we may argue that, if we keep our £100 and spend it at the end of year 1, it will buy the goods that we could buy today for £$(100 - R)$. R is the percentage decline in purchasing power.

If we have £100 now, we need £$(100 + Y)$ in one year's time, to buy the same goods.

If we have £$(100 - R)$ now, we need £100 in one year's time to buy the same goods.

If we write $y = Y/100$, i.e. we treat inflation as a decimal rather than as a per cent

and $r = R/100$,

$$\text{we have } \frac{100 + Y}{100} = \frac{100}{100 - R}$$

$$\text{or } 1 + y = \frac{1}{1 - r}$$

$$\text{therefore } y = \frac{r}{1-r}$$

$$\text{or } r = \frac{y}{1+y} \ .$$

Exercise 7.1
If the purchasing power of the pound declines by (i) 5%; (ii) 10%; (iii) 15%; (iv) 20%; (v) 25%, what are the corresponding rates of inflation?

[(i) 5.263%; (ii) 11.111%; (iii) 17.647%; (iv) 25%; (v) 33.333%]

If the rate of inflation is
(i) 5%; (ii) 10%; (iii) 15%; (iv) 20%; (v) 25%
what are the corresponding falls in purchasing power?

[(i) 4.762%; (ii) 9.091%; (iii) 13.043%; (iv) 16.667%; (v) 20%]

Now if we invest in a project, it is usually in the hope of being able to take out more than we put in.

If $Y\%$ is the rate of inflation and we invest £100 at $Y\%$ for one year, we are able to withdraw £$(100 + Y)$ at the end of that year. While this may be some sort of hedge against inflation we have really gained nothing. Provided the goods that we intended to buy were not perishable, we could have bought them at the beginning of the year and not bothered to invest the money.

If we invest the £100 at less than $Y\%$ we are effectively worse off at the end of the year because we will be able to buy less at the end of the year than we could have done at the beginning.

What we need from a project is to increase our purchasing power.

Example 7.1
Alphonse wishes to invest £100 so that he will be 10% better off in one year's time. He knows that inflation is running at 15%. How much money will he need in one year to be able to buy 10% more goods?

Alphonse invests £100 now.

If he receives back £115 in a year's time he will have only the same purchasing power as now.

As he wants 10% more purchasing power he will need £(115×1.1) back in a year's time.

He will therefore require £126.5 back. Alphonse will therefore look for an interest of 26.5%.

In general, if i_s is the interest that we would require in a period of no inflation, we require to increase our purchasing power from £1 to £$(1 + i_s)$ in one year.

If, however, we have inflation of y, we need to increase our money from £1 to £$(1 + y)$ to have the same purchasing power. To increase our purchasing power we must therefore invest £1 to obtain £$(1+y)(1+i_s)$ in one year.

If i_a is the apparent interest rate in a time of inflation, then,

£1 becomes £$(1 + i_a)$ in a year so that

$$1 + i_a = (1 + y)(1 + i_s)$$

or $\qquad i_a = (1 + y)(1 + i_s) - 1 \quad .$

Exercises 7.2

(i) What apparent rate of return must we seek if inflation, Y, is at 12% and we require a true interest, I_s, (as measured without inflation) of 5%?   [17.6%

	(ii)	(iii)	(iv)	(v)	(vi)
Y	5%	10%	15%	20%	25%
I_s	5%	4%	6%	10%	5%

[10.25%; 14.4%; 21.9%; 32%; 31.25%

Note that we require a slightly higher rate of return than we would obtain by adding inflation to the required increase of purchasing power.

8

Pay back period

A simple method of assessing a project is by its pay back period.

Example 8.1

Alphonse is considering a project which involves buying a machine for £1000. He estimates that with this machine he can make goods which will sell for £600 a year while the annual cost of making those goods (raw material, labour and other annual cash costs) will be £200.

Alphonse does not know how long the project will last but he predicts, confidently, that his estimates will hold for at least the next four years.

Alphonse could argue that he will have a project with cash flows of

$$-£1000; £400; £400; £400; £400 \text{ for years 0 to 4, and}$$

with unkown (but probably not negative) cash flows thereafter.

The rate of return of this project will not be worse than i where

$$1000 = 400 \times (p/a)_4^i$$
$$\text{i.e. } i = 0.22 \text{ or } 22\% .$$

Where the figures are predicted and it is thought that there may be some error in the prediction, we may use crude yardsticks for measuring the usefulness of a project.

One such method is pay-back period.

Alphonse can argue that his investment of £1000 will be repaid in less than 3 years (2½ years if revenues are at a regular rate through the year).

The simple method of determining the pay back period is to accumulate the cash flows, year by year, to determine when the accumulated cash flow first becomes positive.

In Alphonse's case we have:

	Cash flow in year	Sum of cash flows to year end
End year 0	−£1000	−£1000
End year 1	£ 400	−£ 600
End year 2	£ 400	−£ 200
End year 3	£ 400	+£ 200
End year 4	£ 400	+£ 600

We see that the accumulated cash flows become positive between the ends of years 2 and 3.

After 2½ years, any money coming in will be profit.

Exercise 8.1

What are the pay back periods of the projects represented by the following cash flow streams?

(i)	−£1000; +£500; +£500; +£500; +£500	[2 years
(ii)	−£1000; +£600; +£400; +£300; +£100	[2 years
(iii)	−£1000; +£400; +£600; +£800; +£1000	[2 years
(iv)	−£1M; −£1M; +£0.37M; +£0.5M; +£0.6M; +£0.7M; +£0.8M	
		[nearly 5 years
(v)	−£10 000; +£10 000; +£1000	[1 year
(vi)	−£10 000; +£1000; +£9000; +£30 000	[2 years
(vii)	−£10 000; +£1000; +£9000; +£1000	[2 years
(viii)	−£10 000; +£3000; +£3000; +£3000; +£3000; +£3000; +£3000	
	+£3000	[over 3 years but less than 4
(ix)	−£100 000; +£80 000; +£10 000; +£10 000; +£10 000	[3 years
(x)	−£100 000; +£25 000; +£25 000; +£25 000 .... for ever	
		[4 years

Now it is clear that judging a project by its pay back period is crude. By this criterion both (i) and (ii) above are of equal merit although (i) has a rate of return of 35% and (ii) has a rate of return of 20%. Exercise 8.1 (v) actually has the best (shortest) pay back period although its rate of return is 9¼%.

It would be simple to create a project with a short pay back period but which is not worth undertaking at all, for example,

−£1000; +£1000; −£200.

This has a pay back of one year but results in a loss over its life.

Exercise 8.2

The student should calculate the rates of return for the projects in Exercise 8.1.

How does the ranking of projects by their rates of return compare with the calculated pay back periods?

The disadvantages of using pay back period to judge a project are that:

(i)   it may make a bad project (as judged by rate of return or present value) seem better than it really is,

(ii) it may make a good project seem worse than it really is, and

(iii) it ignores the time value of money.

Exercise 8.3
Give examples of projects, defined by their cash flow streams which exemplify the three disadvantages of pay back period that are listed above.

The advantages of using pay back period to judge a project are that:

(i)   it is quick and easy, and
(ii) it can be safe.

It may seem paradoxical to argue that the use of pay back period may make a bad project seem good, while, at the same time, suggesting that it can be a safe criterion.

In fact, provided we recognise the quick and easy (quick and dirty?) nature of pay back period as a criterion, it can be very safe.

Using any method of judging a project requires a prediction of cash flows, and the cash flows for several years hence can be predicted only approximately. If a project is to last 10 years, we may be able to predict the costs involved for the first year or two, but later costs (or revenues) will be predicted with decreasing accuracy. Before the tenth (or even third of fourth) year of the project, the price of oil, the cost of labour, competition, government support, etc. may have changed in a way that could not be predicted.

Generally the pay back period below which a project is acceptable is quite short. A maximum pay back period of three years is typical for project acceptance, and in times of high cost of capital or depression, an acceptable pay back period may be as low as 18 months.

Usually, then, if we use pay back period as a criterion we do not stretch our powers of prediction as far as if we use rate of return or present value. We are expected to predict that once the project has paid for itself, the cash flows will be positive, but this is an easier judgement to make than would be the precise predictions of cash flows required for discounting calculations.

Again, if we appreciate the quick and easy nature of pay back calculations, we will not complain that they ignore the time value of money. Pay back period is a coarse filter. We will accept a project with a short pay back period if subsequent positive cash flows are likely to be large enough for us to believe that the time value of those cash flows will not alter the calculation by enough to turn a good project into a bad one. We will adjust our pay back period and our ideas of subsequent cash flows to such figures that marginal projects will be rejected anyway.

Exercise 8.4
Give examples of projects which may have failed because they required long lives to pay for themselves and their futures were not accurately predicted.
Discuss possible causes of failure of the projects you list.

What happened to the Concorde? Was it late going into production? Was its development cost predicted accurately? Did the cost of oil change between the initiation of the project and the offer of aeroplanes for sale? Was the market for the aeroplane as big as had been predicted?

What happened to Advanced Gas Cooled Reactors?

What factors will affect the profitability of the Humber Bridge?

Would you pay money to electrify Britain's railways?

If taxpayers were asked to support British Leyland, how accurately could the rate of return on the investment be predicted?

In the cases that you have listed and discussed, could the calculation of pay back period be a useful exercise? Would it have been possible to predict cash flows with sufficient accuracy to calculate believable rates of return?

9

Comparing present values and rates of return

We have seen that, although payback period is reasonably used as a criterion by which to judge a project, it does not necessarily accept a project with an acceptable rate of return nor reject a project with a poor rate of return.

This begs the question, 'would a project with an acceptable rate of return necessarily have a positive present value?'

Usually the answer to this question is 'Yes'. Consider the following example.

Example 9.1
A project has the following cash flows. Plot its present value against discount rate and hence find its rate of return.

Invest £250 000 at end of year 0.
Receive £70 000 at the ends of years 1–6
Receive £100 000 salvage at the end of year 6
We may calculate the present values of this project as

$$£270 000 \text{ at } I = 0\%$$
$$£179 920 \text{ at } I = 5\%$$
$$£111 316 \text{ at } I = 10\%$$
$$£ 58 147 \text{ at } I = 15\%$$
$$£ 16 276 \text{ at } I = 20\%$$
$$- £ 17 186 \text{ at } I = 25\%$$
$$- £ 31 429 \text{ at } I = 30\% \quad .$$

These values are plotted on Fig. 9.1, and we see that the rate of return is 22.3% (where the curve intercepts the horizontal axis).

In general we would use the present value criterion if we are borrowing money. We would use rate of return as a criterion if we are investing money.

When investing money we would choose a project with a greater rate of return than available external projects.

When we borrow money we do it at whatever is the cost of capital.

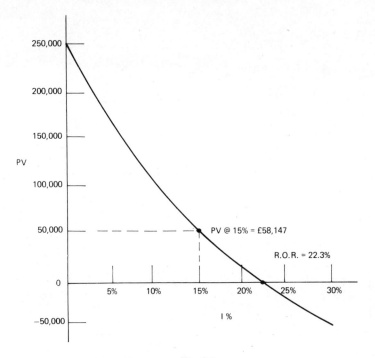

Fig. 9.1

If we believe that borrowing or investing money will be done at the same interest rate then Fig. 9.1 shows that if the rate of return is acceptable (i.e. above the going interest rate) then the present value will be positive at the going interest rate.

If the going interest rate is 15%, we see on Fig. 9.1 that the rate of return is greater than 15% and also the present value at 15% is positive.

Exercise 9.1

Plot the curve of present value against discount rate for the following cash flow streams.

(i)   − £250 000; £70 000; £70 000; £70 000; £70 000; £170 000
(ii)   − £1000; £400; £600; £800; £1000
(iii)   − £1000; £600; £400; £300; £100
(iv)   − £1000; £500; £550; £500; £550
(v)   − £1000; £100; £500; £800; £1100

(ii), (iii), (iv), and (v) are shown plotted on Fig. 9.2.

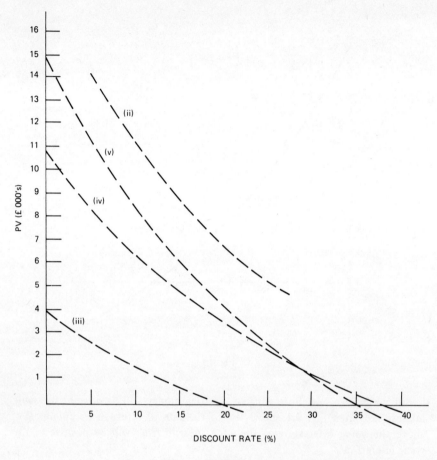

Fig. 9.2

We see that, in each case, at any discount rate lower than the rate of return, the present value is positive.

In all these cases, a project that is acceptable because it has a high rate of return would also be acceptable because it has a positive present value at any discount rate below the rate of return.

(Note that in Chapter 10 we will discover projects for which this would not be true.)

Ranking Projects

We have seen that in many cases, if the present value criterion suggests that a project is a good one, then so will the rate of return criterion. We have now to ask ourselves the question,

'Is one project better than another?'

Example 9.2

Bertram has £1000 which he wishes to invest in projects of his own.

Project A requires an immediate investment of £1000 and returns £500 at the end of each year 1, 2, 3, and 4. (The cash flow stream is − £1000; £500; £500; £500; £500.)

Project B also requires an immediate investment of £1000 and returns £100, £500, £500, and £1100 at the ends of years 1, 2, 3, and 4.

Bertram's immediate observation is that project A has a pay back period of 2 years while project B takes nearly three years to pay off his investment.

His second observation is that in the case of Project A, he invests £1000 to get back £2000, while with project B, for the same investment he gets back £2200.

Bertram eventually rejects both of these methods of judging between the projects.

What reasons might he have for rejecting both of these methods? (There would be some justification for using pay back period if he is not sure of the accuracy of his predictions of cash flows in year 4. There is no reason at all for looking at the total accumulated cash flow over the life of the project.)

Bertram decides to determine the rate of return of each project. He plots the graph of present value versus discount rate for each project and obtains Fig. 9.3.

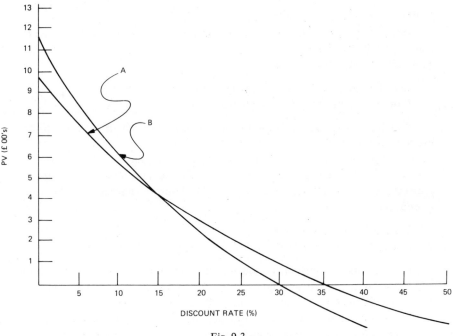

Fig. 9.3

This shows him that project A has a rate of return of 35% while project B has a rate of return of just over 29%.

Because Bertram has £1000 to invest, he can choose only one of the projects and, reasonably, he chooses A because it has a better rate of return. Effectively he is lending £1000 to project A at a better rate of interest than he would get by lending the money to project B.

Example 9.3

Cuthbert finds that he has two projects available from which to select one. By coincidence these two projects have exactly the same cash flows as those from which Bertram had to choose. That is:

Project A: − £1000; £500; £500; £500; £500 and
Project B: − £1000; £100; £500; £500; £1100.

The difference between Bertram and Cuthbert is that Cuthbert intends to borrow the money and finds that he can borrow at an interest of 10%. Cuthbert therefore determines which project has the greater present value at a discount rate of 10%. By studying Fig. 9.3, Cuthbert observes that, at a discount rate of 10%,

Project A has a present value of £585 and
Project B has a present value of £631.

Cuthbert therefore chooses project B.

He borrows £1631, he invests £1000 in project B, and has a holiday on the continent with the other £631. At the end of four years, the project will have paid back the whole of the £1631.

Bertram, using rate of return, thought A was better than B.
Cuthbert, using present value, thought B was better than A.

Clearly, if we wish to choose between two projects (or if we wish to rank many projects in order of desirability) we will not necessarily get the same answer using rate of return as we would using present value.

But why compare projects? Bertram had an obvious reason for comparing projects. He had £1000 to invest and could choose one project or the other, but not both.

Bertram's capital was rationed.
(Capital rationing is a term used to describe Bertram's problem.)

Cuthbert had no obvious reason for choosing only one project. If he could really borrow money at any interest less than about 25%, he could undertake both projects and both would give him positive present values.

There could have been reasons for Cuthbert selecting only one project.
Perhaps his bank manager would lend him no more than £1000.

Perhaps Cuthbert borrowed the money from a building society by increasing the mortgage on his house and was limited by its valuation.

Perhaps the management of either project required Cuthbert's presence and he could find time to manage one or the other (in other words, his resources were limited although he could have borrowed more money).

Perhaps choosing B prevented the choice of A. For example, A and B may have been two alternative ways of doing the same thing. Perhaps A and B were alternative machines to make products to meet the same market.

Exercise 9.2
List families of projects which are mutually exclusive.

Possible examples are:
  (i)   a channel bridge and a channel tunnel;
  (ii) a toy assembly line manned by girls using small hand tools and cheap fixtures and an expensive, highly automated, toy assembly line with almost no manual operations;
  (iii) a milk round using a petrol driven milk float and the same milk round using a battery powered milk float;
  (iv) . . . .
  (v)   . . . .

Exercise 9.3
Postulate two projects, A and B, such that A has a better present value than B at a discount rate of 12%, but B has a higher rate of return.

10

Ranking projects and rates of return

MANDATORY PROJECTS

In some cases we have to undertake a project, whether we wish to or not. For example, if we buy and install a new machine we will have to provide guards on any exposed belts, gears, or shafts so that there is no danger to the operator or to a passer by.

If we set up a plating shop we will have to install means of disposing of poisonous liquids.

A power station would be required to have plant to cool effluent water before it is discharged into a river.

A chemical works would be required to discharge its gases at sufficient height for them not to be a nuisance.

The student will think of many projects of this nature which we will be required to undertake, whether they are profitable or not.

Usually such projects will lose money.

Exercise 10.1
List a number of projects which could be mandatory although unprofitable.

MUTUALLY EXCLUSIVE PROJECTS

We have already discussed (in Chapter 9) the possibility that projects may be mutually exclusive. If two projects, A and B, are mutually exclusive then selecting A means that B will not be wanted and vice versa. This does not mean that we have insufficient resources to select both projects; it means that the selection of one project actually makes the other undesirable.

Exercise 10.2
List a number of groups of projects which are mutually exclusive.

(i)   The Humber Bridge and the Humber Ferry

(ii) Oil fired central heating, gas fired central heating, and coal fired central heating

(iii) A pedestrian bridge across a main road and a crossing controlled by traffic lights

(iv) . . . .

(v)   . . . .

Very often projects are both mandatory and mutually exclusive. Treating factory effluent, for example, may be mandatory, and there may be several plants which will do the job. We would, however, choose only one from those capable of doing the job.

We may have to choose a project from a number capable of doing the job when every one of the projects is a loser.

CAPITAL RATIONING

If we are using rate of return to judge projects that are available, we are in the position of having money to invest. The amount of money that we have to invest will limit the number of projects that we can choose.

All the above situations mean that we must compare one project with another to determine which is the better for our purposes.

Example 10.1

Alan has £100, and there are a number of projects in which he may invest. The projects are independent of one another.

Project A has the cash flow stream

$$- £100; + £15; + £15; + £15; + £110$$

Project B has the cash flow stream

$$- £80; + £12; + £12; + £12; + £80$$

Project C has the cash flow stream

$$- £20; + £5; + £5; + £5; + £25$$

Project D has the cash flow stream

$$- £75; + £15; + £15; + £15; + £90 \ .$$

Any money that Alan does not use on one or other of these projects will be deposited in his building society account where it will earn 10% interest.

The combinations available to Alan may be listed:

(i)   He could invest in A
(ii)   He could invest in B ⎤   remaining cash would
(iii)   He could invest in C ⎬   earn 10% in building
(iv)   He could invest in D ⎦   society account
(v)   He could invest in B+C
(vi)   He could invest in C+D with remaining cash earning 10%

Choice (i) gives a rate of return on his £100 of 14%
Choice (ii) means investing £80 in B and £20 in the building society.

Putting the building society investment on to a four year basis to simplify calculations, it will give a cash flow stream of

$$- £20; \ £2; \ £2; \ £2; \ £22$$

The net cash flow stream from choice (ii) is thus

$$- £100; \ £14; \ £14; \ £14; \ £102$$

which gives a rate of return of 11½%.
Choice (iii) would give a net cash flow stream of

$$- £100; \ £13; \ £13; \ £13; \ £113$$

which gives a rate of return of 13%.
Choice (iv) has a cash flow stream of

$$- £100; \ £17.5; \ £17.5; \ £17.5; \ £117.5$$

which gives a rate of return of £17.5%.
Choice (v) has a cash flow stream of

$$- £100; \ £17; \ £17; \ £17; \ £105$$

which gives a rate of return of 14.75%.
Choice (vi) has a cash flow stream of

$$- £100; \ £20.5; \ £20.5; \ £20.5; \ £10.5$$

which gives a rate of return of 20.5%.

Clearly choice (vi) is the best way for Alan to invest his £100.

In the above solution, no short cuts have been taken, but it was obviously unnecessary to do quite so much work to determine that choice (vi) is best. For example, choice (v) is dominated by choice (iv) and could be eliminated without any significant calculating effort.

Exercise 10.3
Repeat Example 10.1 but attempt to reduce the amount of calculation required to obtain the solution.

CUT OFF RATE OF RETURN

Alan's problem suggests that when a company has money to invest, internal projects are not the only ones available. There is almost always a way of investing money externally, which is usually of low risk (and therefore of fairly low return) and from which money may be withdrawn to invest in good, internal projects if they become available.

We saw this in Example 10.1 in which Alan could always invest money in his building society at 10%. This means that, if any project offering less than 10% return were offered to him, he would reject it.

As far as Alan was concerned, 10% was a cut-off rate of return.

INCREMENTAL INVESTMENT

Sometimes it is convenient to consider the extra return from an extra investment. Consider a situation in which we are already embarked on a project but further investment will possibly improve the return from that project.

Example 10.2

Ben runs a workshop in which he has a mill. The mill has been completely written down but continues to do work which brings in an income (revenue less cash operating costs) of £5000 a year. Ben has been offered a microcomputer attachment which will enable him to take on more complex machining. The attachment costs £10 000 to buy, will cost £500 a year to maintain, but even allowing for this cost the mill will be capable of bringing in an income of £7 500 a year. Should Ben buy the attachment? Ben foresees work for his mill for 5 years. After that the attachment is likely to be obsolete and will fetch no money in salvage. If project A is doing nothing and project B is buying the attachment the cash flows are,

A: £5000; £5000; £5000; £5000; £5000; £5000
B: (£5000 − £10 000); £7500; £7500; £7500; £7500; £7500

These two projects are mutually exclusive because Ben cannot both buy and not buy the attachment. We cannot calculate and compare the rates of return of the two projects because, having completely written down the cost of the mill, project A has only positive cash flows and will show an infinite rate of return. B will have a high, but finite rate of return and by this method, A will be the better project. We overcome this problem by discussing the extra cash flow generated by the extra investment. Our choices are then,

X: do nothing, in which case nothing changes, or
Y: invest £10 000, in which case we increase our present cash flows by £2500

Project Y is really Project (B–A) and has the cash flow stream

− £10 000; £2500; £2500; £2500; £2500; £2500 .

The rate of return of this project is 8%. Ben now knows that the extra investment will bring in 8%. Today, this is probably not enough to justify Ben's buying the attachment for his mill. This extra £10 000 could be invested, more profitably, in a building society or a deposit account (at the time of writing, banks and local authorities are offering well over 10% return on investment).

Example 10.3
Cyril has been left a house in an aunt's will. He has two options:

(a) sell the house as it is for £30 000,
(b) let the house for £3600 a year having first modernised it at a cost of £6000.

Once again, these two projects are mutually exclusive because Cyril cannot both sell the house and let it.

Again, if we consider the projects separately, A gives £30 000 for no effort or expense, and clearly rate of return is meaningless in this case.

B involves an investment of £6000 for a return of £3600 a year for ever and also seems very good, but in taking up B, Cyril gives up the opportunity of having an immediate £30 000.

Cyril must ask himself what is the rate of return generated by the investment implied by choosing B.

Cyril therefore considers the project B–A. Individually the project cash flow streams are

A: +£30 000; 0; 0; ......
B: −£6000; +£3600; +£3600; ......

The project B–A has the cash flow stream

−£36 000; £3600; £3600; ......

This has a rate of return of 10%. If this is above Cyril's cut-off rate (i.e. if 10% is a better return than Cyril can get from other projects available to him) he will make the extra investment required by B.

Notice that this calculation of the incremental investment makes an allowance for giving up the opportunity of gaining an immediate £30 000.

If 10% is below Cyril's cut-off rate then he will not make the extra investment required by choosing B.

Suppose Cyril's cut-off rate is 12%. This means that he knows that he can always invest money (say in Local Authority loans) at 12%. We know that he can find £6000, he will have £36 000 to invest, and he can do this at 12% so he can get an income every year of

£36 000 × 0.12 = £4320

which is obviously better than he would have obtained by modernising and letting the house.

We can use the rate of return on an incremental project even when both projects lose money.

Example 10.4

Douglas wishes to install a central heating system in his house. He is offered three systems although he will obviously choose only one.

System A is gas fired. It costs £1500 to install and £200 a year to run.
System B is oil fired. It costs £1000 to install and £350 a year to run.
System C is coal fired. It costs £1200 to install and £300 a year to run.

Which system should he choose?

Obviously the projects cannot be compared directly on their rates of return. In any case, what is the meaning of rate of return when all cash flows are negative?

We can argue, however, that he could consider the projects in order of their initial investments and then judge the incremental investments.

The project with the lowest initial cost is B, with a cash flow stream of

−£1000; −£350; −£350; −£350; . . . . . . etc.

The project with the next lowest initial cost is C, with a cash flow stream of

−£1200; −£300; −£300; −£300; . . . . . . etc.

Finally, the project requiring the greatest initial investment is A with a cash flow stream

−£1500; −£200; −£200; −£200; . . . . . . etc.

The first question Douglas will ask is, 'Does the extra investment of C give a worthwhile rate of return?' In other words, he will first consider the project C–B, which has a cash flow stream:

−£200; £50; £50; . . . . . . £50; etc.

This has a rate of return of 25%.

Next Douglas will ask if the extra investment of A gives a worthwhile rate of return. This is project A–B, with the cash flow stream:

−£500; £150; £150; . . . . . .; £150; etc.

This has a rate of return of 30%.

Obviously the extra investment in A (beyond B) will be more worthwhile than the extra investment in C (beyond B).

Assuming that Douglas will certainly choose one of the options, he will choose A.

There is an exception to this. If Douglas has a project offered to him which will bring in more than 30%, he will choose B because the extra money (the incremental investment of A over B) will earn 30% if A is chosen but more than 30% if invested externally.

Let us check this. Suppose Douglas will definitely have one form of central heating but has an opportunity to invest money at 35%. He could choose A with the cash flow stream

−£1500; −£200; −£200;......; etc.

This implies that he has £1500 to invest.

Alternatively, Douglas could choose B, investing £1000 and have £500 to invest externally at 35%. There will be two cash flow streams,

B; −£1000; −£350; −£350;......; etc. and
the external project; −£500; +£175; +£175;......; etc.

The sums of the cash flows resulting from these projects is

−£1500; −£175; −£175; ......; etc.

which is clearly better than choosing A.

One way of studying these incremental projects is to draw a vector diagram, as in Fig. 10.1.

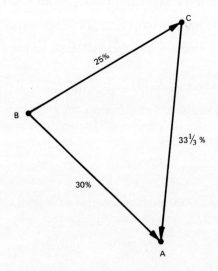

Fig. 10.1 − This vector diagram is used, as follows:
Start at B, the project requiring the lowest initial investment. From B, we can move to C, along the vector C−B, with a rate of return of 25%.
Alternatively, we can move to A, along the vector A−B, with a rate of return of 30%. Clearly, the vector A−B is the better.
BUT
If Douglas can get 35% for his money in some other project which has nothing to do with his central heating system, he will start at B but go to neither C nor A because both C−V and A−B are both poorer investment than the 35% Douglas can obtain externally.

Although it is not necessary for this particular problem, we include the project A–C, which has the cash flow stream:

–£300; £100; £100; . . . . . .; etc.

which has a rate of return of $33\frac{1}{3}\%$.

SEVERAL RATES OF RETURN

All the projects that we have considered so far have been such that their graphs of present value against discount rate have been of the shape shown in Fig. 10.2. Examples of such curves were drawn as Fig. 9.1 and 9.3.

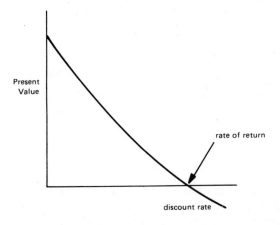

Fig. 10.2

Not all projects give such simple graphs or such obvious values of rate of return. Problems can arise, particularly with incremental project calculations.

Example 10.5

Eric owns a small coal mine, which he works single-handed. He has to operate an old-fashioned pump to drain the mine from which he cuts the coal himself. He get out £20 000 worth of coal every year but after three years the mine will be exhausted.

Eric can buy a more modern pump which will free him to spend more time extracting coal. The pump will cost him £5000, and as a result Eric will extract coal at the greater rate of £30 000 worth a year, but after only two years the mine will be exhausted.

Plot the curve of present value versus discount rate for the incremental investment in the pump. Plot over the range of discount rates between 0 and 200%.

The curve is shown in Fig. 10.3 and is clearly a very different shape from the curves plotted in Chapter 9.

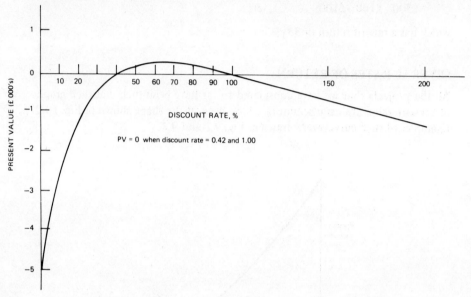

Fig. 10.3

The explanation is clear enough. At zero discount rate, there is a loss of £5000 because, over the life of the project, no more coal is extracted and the pump must be paid for. At a discount rate of 42%, the present value of the loss in the third year has been reduced sufficiently to pay for the pump. Between discount rates of 42% and 100%, the decline in present value of the loss in the third year will more than pay for the pump, but when the discount rate exceeds 100%, all future values convert to such small present values that the pump cannot be paid for.

This example is a fairly artificial one, but situations of this nature can occur in real life and anyone who uses rate of return (or present value) to assess a project must be wary not to draw conclusions which assume that all his projects are necessarily of the type shown in Fig. 10.2.

Example 10.6

Fred has two options in his job as production manager. He can install machine A at a cost of £35 000 or machine B at a cost of £50 000. Both machines will last 6 years. At the end of that time A will have no value but B will have a resale value of £15 000. Both machines are intended to make the same product, but B does a better job. As a result, A makes a contribution (revenue less running costs) of £12 500 a year and B makes a contribution of £15 200 a year.

The alternatives therefore have the cash flow streams:

	A(£)	B(£)
end year 0	− 35 000	− 50 000
end year 1	12 500	15 200
end year 2	12 500	15 200
end year 3	12 500	15 200
end year 4	12 500	15 200
end year 5	12 500	15 200
end year 6	12 500	30 200

Calculate the rate of return of each project.

(27%)   (24¼%)

A gives the better rate of return, but will Fred choose it?

Presumably Fred's employers can afford to invest in B (or Fred would not have the choice). Now Fred's employers will know what they can get for their money from projects outside Fred's knowledge. Suppose they can get 25%. Then the decision must be to accept A which has a better rate of return than the cut-off figure.

But suppose the company's cut-off figure is 20%.

Both projects pass the test, and Fred has to ask if the extra investment in B is above the company's cut-off rate.

The project B−A has the cash flows (£):

− 15 000; 2700; 2700; 2700; 2700; 2700; 17 700

which gives a rate of return of 18%.

If Fred's employers can get 20% for their money then they had better invest in A and put out £15 000 at 20% rather than invest in B (which is the equivalent of investing in A and putting out £15 000 at 18%).

If Fred's choice is only between A and B he can set up the vector diagram of Fig. 10.4. He will start at A because it is the cheaper and move to B if the rate of return of B−A is above the company's cut-off rate.

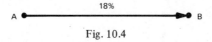

Fig. 10.4

If Fred's choice includes doing nothing, he can set up the vector diagram of Fig. 10.5, in which project 0 is doing nothing. Here Fred starts at 0, the cheapest investment. If the company's cut-off rate is greater than 27%, Fred will choose 0. If the company's cut-off rate is below 27%, Fred will move to A. If the company's cut-off rate is higher than 18%, Fred will choose A. If the company's cut-off rate is lower than 18%, Fred will move to, and choose, B.

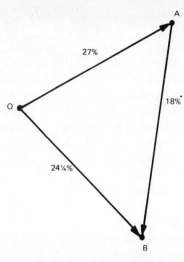

Fig. 10.5

Exercise 10.4

Four investment opportunities are available (A, B, C, and D). Each is assumed to be of an infinite life. The initial investments and annual after tax cash flows are

	Initial Investment (£'s)	After tax cash flow (£'s)
A	10 000	1000
B	6000	900
C	7000	980
D	4000	640

The projects are mutually exclusive, but one must be chosen (because the projects are alternative ways of meeting a HASW requirement).

Arranging the projects in increasing order of investment and calculating incremental rates of return we have

	ROR	ROR	ROR	ROR
D	16%			
B	15%	B–D; 13%		
C	14%	C–D; 11.3%	C–B; 8%	
A	10%	A–D; 6%	A–B; 2.5%	A–C; 0.7%

With this information we set up the vector diagram of Fig. 10.6.

Start at D. If the firm's cut-off rate of return is greater than 13%, choose D because none of the alternatives is better than this.

If the firm's cut-off rate is less than 13% move to B (the best alternative, so far). If the firm's cut-off rate is greater than 8%, choose B. If the firm's cut-off

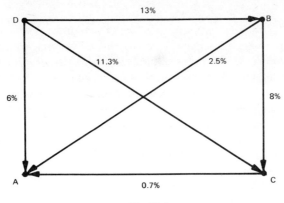

Fig. 10.6

rate is less than 8%, move to C. If the firm's cut-off rate is greater than 0.7%, choose C. If the firm's cut-off rate is less than 0.7% (very unlikely) move to, and choose, A.

Exercise 10.5

George has the choice of building a workshop in an enterprise zone or in the home counties.

If he builds in an enterprise zone, grants, rates relief, advantageous write down programmes, etc. mean that his initial investment is £80 000 and he will make £12 000 (revenue less operating costs) a year.

If he builds in the home counties his initial investment will be £120 000 but he will be nearer his market and will make £16 000 a year.

What should be his choice if he can get a return of 12% on his money if he invests in local authority loans?

Would his choice be altered if he considers going out of business (the do nothing alternative)?

In an enterprise zone (A) the investment is £80 000 and the return £12 000 a year, giving 15%.

In the home counties (B) the investment is £120 000 and the return £16 000 a year, giving $13\frac{1}{3}$%.

B–A is an investment of £40 000 with a return of £4 000, i.e. a rate of return of 10%.

If George can get 12% on his capital without working for it he will choose A.

Draw the vector diagram of the 'do-nothing' alternative is available.
(He will still choose A).

Exercise 10.6

Three mutually exclusive projects, A, B, and C, are listed below. One must be chosen. Set up a vector diagram of the incremental investments and show how the choice of project would depend on the company's cut-off rate of return.

A involves an immediate investment of £1000 and costs £40 a year to run.
B involves an immediate investment of £1500 and brings in £60 a year.
C involves an immediate investment of £2000 and brings in £120 a year.
Assume that the life of any of the projects is infinite.

Rate of Return %

	0	A	B
A	− 4	−	−
B	+ 4	20	−
C	+ 6	16	12

Company's cut-off rate > 20%; choose A
Company's cut-off rate ≤ 20%;
        and > 12%; choose B
Company's cut-off rate ≤ 12%; choose C

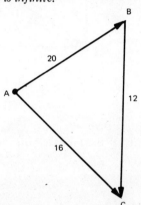

Exercise 10.7

Repeat Exercise 10.6 assuming that the project selector is permitted to choose to do nothing.

Company's cut-off rate > 6% do nothing
Company's cut-off rate ≤ 6% choose C

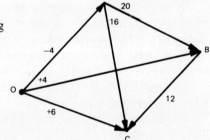

Exercise 10.8

A company has £50 000, and the department heads have proposed the following projects to the Board.

Project	Investment required	Rate of return
A	£10 000	15%
B	£15 000	10%
C	£20 000	8%
D	£ 8 000	12%
E	£ 4 000	18%
F	£10 000	16%
G	£25 000	14%

Any money which is not invested in internal projects is invested in govern-ment stock at 10%.
Discuss the acceptance or rejection of these projects.

Exercise 10.9
A company has £25 000 to invest in internal or external projects. External investment is at 10%.

The board is meeting to select projects proposed by the technical director. The projects have been examined by the commercial department which assesses them as follows:

Project	A	B	C	D	E	F	G	H	I	J
Required investment	£4000	£6000	£2000	£5000	£3000	£7000	£4000	£5000	£1000	£6000
Rate of return	17%	18%	16%	19%	20%	17%	21%	14%	23%	9%

Which projects will be accepted?

Exercise 10.10
With capital rationed to £100 000, three projects are mandatory and nine others are proposed.
The mandatory projects are:

A requiring an investment of £8000 and costing £1000 a year afterwards,
B requiring an investment of £7000 and returning £500 a year afterwards,
C requiring an investment of £5000 and returning £50 a year afterwards.

The expected cash flow streams of the other nine projects are:

D : Initial investment £15 000; return £3000 a year for 9 years and £8000 in the 10th year; life 10 years,
E : Initial investment £10 000; return £4500 a year indefinitely,
F : Initial investment £5000; return £700 a year for 4 years and £5700 a year in the 5th year; life 5 years,
G : Initial investment £20 000; return £3750 a year for 8 years; life 8 years,
H : Initial investment £10 000; return £2000 a year for 5 years and £6500 in the 6th year; life 6 years,
I : Initial investment £15 000; return £3104 for 10 years; life 10 years,
J : Initial investment £12 000; return £2391 for 10 years; life 10 years,
K : Initial investment £20 000; return £4000 a year for 4 years and £24 000 in the 5th year; life 5 years,
L : Initial investment £20 000; return £1600 a year indefinitely.

Discuss the acceptance or rejection of these projects.

Exercise 10.11

How would you cope with the capital rationing system if there were two mutually exclusive ways of coping with a mandatory project?

Let A_1 and A_2 be two mutually exclusive projects which meet a mandatory requirement.

Assume A_2 requires the larger investment. Then we may regard A_1 as being mandatory and $(A_2 - A_1)$ as being optional. When we rank projects, we will certainly accept A_1. We will accept $(A_2 - A_1)$ if it is within the capital budget and has an acceptable rate of return. If we do not accept $(A_2 - A_1)$, A_1 meets our requirement. If we accept $(A_2 - A_1)$, we have already accepted A_1 and so we are effectively choosing $A_1 + (A_2 - A_1) = A_2$.

11

Ranking projects and present value

Because the use of present value as a criterion for judging a project implies that the money for investment is being borrowed, there is no obvious rationing of capital. If a project can be shown to have a positive present value at the cost of borrowing then one might assume that there would be no difficulty in borrowing the required investment.

This argument does, however, ignore the risk. As we have seen, in our discussion of the cost of capital, creditors lend money if they believe that there is no risk involved and shareholders who invest money expect a greater return for a greater risk.

Creditors would limit the amount that they would lend a company if they saw that the debt ratio was high because they would believe their investment to be at risk. Banks, for example, would put a limit on the amount of overdraft that they would allow a company.

In practice, then, we may have two ways in which capital is rationed. There may be an absolute limit to the amount of money that may be borrowed. On the other hand, there may be no clear limit to capital but the more that is raised, the greater its cost. In this case there will be an effective, rough limit when the high cost of capital forces most projects to have a negative present value.

This second case of the cost of capital increasing with the amount of capital raised is difficult to deal with analytically (it is probably best coped with by nonlinear programming, although such methods usually require a refinement of input data that does not accord with the approximation of our predictions). In practice too, companies would usually work to stated limits of investment in new projects.

If we are working to a fixed investment limit, we wish to select projects so that the sum of the present values of the projects selected is a maximum.

Example 11.1
Anthony is managing director of a small company which reckons its cost of

capital to be 12% but which cannot raise more than £25 000 for new projects. Anthony is offered the following four projects by his departmental managers:

	A	B	C	D
end year 0	− £10 000	− £15 000	− £10 000	− £12 000
end year 1	£ 5000	£ 5000	£ 4000	£ 6000
end year 2	£ 5000	£ 5000	£ 4000	£ 6000
end year 3	£ 5000	£ 5000	£ 7000	£ 6000
end year 4	£ 5000	£20 000	£ 7000	£ 4000

At the discount rate of 12% we can calculate the present value of each of these projects and we have:

A; investment £10 000; present value £5187
B; investment £15 000; present value £9720
C; investment £10 000; present value £6191
D; investment £12 000; present value £4953

Anthony cannot choose more than two projects because of our capital limit of £25 000. He would not choose D because it is dominated by the other projects. Clearly he would choose B and C which have a total present value of £15 911 and use up the capital available.

To some extent, we may rank projects in order of present value and then take them from the top of the list until our capital is used up.

This would have worked with Example 11.1 for we would have arranged our projects in the order

Project	Investment required	Present value
B	£15 000	£9720
C	£10 000	£6191
A	£10 000	£5187
D	£12 000	£4953

We could have chosen from the top of the list until we reached our investment limit and we would have chosen B and C.

We must be careful however.

Example 11.2
Bret has a limit of £25 000 to invest, and he has four projects from which to choose. His cost of capital is 12%. The projects are

A; investment required £10 000; present value £5200
B; investment required £15 000; present value £9750
C; investment required £10 000; present value £6200
D; investment required £12 000; present value £7500

If Bret ranks these projects in order of present value, the ranking will be

B, D, C, A

If he chooses B, he cannot choose D because he has insufficient capital.
Bret will choose B and C.

Exercise 11.1
*Capital up to a limit of £100 000 may be raised at 10% to invest in as many as
you wish of the following projects. Which would you choose?*

Project	Initial investment	Present value
A	£33 000	£20 000
B	£20 000	£15 000
C	£16 000	£ 7000
D	£41 000	£20 000
E	£15 000	£10 000
F	£51 000	£26 000
G	£25 000	£12 000
H	£37 000	£21 000

[H, B, E, G but trial and error may find a better combination

Exercise 11.2
*Capital up to a limit of £100 000 may be raised at 14% to invest in any selection
of the following projects. Which would you choose?*

Project	A	B	C	D	E
Cash flows (£'s)					
end year 0	−25 000	−50 000	−60 000	−30 000	−12 000
end year 1	10 000	20 000	20 000	0	4 000
end year 2	15 000	20 000	30 000	0	4 000
end year 3	20 000	20 000	40 000	0	4 000
end year 4	20 000	20 000	50 000	0	4 000
end year 5	15 000	20 000	50 000	75 000	4 000
end year 6	10 000	20 000	40 000		4 000
end year 7		70 000	30 000		4 000
end year 8			20 000		4 000
end year 9			10 000		4 000
end year 10					

[A, C, E

We do have to compare projects if they are mutually exclusive.

Example 11.3

Charles has to choose between two welding machines for an automated washing machine assembly line.

Welding machine A costs £10 000 and will cost £1000 a year to run.

Welding machine B costs £12 000 and will cost £ 800 a year to run.

Money spent on building the line will increase the company's overdraft which carries an interest charge of 17% a year.

The line will last 8 years, at the end of which salvage will be negligible.

The present value of A at 17% is £14 207 while the present value of B at 17% is £15 366.

A is the cheaper alternative because A costs the equivalent of increasing the overdraft by £14 207 now while B costs the equivalent of increasing the overdraft by £15 366.

Exercise 11.3

David has to choose between two storage systems. The first is simple racking with trucks and truck drivers operating it. The second is automated and computer controlled.

The simple system costs £30 000 and £20 000 a year to operate while the automated system costs £137 500 and £2000 a year to operate.

Whichever system David chooses, the money will be borrowed at 16%.

The simple system will last indefinitely.

How long must the automated system last to justify itself?

If the simple system is no longer required for the earmarked project it will be dismantled and used somewhere else in the factory.

[23 years

Exercise 11.4

Edmund has to choose between two mutually exclusive systems. The first costs £30 000 to buy and install and £20 000 a year to run and will last indefinitely. The second costs £125 000 to buy and install and £2000 a year to run. The second system will last 10 years and then have a salvage value of £20 000. Which system should be chosen if money can be borrowed at (i) 16% and (ii) 8%.

Note that in this example, we have to compare two projects with different lives. It is probably best to compare equivalent annual running costs but you could compare over an infinite life by repeating the second project indefinitely.

[At 16% the first project is better; at 8% the second is better

Exercise 11.5

Derek has to choose between two mutually exclusive projects A and B. Both projects will do the required job for 10 years.

Project A requires an initial investment of £125 000, a running cost of £2000 a year for 10 years and gives a salvage value of £18 000 after 10 years.

Project B requires an initial investment of £100 000, a running cost of £5000 a year for 10 years and has no salvage value at the end of that time.

Plot, for each of these projects, the present value of the cost as a function of discount rate. Hence, determine the discount rate at which project B becomes cheaper than project A.

What is the rate of return of project (A–B)?   [11%

                                                                          [11%

Part II

ESTIMATING AND TENDERING

12

The life cycle of a project

In Part I we assumed that a project would be acceptable if it had a positive present value or a rate of return above that of commonly available safe investments. We also suggested that a short pay back period could be a criterion under some circumstances.

We have to modify this view slightly because, as we have seen, some projects may have to be accepted even if they are not profitable, when judged by the above criteria. However, a company's operation will embrace many activities, and we have only to argue that over all the projects, those mandatory projects which do not meet our criteria must be paid for by those that do. In other words, summed over all the projects, the present value must be positive or the rate of return must be above the cut-off level.

Many objectives have been suggested for the firm:

> to maximise profit,
> to capture a good share of the market,
> to survive,
> to please the customer,
> to create employment,
> to provide a social service,
> to provide goods of high quality
> and many others.

However, none of these objectives can be attained unless the firm continues either to:

> achieve a positive net present value when cash flows are summed over all projects, or
> achieve an adequate rate of return from the cash flows summed over all projects.

It can be argued that it is not necessary to meet these criteria in all cases because nationalised industries can continue to run at a loss, companies in enterprise zones can lose money because they receive grants, social projects may not be expected to make a profit, etc. However, if government grants, tax allowances and sums of money from agencies which underwrite social projects are treated as positive cash flows, we still have the need to show positive present values or acceptable rates of return.

Commonly, then, it is argued that a company must make a profit. This is an ambiguous statement because we have to know what is meant by profit. If, however, we are considering after tax cash flows, we will argue that a company is profitable if it can pay (and continue to pay) its shareholders a good return on their investment. This also means that the firm's after tax cash flows will add up to a positive present value at the weighted, tax adjusted cost of capital.

It is sometimes suggested that the object of the managers of a company is to maximise profit, but this is not really necessary as long as their decisions enable them to give the shareholder a competitive return. The return to the shareholder does not have to be the best possible as long as it is enough to please him. This setting of a goal which is acceptable rather than vainly striving after the maximum possible return is known as 'satisficing'.

In the case of a factory, profit is generally made by manufacturing goods that the customers want and will buy at a price which exceeds the cost of manufacture.

Typically the life cycle of a manufactured product will consist of the following activities:

(i) *Market research.* Before any investment is made, the investor must believe that what the company proposes to make can be sold at a price which will permit a profit to be made. This usually means that market research will establish what product the customer wants, how much he is prepared to pay for it and how many he will buy.

(ii) *Specification.* When market research has established what is to be made, it will be necessary to turn the general statement of requirements into a detailed specification which will tell the designer and manufacturing engineer precisely what is required.

The design specification will give such details as required life, maximum permissible maintenance costs, maximum permissible manufacturing cost, the number required, the delivery date, the required performance of the product.

(iii) *Design.* With a precise specification the designers can produce the drawings and process schedules which define the geometry of the product and some of the manufacturing processes.

(iv) *Prototype manufacture.* From the drawings it will be possible to manufacture a small number of the product. These prototypes will be used to develop the product and eventually to demonstrate that it meets the requirements of the specification.

(v) *Development.* When a product has been made for the first time, it is necessary to prove that it meets the requirements of the specification. In fact, when a product is first made it rarely meets the requirements of the specification and changes have to be made until it does. This period of testing and changing is 'development'. Development can be very expensive and often generates a large negative cash flow before any products have been sold and hence, before any positive cash flows have been generated.

(vi) *Tooling.* When a product is shown to meet the requirements of the specification and if calculations suggest that it will be profitable, the decision will be made to make it to sell. This is not a decision that will be taken lightly because, in many cases, the decision to make a product for sale is a commitment to tool up for production. Tooling up for production can mean building a production line costing several hundred million pounds, building expensive jigs, buying special purpose machine tools or, in some other way, making a very large initial investment.

(vii) *Manufacture.* The manufacture of a product involves the purchase of the raw materials, the purchase of bought out components, the use of labour to make and assemble the product, and the use of supervisory labour.

(viii) *Selling.* When the product is fit to sell and available, it may be necessary to spend money on a campaign to sell the product.

(ix) *Distribution.* In the process of selling the product, it must be distributed to the sales outlets and to the customers.

(x) *Product support.* When the product has been bought, the customer will expect it to be supported. The manufacturer or supplier will have to make sure that spares and expert servicing are available for the life of the product. The manufacturer or the supplier may even have to offer free servicing and parts replacement during the early life of the product.

(xi) *Decommissioning or Replacement.* When a manufacturing project comes to an end, the plant used to build the product must be re-used, sold, scrapped, or decommissioned in a way that is acceptable to society.

Exercise 12.1
Give examples of the stages in the life cycle of a manufactured product and suggest some of the costs involved in those stages.

Consider a motor car: considerable sums of money are spent on *market research* to determine what model should be built, this culminates in the *specification* of a model, the model is *designed* at considerable cost, and *prototypes* are built in the experimental shop and *developed* by the technical department to a point at which the company decides to go into *production;* at this point it may be necessary to spend a great deal of money on new plant; manufacture of the car will proceed, using bought out components and raw material and both direct and indirect (supervisors, inspectors, canteen workers, truck drivers, rate fixers, and many others) labour; advertising campaigns will be used to *sell* the car; the new cars will be *distributed* by lorry or rail to the retailers; the manufacturers will *support the product* by making supplies of spare parts available and by training mechanics in the ways of servicing the car and some servicing and spare parts will be offered free during a warranty period. When the company decides to stop making the car the plant must not be left derelict but must be *decommissioned;* some will be re-used, some will be sold for scrap, while the buildings will be modified and re-used for new projects.

In addition to manufactured products, such as aeroplanes, television sets, washing machines, etc. the student should consider industries where the product is not obviously a piece of designed and manufactured hardware.

Do such projects as the mining of coal, the drilling for oil, the generation of electricity, the building of houses, selling ready made clothes have life cycles similar to that described above?

Exercise 12.2
Specify a project and list twelve costs that occur during its life cycle.

In the case of the design and manufacture of a mass produced motor car, we can easily identify

  (i)   the cost of market research (mainly labour),
 (ii)   the cost of design (mainly labour),
(iii)   the cost of the advertising campaign (probably payments to an agency),
 (iv)   the cost of the machine tools which form part of the plant (bought from specialist suppliers),
  (v)   the cost of alternators for the cars (bought from specialist suppliers),
 (vi)   the cost of tyres (bought from specialist suppliers),
(vii)   the cost of steel sheet (bought from specialist suppliers),
(viii)   the cost of assembly labour,
 (ix)   the cost of inspectors (labour),
  (x)   the cost of specialist inspection equipment (perhaps designed and made in house or perhaps bought from specialist suppliers),
 (xi)   the cost of repairs and warranty,
(xii)   the cost of the transport of the new cars to the retail outlets,
(xiii)   the cost of training the retailers' fitters.

Obviously many costs could be added to this list.

Exercise 12.3
Specify a project.
List ten major costs in the life of the project.
Arrange the costs in order of magnitude.

Exercise 12.4
In the end, are all costs labour costs?

Exercise 12.5
How is the cost of assembling a manufactured product (e.g. the cost of the fitter assembling the car) different from the cost of designing the car?
   Try a brain storming session to answer this.

(Design costs the same however many cars are built.
Design costs the same if the car is a failure and is not built at all.
The fitter's costs vary approximately in proportion to the number of cars built.
The fitter's work is much more likely to be paid by the hour.
The fitter's work is much more likely to be measured and his pay varied with his output.
The designer is likely to be paid a fixed annual salary regardless of output.
The output of the fitter per hour is likely to depend on the investment in tools for him.
And so on.)

Exercise 12.6
What labour skills (or other classifications) will exist in the production department of a factory making motor cars (or any other product of your choice)?

(Assemblers and fitters, inspectors, tool room fitters, tool room machinists, charge hands, foremen, progress chasers, time clerks, rate fixers, overhead crane drivers, fork lift truck drivers, maintenance fitters, maintenance electricians, and so on.)

13

The corporate plan

In Chapter 12 we argued that a company has to make a profit (in the sense that the total of its cash flows must be given a positive present value or an acceptable rate of return) but clearly, if this is a major objective of the company, profit cannot be left to chance.

In any company the managers must set the goals, and this is done by the establishment of a corporate plan (or corporate strategy). The way a company establishes its corporate plan will obviously differ from one company to another but, with some simplification, the procedure will approximate to the following.

(i)   The managing director will set an approximate profit goal for, say, one year.

(ii) The marketing and the finance directors will relate the profit goal to a revenue from goods sold.

(iii) The marketing director will be able to say whether he can sell the required turnover of goods and will be able to identify the goods which will sell in the required quantity.

(iv) The production director will be able to say whether his department can make the required goods in the time available.

(v)   The technical director will be able to say whether his departments can design and develop the goods in the time available.

Steps (i) to (v) are repeated until, by a process of iteration, the board reaches a programme of designing, manufacturing, and selling a quantity of products which will

give the required profit,
can be made, and
can be designed.

During this iterative process, the production director will determine what resources he needs in terms of men and machines to meet the requirements of the programme, and he must believe that he can obtain any resources that he does not already have.

The finance director will determine what money is required to meet the needs of the programme, and he must believe that he can raise any capital that is not immediately available and at a cost that is acceptable.

When the corporate plan is agreed, the directors and managers will agree that their departments can produce what is needed with the resources that will be made available.

In particular, the production director will know what money he will get for capital investment, what money he will get for wages, raw materials, and other necessary expenses, and he will have agreed that with these resources the production department will make the products in the mix and at the times demanded by the corporate plan. He will, in short, have a capital budget and a revenue budget, and he will have a programme which commits him to produce a predetermined mix and value of products each month (or whatever the accounting period is).

In essence, the production director's job is to keep his department's spending within its budget and its output up to the planned mix and value each month.

This is, of course, the function of every department manager within the corporate plan. His department must keep its spending within budget and its output up to the required mix and value. It is not always as easy to identify the value of the output as it is in the case of the production department. The design office will produce drawings which have a value and which must be produced on time; the sales department must produce sales according to the plan; the commercial, service, and other departments must produce services which can be evaluated and which contribute to the plan.

Example 13.1
The production director of a company which mass produces motor cars has agreed to and has been allocated a budget for the forthcoming year. The budget is divided into a capital budget and a revenue budget.

How is the production director likely to spend his budget?

The capital budget may be spent on new buildings, new machine tools, new storage systems, new materials handling systems, etc.

The revenue budget may be spent on raw materials, bought out components, power, labour for assembling, labour for machining components, labour for collecting swarf, labour for inspecting work, etc. In Part I we tended to call these the annual operating costs to distinguish them from the costs of investment in plant. The major difference between capital costs and annual operating costs is that capital equipment is expected to last several years whereas when labour or raw materials are bought, their translation into saleable goods is hoped to be almost immediate. The term 'revenue budget' is used in industry, although it can cause some confusion because revenue is often thought to suggest income.

Exercise 13.1

Specify a company and the products it makes.

List four capital purchases that the production director might make as part of his capital budget (which is, in turn, part of the company's corporate plan).

List ten payments that the production director might make as part of his revenue budget.

What might be the production director's target production in a month?

What costs would be generated if the production director did not meet his target in a month?

14

Costs

What costs are involved in manufacturing a product? We have seen that plant has to be paid for, although usually over several years, and some fraction of the price of a product must pay for the plant. Part I showed how any capital investment may be converted into an annual equivalent cost and hence spread over the products made.

We have also seen that labour, raw materials, and bought out components must be paid for, and these costs too will contribute to the price of the product.

The costs of making a product are classified in many ways, and the way they are subdivided depends on the problem that we are attempting to solve.

One commonly used subdivision is into fixed and variable costs; another is into direct and indirect costs; another is into the cost of direct labour and overheads, while yet another is into the cost of direct material and overheads.

FIXED AND VARIABLE COSTS

In this subdivision of costs, we classify as fixed those which are independent of the number of products made. The variable costs are those which vary, more or less directly, with the number of products made. In some cases we call the fixed costs 'non-recurring costs'.

Examples of fixed costs are the costs of design and development, the cost of plant and buildings, and the cost of tools (although tools may, with long product runs, need refurbishing from time to time and therefore may be regarded as having semi-variable costs). The use of fixed and variable costs enables us to calculate the break-even number of products, that is the number of products which must be made before a profit can be made.

If the selling price of a product is $£P$
 the variable cost of a product is $£V$
 the fixed cost of a product is $£F$ and
 the number of products made is N

we define the *contribution* of each product as

$$C = P - V$$

This means that each product sold makes a contribution C to the fixed cost. The total contribution from N products sold is

$$NC = N(P - V) \text{ and the}$$

project is profitable if

$$N(P - V) > F \quad .$$

Another way of looking at fixed and variable costs is shown in Fig. 14.1.

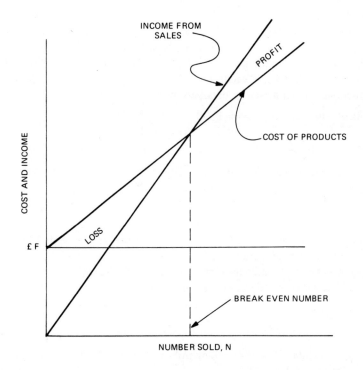

Fig. 14.1

If the number sold is N, the total income is £NP and this is shown plotted in Fig. 14.1.

The variable cost per item is V so that the total variable cost is £NV.

But there is a fixed cost, regardless of the number sold, so that the total cost is

$$£(F + NV) \text{ and this is shown plotted as cost of products on Fig. 14.1}$$

Clearly there is a profit if the income from sales exceeds the cost of the products sold, i.e. if

$$NP > F + NV \text{ or}$$
$$N(P - V) > F .$$

The number of products for which

$$N(P - V) = F, \text{ i.e.}$$
$$N_B = F/(P - V) \text{ is called the break-even number.}$$

If the number of products sold exceeds the break-even number, there will be a profit; otherwise there will be a loss.

Example 14.1
Arthur buys a machine for printing slogans on T-shirts. The machine costs £100. He buys white T-shirts from a Hong Kong supplier at £1 each and he reckons that his labour and materials cost £1.30 for every T-shirt he prints. He sells the printed shirts for £2.50 each.

How many must he sell to break even?

Fixed cost	= £100	= F
Variable cost	= £ 1.30	= V
Selling price	= £ 2.50	= P

$$\begin{aligned}
\text{Break-even number, } N_B &= F/(P - V) \\
&= 100/(2.50 - 1.30) \\
&= 100/1.20 \\
&= 83.3 .
\end{aligned}$$

Clearly Arthur cannot sell a fraction of a shirt, and he would have to sell 84 shirts before he makes a profit.

Plot the graphs of income versus number sold and total cost versus number sold on the same axes and confirm the above answer.

Exercise 14.1
Calculate the break-even sales with the following data:

  (i) Fixed costs = £30 000; selling price per item = £10; Variable cost per item = £7 [10 000

 (ii) Fixed costs = £60 000; Selling price per item = £80; Variable cost per item = £40 [1500

(iii) Fixed costs = £225M; Selling price per item = £10M; Variable cost per item = £7M [75

Exercise 14.2
How much would a company have to charge for an aeroplane if the costs for design, development and tooling were £225M; the cost of labour, material and

*bought out parts were £7M per aeroplane, and it was believed that 100 aero-
planes would be sold?*   [£9.25M

How much would the company lose if only 75 aeroplanes were sold?
                                              [£56.25M

How much would the company gain if 150 aeroplanes were sold?
                                            [£112.5M

The above examples have been over-simplified because they ignore tax and
they ignore the time value of money.

We will continue to ignore tax in this chapter because

(i)   at the break-even point, no profit is made and so tax is not relevant, and
(ii)   allowing for tax when a profit or loss is made adds complication to the
exercise but does not require any new ideas beyond those of chapter 5.

The problem of the time value of money may be taken into account by
using annual equivalent values.

Example 14.2

An aeroplane company spends £300M designing, developing, and tooling up for
the manufacture of an aeroplane. The company estimates that it can produce
the aeroplane for 10 years before it becomes obsolete. The costs of labour
and materials to make an aeroplane are £3M. The company's cost of capital is
15%. It is forecast that the company will be able to make and sell one aeroplane
a month during the 10-year life of the project.

How much must be charged for an aeroplane if the company is to break even?

The cost of capital given in the question is an indication that we must take
into account the time value of money.

Consider the problem on an annual basis. The fixed cost for the whole project
is £300M, but at 15% the annual equivalent cost is £300M/5.019 = £59.773M.

As 12 aeroplanes are made and sold in a year, they must contribute at least

	£59.773M
i.e. at least	£ 4.981M each
But variable costs are	£ 3.000M each
So that, to break even, the company must charge at least	£ 7.981M each

Exercise 14.3

(i)   *A company making washing machines needs 10 000 grommets a year.
B & Co. offer to supply the grommets and estimate that to do so they
must buy an automatic lathe which costs £10 000. This machine has an
estimated life of 10 years, and the company has an overdraft which
costs 20% a year.*

The labour and power costs in making a grommet will be 20p each and the raw materials will cost 10p.

How much must B & Co. charge for a grommet to break even?

[*53.85p*

(*ii*)   *If, after B & Co. have quoted a price of 60p a grommet, the washing machine company reduce their requirement to 5000 a year, how will B & Co. be affected if they do not re-quote?*

[B & Co. would lose £885 a year

(*iii*)   *If the project lasts 6 years and the lathe can then be sold for a second-hand price of £3000, how should B & Co. fix the price of a grommet to break even at a production rate of 8000 a year? Again assume the cost of capital to be 20%, labour costs per grommet to be 20p and raw material costs, 10p.*   [61.26p

DIRECT AND INDIRECT COSTS

With any manufactured articles, there are labour and materials costs that can be associated directly with the article.

Direct labour costs are often easy to identify, and examples could be:

the man hours spent assembling a motor car. Clearly the cost of those man hours can be seen directly in the cost of making the car;

the cost of the time of the girl who assembles toys may be seen directly in the cost of the toy;

the cost of the time of the man who machines the base plate of a digger may be seen directly in the cost of the digger;

the cost of the time of the inspector who spends all his time on the inspection of one product may be seen directly in the cost of that product.

Sometimes direct labour costs are not easy to identify.

Suppose a toolroom fitter spends his time refurbishing dies for the casting of toy motor cars. Sometimes he will be working on a die for one product, sometimes on the die for another. He can record the time that he spends on each job, and the cost of this time can be regarded as a direct labour cost of the product concerned. On the other hand, recording times may be a complicated procedure that does not warrant its cost.

Sometimes we make no attempt to record times and simply classify the cost of a man's time as an indirect labour cost.

Supervision may be an example of labour which is classified as indirect. A foreman or a managing director may spend his day dealing with many jobs, so that he cannot determine precisely how his costs should be allocated to the different products. The managing director may be working on the corporate plan − how is his time to be allocated to products? The foreman may be trying to determine the space required by a new horizontal borer − how is his time to be allocated to a product?

Many administrative jobs have labour costs that would be difficult to allocate directly to products. How would the cost of the time of a man writing the computer program which determines weekly wages be allocated to a product?

The real distinction between direct and indirect labour costs is arbitrary and depends on the degree of difficulty with which a man's time may be associated with a particular product. There is also a problem associated with status, for there is no doubt that some men at middle management level regard it as beneath their dignity to fill in a time sheet from which may be determined how their time was spent.

Direct material costs are often easy to identify, and examples could be:

the cost of light alloy which is used in the casting of a chassis on which are mounted the printed circuits of an electronic instrument;

the cost of the titanium billet from which is machined part of an aeroplane wing. Note that, in this case, the swarf may be salvaged or may be lost and be regarded as part of the direct material;

the cost of the granules from which a plastic washing-up bowl is moulded.

Again, some materials cannot easily be associated directly with a particular product. The cost of the lubricating oil used in the machines of a gear cutting section could not easily be allocated to particular products (unless the gears cut were all for one product); the cost of the paper used by the computer could not easily be allocated to a particular product; the cost of components used to repair an overhead crane could not easily be allocated to particular jobs.

Once again we have a fairly arbitrary division of the cost of materials into direct and indirect, depending on how easy it is to allocate the cost of the material to a particular product.

DIRECT LABOUR COSTS AND OVERHEADS

Once we accept the idea that some costs are direct and some are indirect, we must find a way of allowing for the indirect costs. Sometimes this is done by calculating the indirect costs as a fraction of the direct labour cost (this fraction is called the 'overhead'). We may distinguish between the costs incurred in each department, or we may lump all costs together over the whole factory.

Commonly, though not invariably, we will assume that the cost of a product is made up of

See fig 14.2

(i)   direct materials
(ii)   direct labour   *+ cap. investments*
(iii)   shop overhead made up of indirect materials/used in the shop and indirect labour used in the shop
and (iv)   company overhead made up of materials used outside the shop and labour used outside the shop.

(iii) would be calculated as a percentage of (ii) and called shop overheads, while (iv) would be calculated as a percentage of (ii) and called company overheads.

Sometimes the sum of direct labour cost and direct material cost in a product is called the 'prime cost'.

Often when we think of overheads, we think of the cost of providing the direct operative with warmth, light, a canteen, and such similar aids which do not amount to much cost. In fact, overheads amount to a very high proportion of the total cost of a product and lumping so many costs together as an overhead can be very dangerous if it conceals where our true costs of production lie.

Even a direct operator's wage contains a high overhead content.

Consider a man who is paid £2.50 an hour, i.e. £100 for a normal working week of 40 hours.

The operator will probably have a holiday of 20 working days in a year (summer holiday plus bank holidays), and he may well have 15 days away from work through sickness (many firms would pay a basic rate during some sickness).

Further, the company might contribute towards a pension for the operator and would certainly pay for part of his National Insurance stamp.

Even when the employee is at work, it may be reasonable for him to use some time on work which is not directly associated with the products he is making — he may be allowed some time to clean down his machine, he may be allowed some time to attend union meetings, he may be waiting for a tool to be supplied.

Altogether we may assume that the man is working 52×40 hours a year for £5200 (i.e. £2.50 an hour), whereas he is providing 45×37 hours of direct labour at a cost of, say £6240 (i.e. £3.75 for each hour of direct labour).

This means that if we work to the man's nominal pay per hour, we must assume 50% overhead before we provide him with a working environment, supervision, or any other type of support.

If we consider indirect labour in the shop, we will be surprised to find that, between the production director and the girl who brings round tea, there are at least as many people in the shop providing indirect labour as there are providing direct labour. Each of these persons who provide indirect labour also has holidays, suffers from sickness, etc. and we see that, considering labour alone, the shop overheads are likely to cost at least twice as much as the direct operator's wage per hour.

The nature of the company's business will, of course, determine the distinction between direct and indirect labour but if we include tool room operatives, fork lift truck drivers, inspectors, maintenance men, and production controllers, the indirect workers in a shop may exceed the direct workers several times over.

We have to add the cost of the capital investment (the buildings, the machines used by the operator, the trucks, the racking, the moving belts, the overhead conveyor, the cranes, etc.) and this will probably be done on the basis of an equivalent annual cost. We have to add to them those comparatively small items of heating, lighting, and power.

All in all, we will be lucky if the shop overheads are less than about 400%, e.g. if the operator is paid £2.50 an hour, the cost of an hour's direct labour in the product is a total (direct labour plus overheads) of £2.50 + (4 × £2.50) = £12.50.

High overheads are not necessarily a bad thing because a direct operator is much more productive if he is supported with good, but expensive, machinery, good production control, a good toolroom, good staff relations, etc. High overheads may be attributable to these useful expenses which may more than pay for themselves.

High overheads may be bad if lumping many costs together as overheads obscures their source. Suppose we have a production control team which is too large, too little skilled in modern production control methods, and generally too expensive for the job it does. If the cost of this team is lost in an overhead figure, and the commercial director sees only the total overhead, there may be no way of knowing that production control is costing too much.

In addition to the shop overheads, we must add the company overhead. That is, we must pay for those departments which are not directly involved in production. There is the commercial department, concerned with keeping track of costs, the wages and salaries department concerned with calculating and paying wages, the sales department concerned with selling the products, the service department concerned with providing product support in the field, the technical department concerned with designing and developing new products, the research department concerned with exploring new ideas, the publication department concerned with providing service and operating manuals to the customer, the personnel department, and probably others. The total cost of all these departments must be added in to the cost of the product, and one way of doing this would be to treat them as overheads.

For example, if the total costs of running the production department were £10M and the total costs of running all other departments were £5M, and if the shop overheads on direct labour were 400%, what overheads must be added to pay for the remainder of the company?

If the total cost of running the shop is £10M and shop overheads are 400%, the cost of direct shop labour is £2M.

The total overhead (shop and company) will therefore be $(15 - 2)/2 = 6.5 = 650\%$.

PRIME COSTS AND OVERHEADS

Sometimes indirect costs are calculated as a percentage of prime costs. That is, to the cost of the direct labour in a product is added the cost of the direct material. All other factory costs — all labour other than direct, all materials other than direct — are determined as a fraction of the total cost of direct labour and materials. For example, if a company making trousers costs £1 000 000 to run — that is the total annual bill for wages, materials, and equivalent annual capital costs, if the cost of direct labour is £200 000 and the cost of direct material (almost wholly cloth from which the trousers are made) is £300 000 then the overheads are 100%.

COMBINATION OF COSTS

There are many ways in which costs may be combined to determine the total cost of a product. One commonly used method is to keep separate the direct material and direct labour costs. Thus the direct labour costs of a product could be loaded with all the indirect costs to give an overhead on the direct labour. To this, however, must be added the cost of materials and bought out parts. This method could be relevant where the products of a company were, say, electronic systems containing bought out sub-assemblies. The direct materials could account for much of the cost of the product, and where products would differ considerably in their bought out content, a fair measure of the difference in the cost between one product and another would be accounted for.

THE ALLOCATION OF COSTS

The different ways of allocating costs to the product are shown summarized in Fig. 14.2. Notice that we have added profit to the costs to give the selling price.

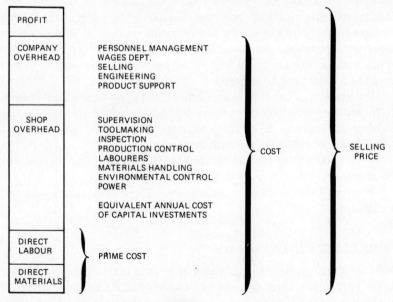

Fig. 14.2

The method of allocation will differ from company to company, depending greatly on what is manufactured or on what business the company is in.

Again, the proportion of each cost to the whole selling price will depend on the company's business.

Direct material costs could range from a few per cent to over a half of the selling price.

Direct labour costs could be typically, between 10 and 20 per cent.

Shop overheads could vary between 100 and 500 per cent.

Company overhead could be very small where only a little administration is required, to 30 per cent when engineering (design and development) is a very important part of what the company is selling.

Ten per cent of the selling price could be profit.

Exercise 14.4

(i)   *Give an example of a direct labour cost.*

(ii) *Give an example of a direct material cost.*

(iii) *Give five examples of labour cost which might be considered as indirect.*

(iv) *Give two examples of fixed cost.*

(v)   *A director thought that direct labour accounted for about 14% of the cost of building an aeroplane. What might have contributed to the other 86%?*

(vi) *Give examples of products in which the direct material cost is high.*

(vii) *Give examples of products in which the direct material cost is low.*

(viii) *In Fig. 14.2, design and development was not regarded as a shop over-head. Most textbooks treat design as a shop overhead. Use examples to justify both procedures.*

(ix) *Most companies like to treat as much labour as possible as direct labour. Suggest why.*

(x)   *If a man works on several jobs in a week how can he be treated as direct labour? (If he fills in a time sheet to say how many hours he spent on each job, his time may be distributed reasonably accurately).*

15

Work measurement

We have seen, in Chapter 14, that the direct labour cost in a product may be the base from which we determine first its total cost and then its selling price. If we are to base the cost of a product on its direct labour cost, we must be very confident of our estimate of direct labour.

We also need to study the direct labour content of a product because only by such study are we able to improve (cheapen) our manufacturing methods.

We may also need to study the direct labour content of a job if we wish to pay the operator according to the work he does (payment by results or PBR), and an essential ingredient of this is to provide the worker with the incentive that, if he works hard, he can add a bonus to his basic wages.

If we are to design work so that it is done efficiently and if we are to make sure that we know the labour content, we may use time and motion study.

Time and motion study has to be an iterative procedure, but it must start with a first attempt to design the operation that we are expecting the man to perform. The operation is broken down into a number of fairly basic motions; getting the raw piece from a pile, putting it into the machine, switching on the machine, removing the part from the machine, inspecting the part, putting it on the pile of finished parts, for example. In fact, if the motion study is performed properly, the operator's movements will be broken down into even more simple motions than the above example suggests; such elementary motions as reach, grip, lift, etc.

The number of motions, their complexity, and their difficulty will be different from job to job and from one quantity to another. Large batches or mass production will justify a large investment in tools which reduce the difficulty or extent of the direct labour input.

We must allow for necessary idle time because it is virtually impossible to design a job so that the operator is usefully employed for the whole of his time. If he is operating a machine, he may have to wait, from time to time, while the machine completes a cut. If to avoid waiting time, we ask the man to operate several machines, we will still find that it is almost impossible to arrange for idle times on one machine to coincide with an operator's work on another.

We must also design the job so that the operator's method of working contributes most effectively to the whole shop effort. That is, the equipment he uses may be standardised with that used by other operators in the shop. The general purpose tools that the operator may call up from the tool stores will be a standardised set of most use to the generality of the shop; the materials handling systems will apply to the whole shop, etc.

Perhaps most important of all is that, if the operator is performing one task in a sequence, the time he takes will have to be balanced with the time taken by the other tasks. Consider the assembly of a line of washing machines. One part of the line will consists of a sequence of welding operations, each weld being performed by an operator using a specially designed welding machine. If one operation takes 3 minutes and all the others take 2 minutes then the result will be as if all operations take three minutes because the jobs can only come off the slower operation once every three minutes. Clearly there would be considerable saving if the slower operation could be redesigned so that it took 2 minutes (this is known as 'line balancing').

The design of work involves considerable skill, and many factors have to be taken into account — handling, setting up, adjusting, idle time, setting up methods related to batch size, the nature of the support from the toolroom and by capital investment, the relation of the operation to other work in the shop, and so on. When the operator's work has been designed it will be necessary to determine how long it will take him.

Commonly, it is assumed that an operation will be timed by the use of a stopwatch. This timing requires considerable skill because motion times are not fixed. Even for one man the time taken over a simple motion will vary. Generally, the simple motions are repeatedly timed so that the time of the whole operation is the sum of the motion times which are, in turn, times that are distributed in a probabilistic fashion (usually it is assumed that motion times are normally distributed). Times must be included that are outside the operator's control — waiting times, machine operation times, for example. Allowances must be made for rest breaks, for fatigue, or for the job not going according to plan. If payment by results is intended, there must be some policy by which hard work earns the operator a bonus. The man making the time study must also determine whether the operator is working at a standard rate or whether he could be expected to work faster (or possible even slower) when he is not being observed.

Such direct time study also creates difficulties because
most men object to being timed,
most men will make the job seem more difficult than it really is if their pay is to be linked with the observed times,
most operations are possible by so many combinations of motions, idle times and machine operations that experience often produces a better way of working than that designed by the expert.

In addition to timing an operation, the time study man must determine the operator's rate, usually on a percentage scale. An operator working at a rate of 80 would be producing, in an hour, only 80% of what we could expect an average man to produce. An operator working at a rate of 110 would produce in an hour, 110% of what the average operator would produce. If the observed time were t seconds and the operator were rated at 80% then the allowed time for the operation would be $0.8t$ (plus, of course, all allowances).

Times can, of course, be converted to the number of parts that can be made in an hour. If it takes t hours to make one part then the number of parts made in an hour will be $1/t$. This conversion is often necessary if the operator is paid by by the piece (piece-work).

Where there is some reason for not timing the man directly, perhaps because industrial relations are sensitive or perhaps because the part has not yet been made and the company are trying to predict its cost from drawings, use may be made of synthetic times or Predetermined Motion Time Study (PMTS). Here, again, the method of manufacture is designed, down to the small motions of the operator. Standard data have been published (e.g. MTM) which give the times that elementary motions (reach, grasp, etc.) might be expected to take, and with some experience, time study men can predict the direct labour content of a product with acceptable accuracy.

There are methods, then, by which the direct labour content of a component may be determined, although those methods carry with them some difficulties.

Motion study which leads to the best way of doing a job, and time study which tells us how long the job should take, are iterative procedures. Motion study must precede time study, but time study will usually lead to changes in work design and so will the experience of the operator. This leads to further difficulties because, if a man is paid by results, he will not be willing to see his allowed time reduced as his own experience makes the job easier.

Time and motion study may well be necessary if we are to know (i) how much a job will cost, and (ii) how much a job *did* cost. There is, however, a move away from the linking of time and motion study with the way a man is paid. PBR is believed to cause industrial problems, particularly where the operator sees little correlation between his wage and how hard he works. Shortage of parts (resulting from poor production control), shortage of tools (resulting from poor support from middle management), and the degree of investment are all seen by the operator to be more significant factors in productivity than his own efforts. Almost by definition, those jobs to which time study is most easily applied are those jobs which are most easily automated.

If PBR is used, we have a further complication in cost prediction. Usually a PBR system is not the simple piece-work in which the operator's wage is directly proportional to the number of pieces he produces. It is much more likely that the operator will be paid by the hour but with a fall-back (or basic) pay. The fall-back hourly rate may be paid to a man if his rated performance is 80 or below (or 100 or below), while if his output rises above this rating level, his hourly rate of pay will increase. This type of PBR is shown diagrammatically on Fig. 15.1. An operator's bonus may be anywhere between the line on which his bonus is the actual value of his extra output or some lower line on which he earns a bonus that is a fraction of his extra output (on the grounds, presumably, that the company wants to benefit from extra work and may deserve to do so if its management has made the extra output possible).

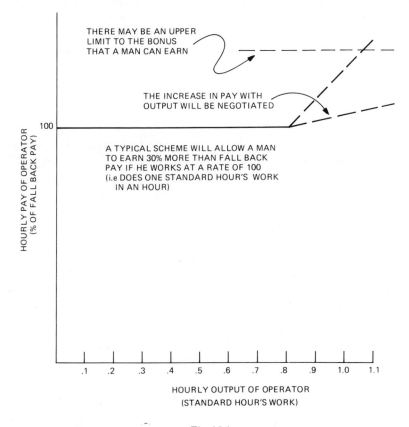

Fig. 15.1

Whenever PBR is more complex than simple piece-work, the estimator cannot simply determine costs from the direct labour content of a job in terms of standard hours.

So far we have been discussing the direct labour content of a job in terms of the work (motions) of a single operator. But a complex product is not made by a single operator. A motor car, a washing machine, a radio set, or an aeroplane is made up of hundreds of sub-assemblies; each sub-assembly is made up of many components; each component is made in a sequence of many operations. When, therefore, we want to know how much a product will cost (or how much it *has* cost), we need to know the whole sequence of operations on each component, the ways in which components are built into sub-assemblies, and the ways in which sub-assemblies are built into the main assembly. These procedures must also be designed and are best demonstrated by examples.

Fig. 15.2 is the process schedule which describes how a detail is made. Note that the schedule describes the raw material which must be taken from the stores, gives the number of parts required, gives the required delivery date, and then lists the sequence of operations. Against each operation is shown the resource or facility required and, where applicable, the set-up time, the time per piece, and the expected wastage.

PROCESS SCHEDULE

DESCRIPTION Coil Lock Ring				ORDER WK 42	PART NUMBER 54321
Tools Available	Material Available		Quantity 500 + 50	Req'd Wk 50	Batch Number 44066

Material Specification: 1¼ Dia. Bright Mild Steel BSS S.32		Qty Per 100 5 Ft	Part Number 54321	Issue						
Operation Number	10	20	30	40	50					
Machine Group	2	2	16	4	43	90				

OP. No.	M/C GP	DESCRIPTION OF OPERATION	T/A EACH (MINS)	SETTING TIME (MINS)	M/C TIME PER 100 (HRS)	TOTAL LOAD	QTY SCRAP	QTY GOOD	DATE COMPLETED
10	2	Cut to length and face	4.00	4½	6.70			550	13/2
20	2	Turn thread blank	0.95	210	1.58			550	20/12
30	16	Form thread	2.80	3	4.70			550	31/12
40	4	Turn Profile	0.80	2	1.33		3	547	6/1
50	43	Nickel Plate (to DTD 919)						547	10/1
	90	Deliver to Stores						547	10/1

Fig. 15.2 – Extract from a Process Schedule.

Fig. 15.3 is an assembly schedule which describes how a sub-assembly is put together and, in particular, what components are required, what facilities are required, and how much time should be taken.

ASSEMBLY SCHEDULE							
DESCRIPTION Spring Assembly				ORDER WK 40		PART NUMBER 12345	
TOOLS AVAILABLE	MATERIAL AVAILABLE		QUANTITY 10	REQ'D WK 50		M/A NUMBER 10345	
PART NUMBER	DESCRIPTION	SOURCE	No. OFF PER ASS	OPERATION	TOOLS REQU'D	SET UP TIME	TIME ALLOWED (EACH)
54321	coil lock ring	X stores	1	Grease coils with FS XYZ.	Fitter's bench	N/A	13 mins
65432	spring	X stores	1	Screw rate adjustor on to spring until measured rate is 10 lbs/in ± 0.01.	Fitter's hand tools		
64253	rate adjustor	X stores	1		Rate test rig (EXP 4321)		
"	compound DTD ABC	S stores		Apply locking compound (DTD ABC) to thread and lock adjustor to spring.			
	paint, grey DTD PQR	S stores					
	compound FS XYZ	S stores	"	Paint machined end of coil with DTD PQR.			

Fig. 15.3 – Extract from an Assembly Schedule.

Exercise 15.1 (for group discussion)

(i) *Why do we need to know the direct labour content of a job?*

(ii) *How important is it to know the direct labour content of a job compared with other costs?*

How, for example, is the direct labour cost likely to compare with the material cost?

(iii) *How dependent on the operator is the amount (and cost) of the direct labour cost in the total cost of a product?*

Is the answer dependent on the quantity of products being made?

(iv) *What are the difficulties in determining the direct labour cost of a product?*

How accurately would you expect to be in

(a) predicting the direct labour cost of a product; and

(b) determining how much the direct labour in a product has actually cost?

(v)   *Could PBR actually increase the cost of a job?*

(vi)   *What do you suppose is meant by the suggestion that operators 'hold back' before a job is timed?*

(vii)   *What technical skills are required in the production of process and assembly schedules?*

(viii) *It has been suggested that PBR is used more in the UK than in the USA, and more in the USA than in Japan. Discuss why this might be the case and what you would expect the results to be.*

16

Estimating

There is no point in making an article to sell unless it can be made at a cost which is less than the selling price. The selling price is usually the price that the customer is prepared to pay and is determined by the customer's own business and by competition much more than by the manufacturer. Determining the selling price by adding a profit margin to the cost of manufacture will not serve if this gives a price which is greater than the customer will pay.

The fact that the selling price of a product is under the control of the manufacturer to a very limited extent makes it imperative that he estimates his manufacturing cost very carefully because he will not often be able to turn a loss into a profit by raising prices. In any case, with a product of any complexity, the price is negotiated with the customer long before the product has been made. Estimating costs in advance of production is very important because, however good are design and manufacture, if the price which has been negotiated is too low to cover costs, the company will lose money. In addition to forecasting costs we have to know how much a job *has* cost to make because

(i)   such knowledge is necessary if we are to be able to predict future job costs, and

(ii)   comparing actual costs with predicted costs tells us where managers have not done their job properly and where we should mount cost reduction exercises.

In Chapter 12 we discussed the life cycle of a product, and in Chapter 14 we discussed ways of allocating costs. We can use these ideas to build up methods of cost forecasting.

NON–RECURRING COSTS

Market research, specification, design prototype manufacture, development, and tooling are mainly non-recurring costs. There are costs incurred by the introduction of specification changes (but these are development costs if the changes are the result of putting things right or costs which the customer must pay if he has changed his mind), and there are costs caused by the refurbishing of tools (but these should be taken into account as future negative cash flows). Generally, we can argue that, however many products we manufacture the costs of these functions will not occur again, and they may be regarded as fixed costs. We generally divide these non-recurring costs into

(i)   market research which is covered by the budget of the marketing director,

(ii)   specification, design, prototype manufacture, and development, which are covered by the budget of the technical director, and

(iii) tooling, which is covered by the capital budget of the production director.

Market research may well be treated as an overhead since few manufacturers would employ many people in this role. In such a case, the salaries and other expenses of market researchers are simply added into the company overhead which will ultimately be carried by the direct labour content of all the products made.

In some cases, when it is believed that market research is going to be very expensive (as it may be when launching a new car, defining a major civil engineering project or an aerospace project), a sum of money will be set aside for the work. This means that the marketing director must predict the number of man hours that he expects to employ on this phase of the project. Even if the marketing director is able to do this, a further difficulty arises because, by its very nature, the time spent on market research may have to be written off. If market research discovers that the world does not want the suggested motor car, Channel Tunnel, or supersonic transport then the money spent on that market research will have to be paid for by the products which do find customers.

Where it is hoped that the market research will be paid for directly by the product under discussion, the costs will be predicted, then recorded and charged against the job, if it is a success, or written off as an overhead, to be paid for by other successful jobs.

Design, prototype manufacture, and development may be treated as an overhead when they form a very small part of the total cost of a product. Many companies spend only about 1% of their total costs on design and development, and there would be little point in attempting to allocate these costs to individual products when even a hundred per cent error in estimating would be negligible in the amount it added to the selling price.

In some cases, however, the design and development costs are far from negligible. Whether they must be estimated specifically for each product depends on the extent of the work involved and the number of products made. The design and development costs of an aeroplane at over £1000M contribute the major part of the cost of each aeroplane if only about a dozen are sold; the design and development costs of a satellite are much more significant than the manufacturing cost of the satellite itself.

Sheet 1
Design and Development

Engineering Division Estimate

Description..

Customer..

Drawing number and issue
on which estimate is based...

Specification number and
issue on which estimate is based ....

Office	Description of Work	Man hours	Costs	Remarks
Technical	Preparation of specification Performance analysis Stress analysis			
	Sub-total			
Drawing Office	Scheme drawing Detail drawings Sub-assembly drawings Work arising from development			
	Sub-total			
Development Dept.	Development Endurance tests Manufacture of test rigs			
	Sub-total			
	Material for test rigs Bought out test equipt.			
	Sub-total			
	Number of prototypes required for testing			

Fig. 16.1

Sheet 2

Prototype Shop

Engineering Division Estimate

Description. . . . .

Customer . . . .

Drawing number and issue
on which estimate is based . . . .

Specification number and
issue on which estimate is based . . . .

Description of work	Man hours	Costs	Remarks
Machining Assembly Inspection Tool design			
Sub-total			
Materials Bought out parts Parts from Production Dept.			
Sub-total			

Fig. 16.1 – continued

Fig. 16.1 is a form which is used in one company for predicting design and development costs, and it will be seen that

> designers are required to predict the *man hours* that will be required to design the product,
>
> development engineers will be required to predict the *man hours* that will be required to develop the product and how many prototypes they will require for testing,
>
> the experimental shop foreman is required to predict the *man hours* that will be required to make the prototypes that will be used for development, and
>
> the cost of the materials and *bought out parts* that he will need.

Tooling costs also vary in their importance from one type of manufacture to another. To embark on the manufacture of a mass produced car may require an investment in a production line at a cost of several hundred million pounds. Even without considering the time value of money, the cost of the production line will contribute several hundred pounds to the cost of each car that is sold.

At the other extreme, in a jobbing shop making small batches of products to order, there will be few expensive tools that are designed especally to make a particular product. The machines in the factory will be general purpose machines (centre lathes, mills, borers, etc.) which may be used whatever product is made but perhaps with the help of small, inexpensive, fixtures for each product.

In such a case, the cost of the plant will not be treated as a non-recurring cost of the product but be broken down into hourly costs of running so that the use of any machine may be incorporated into the direct manufacturing cost of the product. This incorporation of machine costs into direct manufacturing costs will be discussed later.

The problem of fixed cost has been discussed in Chapter 14, and the following numerical example will serve as revision.

Example 16.1

A production plant is built at a cost of £100M with the intention of building 1M cars at the rate of 100 000 a year over 10 years. The cost of capital is 12% and the scrap value at the end of ten years will just pay for site clearance. How much does the plant contribute to the cost of each car?

At 12%, the effective annual cost of the plant over its life will be

$$\text{£100M}/(p/a)_{10}^{0.12}$$
$$= \text{£100M}/5.65 = \text{£17.699M}$$

Spreading this cost over 100 000 cars gives a contribution of £176.99 to the cost of each car.

Allowing for the cost of tooling in the cost of the product does not present many problems except for the difficulty of predicting the cost of the tooling. When it is worth treating tooling costs as a fixed cost of the product, the specification of design and manufacture of the tooling will itself be a major project.

The design of tooling is itself a major task both from the point of view of the man hours that it takes and also because the planning of manufacture determines both the tools and the operations that are required to manufacture the product.

VARIABLE COSTS

The variable costs consist of the direct labour costs, the direct materials costs, and the overheads that one or other (usually direct labour) of these direct costs must carry.

The direct material costs may be calculated from the manufacturing drawings. Each detail drawing will specify the material from which the detail is made, and it is straightforward to calculate the raw material which must be bought and from which the detail will be cut (or forged, moulded, cast, or whatever process is to be used).

The bought out, manufactured components are also listed on the manufacturing drawings. The buying of these components is a skilled job because, whether they are purchased from a catalogue or made to order through a sub-contract, there is a need to negotiate the best price. Within this is the need to determine the best ordering quantity. To buy too many components before they are required means that capital is invested earlier than necessary, with the cost that that involves. On the other hand, buying a large number of the components usually attracts a discount.

The direct labour cost will be calculated in ways that have been discussed in Chapter 15. That is, each job will be broken into the sequence of operations and the time of each operation either measured by time study or predicted by some Predetermined Motion Time Study (PMTS). Measuring the time when the cost has to be predicted may seem to be a contradictory suggestion because, if the cost has to be predicted, it is unlikely that manufacture will have started; but most companies who need to predict operation and job times keep records of measured times, and it is frequently possible for such a company to base time predictions on the records of times taken to perform similar operations in the past.

Of course, as we have seen, an operator's job time will not be determined only by his own motions. He will frequently have to wait for the machine that he is operating, to finish a cut. Generally, the calculation of the time taken by a machine to cut the part from the raw material is reasonably straightforward. The estimator will know how to make the part by studying the drawing. He will know how to set it up in the fixture (operator's time), how great a thickness the machine will cut away at each cut, how fast the detail will travel, and hence how many cuts will be made by the machine (hence he can calculate machine time), he will know whether the part must be removed from or moved in the fixture for measurement or further machining (operator time), and he will be able to determine the total time taken by the machine to cut away the metal which leaves the detail as required by the drawing. This type of estimating applies to prototype and very small batch manufacture, but when large enough quantities justify investment in more special purpose tooling, the machine virtually takes over, and the man's time in an operation becomes more calculable but less significant. With, for example, a numerically controlled machine or a specially designed spot welding machine, every effort is made to reduce the operator's time, although the time saved must clearly more than pay for the extra investment.

We see, then, that for any job we should be able to estimate the operator's time and the machine time. We must remember too that both the operator and the machine are necessarily idle during part of the work, but this idle time must be paid for as much as useful motions. There will also be occasions when the operator and the machine are idle between jobs.[†]

Fig. 16.2 is an example of a typical operation in the manufacture of a washing machine and we see that the whole operation takes 33 seconds of which the operator is working for 21 seconds and the machine for 12 seconds although each is occupied for the full 33 seconds. In addition, there will be times when the line is changed from one model to another and while the fixtures are being changed the machine is necessarily idle. We have already discussed (in Chapter 15) the fact that the operator will not be able to give 100% of his time to useful work, and even when directly concerned with (and clocked onto) a job, he will sometimes have to wait for the job to come from the previous operation, he will need to clean down the machine, he will need to make adjustments, he will need to wait for an inspector to check his work, he will need to clock on and off, he will need to record his work, and so on.

Operator lifts washing machine shell off overhead conveyor, puts it into the welding machine, centres it in the fixture, closes gate and then switches on the machine	13 seconds (operator working, machine idle)
The machine logic moves the welding calipers to four points of the shell in turn, making a spot weld at each. The job is released and gate opened.	12 seconds (machine working, operator idle)
The operator lifts the job off the machine, checks it and puts it onto the overhead conveyor.	8 seconds (operator working, machine idle)

Man/machine interaction

Fig. 16.2

[†] Simple queing theory demonstrates that it is virtually impossible to use more than about 80% of the available time of any resource if reasonable delivery dates are to be met.

We have seen (in Chapter 15) that some overhead on direct labour is accounted for by necessary idle time of the operator. If we intend to calculate the machining costs to allow for both the operator's time and the machine time, we must allow for machine idle time too.

Example 16.2

An operator who is paid £100 a week operates a machine which cost £10 000 and has a five year life. Capital costs 15%. The machine and operator perform one operation on a product which takes 33 seconds. If it is assumed that the man and the machine can be employed usefully for only 75% of the time available, what is the cost of the operation in terms of

(i) direct labour, and
(ii) paying for the machine.

Assume that five eight-hour shifts a week are worked.

(i) The man costs, initially £2.50 an hour, but since only 75% of his time is useful, this becomes £2.50/0.75 = £3.33 an hour.
The operation thus costs

$$100 \times 33 \times 3.33/(60 \times 60) \text{ pence for direct labour}$$
$$= 3.05 \text{ pence.}$$

(ii) The machine costs £10 000, and at 15% the equivalent annual cost is

$$£10\,000 \ / \ 3.352$$

The hourly cost (allowing for waiting, etc.) is

$$£10\,000/(3.352 \times 40 \times 50 \times 0.75) \text{ so that}$$

the cost for the operation is

$$(100 \times 33 \times 10\,000)/(3.352 \times 40 \times 50 \times 0.75 \times 60 \times 60)$$
$$= 1.82 \text{ pence.}$$

These costs are only for direct labour and for paying for the machine. They do not include overheads (other than the man's idle time), maintenance, power, or materials.

This example demonstrates that we can determine the direct costs of man and machine for an operation, and by summing these costs over all operations we can determine the cost of man and machine for the whole product. Note, however, that while the man's time and machine's time which are directly concerned with the operation can be calculated with some accuracy, the allowances for idle times and the estimate of the cost of capital introduce elements which cannot be predicted with accuracy.

The further problem occurs when we attempt to bring in other costs as overheads on the direct labour cost of the operation. We have seen that the cost of the machine can reasonably be added as overhead, for in Example 16.2 we calculated that the man cost 3.05p for the operation while the machine cost 1.82p. This could have been regarded as 3.05p plus $(1.82/3.05) \times 100\%$ overhead = 3.05 + 60% overhead, or we could have argued that the man's time on that particular machine

cost £3.33 + 60% overhead
= £5.33 an hour

(Note that this accounts only for some idle time and for the cost of the machine.)

Such an example suggests that if a job is done on an expensive machine the overhead will be greater than if the operator uses only simple, cheap tools, but accountants find differential overheads complicated to use and prefer to charge one price per hour regardless of the skill or equipment complexity required.

More difficult is the fact that generally, the direct labour cost of a product is a small part of its total cost. It is not common for the direct labour content of a product to exceed about 20%, and it could be as low as 5%. One company believes that about 14% of the cost of an aeroplane is attributable to direct labour costs when the production run is about 200; with shorter runs, the direct labour costs are an even smaller percentage of the total cost. As we saw in Chapter 14, this implies that the overhead is several hundred per cent, and so we must be careful that we do not calculate our direct costs meticulously and then add an almost arbitrary large overhead which is several times more important than direct costs but which has not been analysed.

Exercise 16.1
Give examples of costs which may be regarded as non-recurring costs or fixed costs. State the product that you are considering.

(Development cost of an aeroplane;
the cost of an oil rig is a fixed cost on the cost of oil;
the cost of an oil refinery is a fixed cost on the petroleum products;
the cost of a van to a milk roundsman;
. . . .)

Exercise 16.2
Give examples of capital investment that may be treated as an overhead on direct labour. State the product that is being made.

(Centre lathes in a jobbing machine shop doing small subcontract work;
the plating bath used for plating many of the firm's products;
small tools such as power drills used by fitters during aircraft assembly;
. . . .)

Exercise 16.3
How would you predict the man hours required to develop a product.

(Comparison with similar, previous jobs: note that this means that records of times spent must be kept.)

Exercise 16.4
List some necessary company activities that may be treated as overheads on direct labour.

(Time and motion study; wage calculation; personnel management;
. . . .)

Exercise 16.5
Why is it desirable for as many workers as possible to account for their time?

(This increases the direct labour content of a job and reduces the overheads which cannot be properly analysed.)

List some jobs which might be possible to treat as direct labour even though the worker concerned is not either making a detail of the product or assembling it.

(There is no reason why some supervisors should not record their time so that it may be apportioned directly to jobs; inspectors could sometimes record their time so that it could be allocated directly;
. . . .)

Exercise 16.6
Suggest a methodology for predicting the direct labour content of a product.
Design a form which could be used to predict the direct labour content of a job.

Exercise 16.7
Suggest a procedure for determining the overheads that will be added to direct labour.
Assume that the overheads (as a percentage) are being calculated once a year in a production department.

Exercise 16.8
What factors make it difficult to calculate, precisely, the overhead that will add to direct labour costs?

(Idle times of machines; idle times of workers; the different values of different workers; the different facilities required by different workers;
. . . .)

Exercise 16.9

What factors might affect the price of bought out components, sub-assemblies or materials?

(Quantities bought; promise of further orders; required delivery date; level of inspection required; . . . .)

17

Learning curves

It has been shown that, with many products, the cost of manufacture reduces as more and more products are made. This was first demonstrated, before World War II, to apply to the manufacture of aeroplanes, but it is now known to apply to almost any manufacture in which numbers of products are involved.

In one version, when we speak of 80% learning, we mean that if the first product costs   £a to make,
the second costs   £(0.8)a,
the fourth costs   £(0.8) (0.8)a
the eighth costs   £(0.8) (0.8) (0.8)a,
etc.

Every time we double the number of products made, the time taken to make one product is cut to 80% of what it was.

In another version (still assuming 80% learning) when we double the number of products made, the average cost of the product reduces to 80% of what it was.

Thus if the first product costs £a;
the average product cost over two products is £(0.8)a;
the average product cost over four products is £(0.8) (0.8)a,
etc.

We will consider the use of the first of these versions because recent publications show it to be used in estimating costs.

Consider a learning rate of k (where $0 < k < 1$)
The first product costs   £a
the second product costs   £ka
the fourth product costs   £k^2a

. . . .

the (2^n)th product costs   £k^na
If $m = 2^n$ then the cost of
the mth product is £k^na

where $\log m = n \log 2$

or $n = (\log m)/(\log 2)$,

therefore the cost of the mth product is $£k^{(\log m)/(\log 2)}a$

If we write

$$C_m = \text{the cost of the } m\text{th product}$$
then $\quad C_m = k^{(\log m)/(\log 2)}a$

or $\log\ C_m = (\log m)\,(\log k)/(\log 2) + \log a$

or $\quad C_m = am^{(\log k)/(\log 2)}$.

If the rate of learning is 80%

i.e. $\quad k = 0.8$
$$C_m = a\,m^{(\log 0.8)/(\log 2)}$$
$$= a\,m^{-0.322}\ .$$

If the rate of learning is 70%

$$C_m = a\,m^{-0.515}\ .$$

Exercise 17.1
If $C_m = a\,m^{-b}$, calculate b for learning rates of 0.65; 0.70; 0.75; 0.80; 0.85; 0.90; 0.95.

[0.622; 0.515; 0.415; 0.322; 0.234; 0.152; 0.074

Exercise 17.2
If the first aeroplane costs £10M to build and the learning rate is 80%, what does the 100th aeroplane cost? What does the 200th aeroplane cost?

[£2.269M; £1.815M

What does the 100th aeroplane cost if the learning rate can be pushed to 0.75?

[£1.479M

What does the 100th aeroplane cost if a learning rate of 0.9 is all that can be achieved?

[4.966M

Learning is often assumed to result from the the increased dexterity of the operator as he learns to do his job, and there is a great deal of evidence (dating at least from the Hawthorn experiment) to show that the operator can reduce his time on an operation as he gets used to performing it. There are, however, many other factors which contribute to learning; production support improves so that the fitter is less often required to assemble with shortages (parts not available); the methods engineers sees ways of improving the way a job is done or devises better tools; the designer finds ways of simplifying the component, etc.

Learning is typically at about 80%, but the above example shows how improving learning from, say, 80% to, say, 75%, reduces costs very considerably.

Learning may be used to demonstrate the distribution of fixed costs among products. If we ignore time values of money we know that the cost of making m products is

$$C_m = F + Vm \text{ where } F \text{ is the fixed cost and}$$
$$V \text{ is the variable cost per product.}$$

If the fixed cost is distributed equally over all products then the mth product must contribute $£F/m$ to the fixed cost.

If f_m = portion of fixed cost carried by each product when m are made

$$f_m = F/m = Fm^{-1}$$
$$= F^{(\log k/\log 2)}$$

when $(\log k/\log 2) = -1$

or $\log k = -\log 2 = \log \frac{1}{2}$
or $k = \frac{1}{2}$.

The distribution of fixed costs is thus comparable to a 50% learning curve.

We may draw the learning curve, that is we may plot the graph of cost/product as it reduces with the number of products made.

Example 17.3
Plot the 'learning curve' which shows the cost of the mth product when the learning rate is 80% and the first product costs £100. Plot over the range $m = 1, \ldots, 100$.

Referring to Exercise 17.1 we see that, for 80% learning, the cost of the mth product is given by

$$C_m = a\, m^{-0.322} \text{ where } C_m \text{ is the cost of the } m\text{th product and } a \text{ is the cost}$$
of the first.

We may construct the following table:

m	1	5	10	15	20	25	30	35	40	45	50
C_m	100	59.6	47.6	41.8	38.1	35.5	33.4	31.8	30.5	29.4	28.4

m	55	60	65	70	75	80	85	90	95	100
C_m	27.5	26.8	26.1	25.5	24.9	24.4	23.9	23.5	23.1	22.7

This is shown plotted on Fig. 17.1.

An alternative method is to remember the way in which learning was defined. 80% learning implies that the cost of the 2nd product is 80% of the cost of the first, and the cost of the 4th product is 80% of the cost of the second, and the cost of the 8th product is 80% of the cost of the fourth, etc.

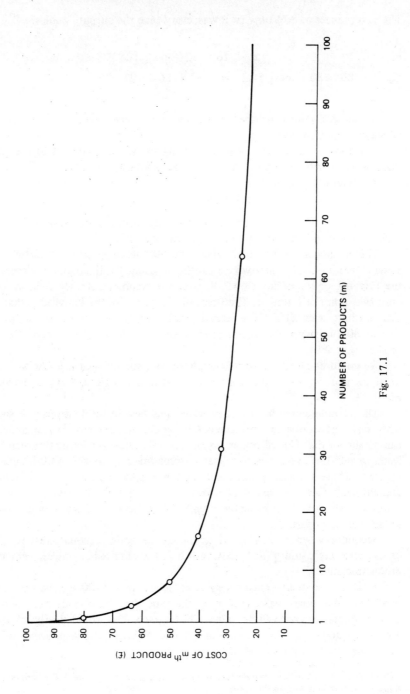

COST OF mth PRODUCT (£)

NUMBER OF PRODUCTS (m)

Fig. 17.1

The cost reduces to 80% of what it was, every time the output doubles.

m	1	2	4	8	16	32	64	128
C_m	100	80	64	51.2	41	32.8	26.2	21

It can easily be confirmed that these points give the same curve as that already shown plotted in Fig. 17.1.

Yet another, and easier, way of plotting the learning curve is to use graph paper with logarithmic scales (vertical and horizontal).

Consider $C_m = a\,m^{-b}$

then $\log C_m = -b \log m + \log a$,

therefore if we plot $\log C_m$ versus $\log m$ we expect to obtain a straight line with a slope of $-b$ and an intercept on the vertical axis at $\log a$[†].

This is shown on Fig. 17.2 where the 80% learning curve is plotted as a straight line on graph paper with logarithmic scales. On this figure the costs for the first ten products are shown. Because the graph is a straight line, we need only two points to draw it. The first point is given by the knowledge that the first product costs £100. The second point may be determined from the fact that at 80% learning, the second product will cost 80% of the cost of the first product (i.e. £80).

We could easily continue this graph on to a second sheet because we know its slope and we know the cost at 10 products. A continuation is shown in Fig. 17.3.

The learning curve has two important qualities. In the first place, it shows what cost reductions can be achieved by good management. For example, it can be shown that United States aircraft manufacturers achieve better than 80% learning and this continues over many (sometimes up to the 1000th aircraft) products whereas British aircraft manufacturers achieve poorer rates of learning and although they are capable of making the first few aeroplanes at costs which compare well with those made by foreign competitors, the costs are not reduced as fast over long runs.

Secondly, when estimating prices in order to tender, account must be taken of the company's ability (and a competitor's ability) to reduce prices over a long production run.

Thus if a company makes a product at a cost of £100 for the first to be produced, they might assume that by the time they have made fifty or sixty such products the cost will be under £30 for each. This would clearly influence the price quoted to the customer and would highlight the significance of the size of any order or the size of the market.

[†]This follows from the well known formula for a straight line; $y = mx + C$ where m is the slope and C the intercept on the y axis.

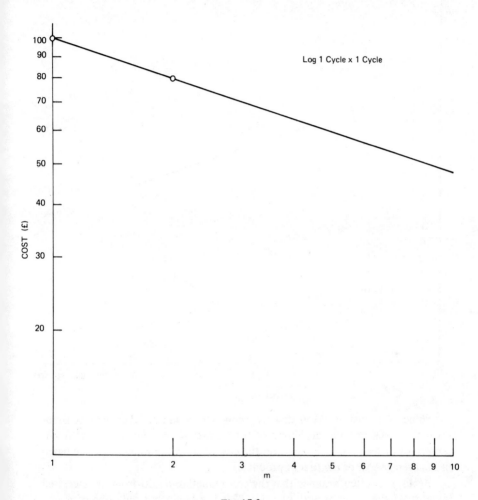

Fig. 17.2

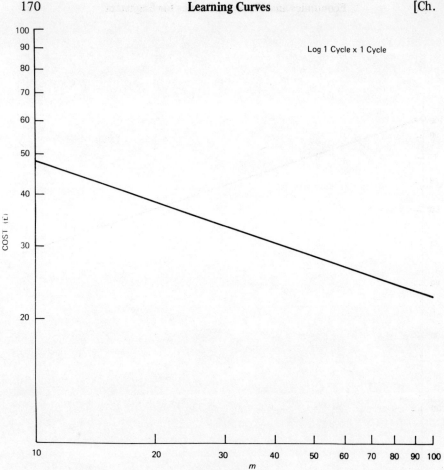

Fig. 17.3

Some care must be taken that we know what we mean when we talk about 'learning curves'. At the beginning of the chapter we considered two different definitions of learning, one based on the cost of the mth product and one based on the average cost of the first m products.

Again, it is often assumed that the cost reduction results from the increased dexterity of the operator with practice. This is a factor but only one of many, and it may be of low importance against improvements in process design. Attempts to improve learning should not be aimed at the operator only. It is true that most companies derive their learning curves from their records of direct labour hours booked to each product, but this must not lead us to assume that the reduction is wholly the result of the operator's learning.

We must also be careful in our interpretation of learning because, as we know, direct labour contributes only a small percentage of the cost of a product. If, say, direct labour initially contributes 14% of the cost of the product and we reduce direct labour by half, we will have reduced the total cost of the product by 7% unless we have also reduced overheads. Any interpretation of learning curves requires us to be careful to know exactly what costs have been reduced.

If a factory has 1000 employees of whom 140 are direct workers and if output is doubled, then product costs are halved.

If a factory has 1000 employees and the doubling of the productivity of the direct workers enables their numbers to be reduced from 140 to 70, then product costs are reduced by 7%.

Exercise 17.3

Plot the 90%, 80%, and 70% learning curves on the same axes, over the range 1 product to 200 and where the cost of manufacturing the first product is £100. Use ordinary graph paper.

Repeat the exercise using 3 cycle, log-log graph paper.   [see Fig. 17.4

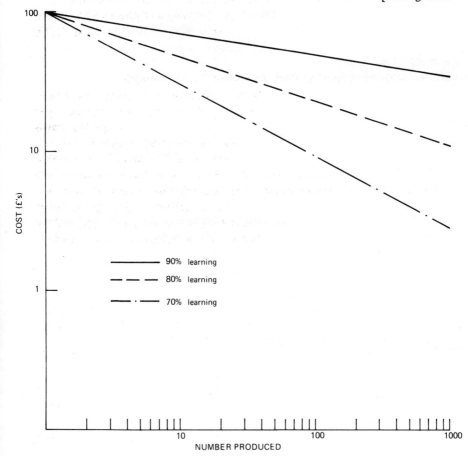

Fig. 17.4

Exercise 17.4

Aeroplane manufacturer A makes the first aircraft of a particular design for £50M and has a 90% learning curve.

Aeroplane manufacturer B makes the first aircraft of a competing model for £80M and has an 80% learning curve.

At what size order will B start to make cheaper aircraft than A?

[at about the 16th aircraft

Exercise 17.5

A company designs and makes atomic power stations. So far they have built three to the same design. The first cost £200M to build, the second cost £160M to build, and the third cost a little over £140M to build.

If the company quotes £138.24M for building the fourth power station to the same design, how much profit would they expect to make on the deal?

[about 8%. The figures suggest an 80% learning
curve with the fourth costing £128M

Exercise 17.6

List and discuss five factors which might contribute to learning.

[Better production control reduces shortages;
design changes make manufacture easier;
the operator learns;
the manufacturing method is improved;
experience leads to better tool design;
experience permits the elimination of some inspection procedures;
insistance on better quality components from suppliers reduces rejection rates;
experience leads to better plant layout;
experience leads to improved materials handling;
preventive maintenance reduces down time;
. . . .
. . . .)

18

Standard costs

Standard costs are the costs that we have predicted for each of the elements in the total cost of a product. Thus as we have seen in Fig. 14.2 or as we may determine from the process schedule of Fig. 15.2 the cost of any component may be divided into

direct material cost,
direct labour cost,
shop overhead and
company overhead.

Material cost will be determined by

the amount of material used,
the cost of the material, and
the amount of material scrapped through failure to make the component properly.

If, then, the cost of the material is predicted and if records are kept of the cost of the material used, the manager (prompted by the accountant) will know whether the material in a component has cost more or less than it should have done.

The predicted cost of the material is the standard material cost;
the amount by which the actual cost exceeds, or is less than the standard cost is known as the 'variance', and if the variance is large and positive, the manager knows that he must investigate the manufacturing process.

If the variance is small or zero, the manager may assume that the process is acceptable. We have, in fact, provided the manager with a tool with which he can

MANAGE BY EXCEPTION

If the manager discovers a positive variance he will investigate whether

(i)   the material is being bought at a price greater than had been allowed, or
(ii) more material is being used than had been allowed for. This could be because of having purchased raw material of the wrong size or specification or because bad workmanship is causing too much scrap.

Direct labour cost will be determined by the

the wages paid and
the efficiency of the operator.

If there is a payment by results scheme, then there is no problem in determining the standard cost because a time will have been allowed for each operation. From this can be determined the number of components that should be made in any fixed period — the required number per hour, per week, or per accounting period. If payment is not by results, there must still be some means of controlling production, and normally this will be the production schedule. The production schedule, as we have seen, gives the time allowed for each operation (and time allowed for setting up, etc.). The standard time must be available then if production is being controlled.

By keeping records of time spent, it is straightforward to compare the actual cost of direct labour with the standard cost, and if there is a large positive variance, the manager will be required to determine the cause.

The cause is likely to be

(i)   the wage being paid per hour is greater than has been budgeted. This is unlikely to happen casually except in cases where a PBR scheme is not being properly maintained, or
(ii) the time taken by the operator is greater than the standard time.

Of course, the first intimation of a positive variance will be in terms of cost only. There will be a need for some analysis to find out where the extra cost has been incurred, and it may be that several factors contribute to the variance.

Most of the costs of a product are, of course, overheads, and they do not show easily in the standard costs or the variances. If a shop is making only one product the actual cost of the product may always be determined by simply dividing the number of the product made in any accounting period into the total costs incurred by the shop. The overheads will simply be those costs not accounted for by either direct labour or direct material. This will yield a variance (either positive, zero, or negative) which may have to be investigated, but it does not point readily to the cause of any excess overhead.

If a shop produces many different products, the allocation of overheads within any product cost may be almost arbitrary. If one product is harder to sell than another, would a greater portion of the cost of selling be added to its overhead?

Perhaps, where there is any complexity in the production process, where many different products are made and where many manufacturing methods are used, there needs to be a regular analysis of overheads. Most companies determine their overheads at least once a year — this is made necessary by the setting up of a corporate plan, the establishment of departmental budgets and of departmental targets. The checking of these targets and budgets every accounting period does permit some sort of variance analysis although it does not direct the manager to the cause of the variance.

Exercise 18.1
Discuss the ways in which variances in material costs might be detected.

Discuss the ways in which variances in direct labour costs might be detected.

Exercise 18.2
Suggest examples of products where standard costing of materials might be easy and useful.

Suggest examples of products where standard costing of direct-labour might be easy and useful.

Exercise 18.3
Discuss the ways in which overhead costs may be controlled.

19

Tenders

The business of manufacturing and selling goods falls into two broad areas. In one of these, the company decides what the customer will buy, designs it, makes it, and then tries to sell it. This is commonly the case where the goods are made in large quantities for the consumer market. A motor manufacturer or a washing machine manufacturer is usually in this situation. This situation is usually (but not necessarily) associated with mass or large batch production.

The other situation is that in which the manufacturer responds to invitations from a prospective customer to tender. Market research and some design are carried on before tendering, but the major costs of design, development, and manufacture are not incurred until the customer has accepted the tender and committed himself to buying the product. This situation is usually (but not necessarily) associated with unit or small batch production.

Determining the selling price of a product which is not sold until after it has been built is a matter entirely for the manufacturer. In ways that have been discussed in Chapters 15, 16, 17, and 18, the manufacturer can establish the cost of making the product and add to that cost a profit which will give a selling price that his marketing department believes that the customer will pay.

In the case of the manufacturer who obtains work by tendering, the selling price of the product will be the subject of detailed negotiation with the customer, although it will follow the initial offer by the manufacturer to sell at a price that the customer finds competitive.

Usually when a manufacturer is tendering for a major product, he is offering a high degree of expertise and the product is likely to have a high technological content.

When a customer wishes to buy a particular product he will invite suitable firms to tender for the work and his invitation will be accompanied by

(i) a technical specification which describes the performance requirements of the required product,

(ii) a statement of the required delivery date(s),

(iii) a statement of the required product support (which may be operating manuals, servicing and maintenance manuals, training for operators and service engineers, and guaranteed spares availability) and

a statement of the maximum permissible costs of breakdown.

Appendix 4 discusses a design specification pro forma in the context of some of the above factors.

It is usually assumed that the manufacturer who tenders the lowest price will get the job, but this would occur only in the case of the simplest of products or where the tender is for products which are already being built.

In the case of a product of any technical complexity the customer will first examine the manufacturer's proposal to convince himself that it will meet the technical requirements, and he will examine the manufacturer's resources to convince himself that they are capable of doing the job.

Most customers are aware that when they buy a product of any complexity, the purchase price will be only a small proportion of the cost of owning the product over its whole life cycle. In the case of buying a car or an aeroplane, a customer will spend, as the purchase price, perhaps 20% of the total cost to him of buying, running, maintaining, and eventually getting rid of the product. It may be much more worthwhile for the customer to haggle over fuel consumption, ease of operation, reliability, life, spares availability and cost, and skilled service support than over the purchase price.

The ability of the manufacturer to deliver on time will be worth money to the customer. This is partly because of the time value of money but also because any delay to the customer's operation will cost him money. What happens if a factory is built but the approach roads to it are completed late? What happens to a shipping line if a holiday cruise liner that it has ordered is delivered late? What happens to the output of a motor car manufacturer if the conveyor system he has ordered for the production line of a new model is delivered late?

The following, at least, has to be agreed between supplier and customer during the negotiations which precede a firm tender:

(i)   Required performance
(ii)   Proof that the required performance will be met. This is not a simple matter of endurance testing, because no testing (or even records of performance in the field) can provide absolute proof that, e.g. the life will be what is required, that the environmental conditions will never be more extreme than those specified, or even that the stated performance is really what the customer needs.

Usually, then, there must be agreement on what the testing will consist of, and it may be that the customer will want his own engineers or inspectorate to be involved.

Sometimes performance can be proved only in service, and the time allowed after delivery for the manufacturer to prove compliance with the specification must be agreed.

(iii) Proof that any particular product meets the agreed standard. This means that there must be agreement between manufacturer and customer about the inspection procedure and the inspecting authority.

(iv) Delivery dates. This is not simply a single date for the delivery of the product but will be a programme for delivery of a number of products to different, improving standards; a programme of development; a programme for spares availability; a programme for operator training, etc. The contract may include a penalty for late delivery.

(v) The price. This again will not be a simple sum to be paid on delivery of the product. There will be a programme of payments tied to various stages of completion of the contracted requirements.

Some parts of the contract may be subjects for separate negotiations — training programmes, test equipment, operating and service manuals, etc. Some contracts carry allowances for inflation and the consequent increase in employees' salaries.

Some contracts permit the renegotiation of prices if environmental conditions do not turn out to be as predicted.

(vi) Any warranty period and what the supplier will be responsible for during that period. Will he be required to replace parts free of charge, supply free labour, or even pay for the customer's cost of down time?

(vii) What the customer is buying. He has certainly bought an engineered product. Has he bought the drawings? Will he own the patent?

(viii) How the goods will be delivered and who will be responsible for damage during transit.

When the tendering company determines the price(s) that it will charge for the product the following approximate procedure will be followed:

(i) Determine the cost of tendering. This may be sufficiently small to absorb as an overhead but in some cases will amount to about 10% of the development costs. Certainly the cost of the tendering process must be considered.

(ii) Determine the cost of design, prototype manufacture, and development. This has been discussed in Chapter 16.

(iii) Determine the cost of tooling. This has been discussed in Chapter 16.

(iv) Determine the cost of manufacture. This has been discussed in Chapter 16.

(v) Determine the cost of product support over the life of the product. These are the costs of having spares and service engineers available.

(vi) Determine how the cost may be modified with the quantity of products ordered. This has been discussed in Chapter 17.

Exercise 19.1
List 10 costs that must be taken into account by the sales director when he is tendering the price of a complex, technical product.

Exercise 19.2
List 4 costs that must be taken into account when tendering but which cannot be determined precisely.

Exercise 19.3
Give 3 reasons why a customer might not accept the lowest tender.

Exercise 19.4
What do you understand by the expression 'Life Cycle Costs'?

Exercise 19.5
Obtain and discuss the recommended forms of contract that are suggested by one of the major engineering institutions.

Part III

SUPPLY AND DEMAND

20

Cost, price and profit

Up to now we have assumed that the marketing director knows the market and knows what the customer is prepared to pay for the product, or else that he negotiates a price with a single customer. This is generally true of large and complex engineering products but it is a matter of common knowledge that the number of products sold may depend on their price. If a seller negotiates with Mr Jones to sell him a car, it is true that Mr Jones should know how much he is prepared to pay; but if he could get it for less he would, and if the price of the car is reduced, more men like Mr Jones will buy it.

We can modify our break-even curve as shown in Fig. 20.1. Here we have

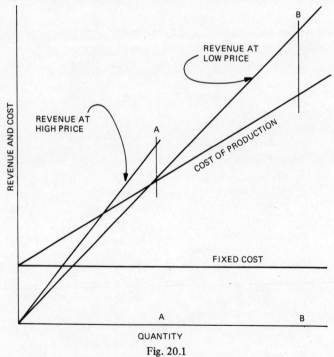

Fig. 20.1

the usual cost of production which is the sum of fixed and variable costs but we have two possible revenue curves. The higher of these curves shows the revenue if a high price is charged for the product and at the price charged *A* units will be sold. The difference between revenue and costs gives the profit, which is shown.

Suppose now that by reducing the price of the product, sales can be doubled so that *B* units will be sold. Although the revenue per unit is less, the increased sales at the lower price actually mean that profit is increased.

Of course, whether total profit is increased or not does depend on how much sales are increased by the reduced price.

Exercise 20.1
The fixed costs of making a product are £2000 and the variable costs are £10 per unit. The product is sold for £12 and 2000 are sold.

If the selling price is reduced to £11, how many of the product must be sold before the reduced selling price increases profit?

Draw the break-even curves.   [4000

Exercise 20.2
The fixed costs of making a product are £2000 and the variable costs are £10 per unit.

The selling price is £12 per unit and 2000 units are sold.

The marketing director believes that he could sell 3000 units if the price of the product were reduced. To what level could he afford to lower the product price in an attempt to sell 3000 units?

Draw the break-even curves.   [£11.34

The problem of break-even is made slightly more complex by the fact that a larger market may justify a larger investment in capital equipment. If a company intends to build 4000 cars a week it will invest in much more expensive tooling than if it intends to build 40 cars a week. The more expensive tooling will reduce labour costs and hence variable costs.

The value of higher investment with larger markets is demonstrated on Fig. 20.2. Here we see the total cost of making a product when

  (i)   cheap tooling gives low fixed cost but high variable cost, and

  (ii) expensive tooling gives high fixed cost but low variable cost.

When quantity *A* is sold, policy (i) breaks even, and at higher quantities policy (i) is profitable.

When quantity *B* is sold, policy (ii) breaks even, and at higher quantities policy (ii) is profitable.

When quantity *C* is sold, policies (i) and (ii) are equally profitable, and at higher quantities policy (ii) is more profitable than policy (i).

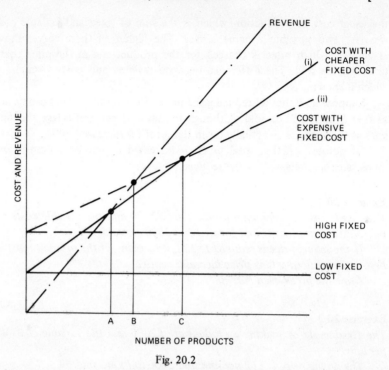

Fig. 20.2

It can be seen that it is very important for the marketing director to predict the size of the market. If he underestimates (perhaps to give himself an easy sales target) the company may well invest in the wrong tooling.

We can have a combination of factors so that we need to know how a price reduction will increase the market and how more expensive tooling will reduce the cost. This is shown on Fig. 20.3. Using cheaper tooling, and a related price, quantity *A* is sold. Increasing the cost of tooling reduces the variable cost and will permit a price reduction and increase the quantity sold to *B*. It is not always the case that increasing tooling costs will increase the profit, and the relationship between price and number sold must be known before we know whether we should do so.

Exercise 20.3
With fixed costs of £2000, variable costs of £10 a unit and a selling price of £12 a unit, 2000 of a product are sold.

The company is considering improving its tooling. This will raise fixed costs to £4000 but reduce variable costs to £8 a unit. If the selling price is reduced to £10, to what figure must sales be increased to justify the extra investment on tooling?

Draw the two break-even curves.   [3000

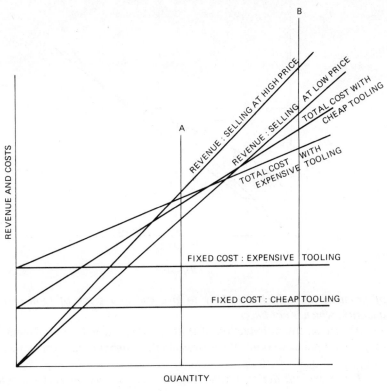

Fig. 20.3

The above examples show us that, in order to make investment decisions, we need to know something about the behaviour of the customers. We certainly wish to know how demand is affected by price.

The simple curve of total cost which is derived from fixed cost and variable cost has to be modified in most situations. A possible shape to the modified curve is shown in Fig. 20.4. Here the so-called fixed cost does increase slightly with the quantity of goods made because, with more goods made, more direct labour is used, and eventually more indirect labour (wage clerks, time clerks, supervisors, etc.) will be required. Again the variable cost per item will not necessarily be constant so as to give a line of fixed slope. At low output, the plant will be running at well below its optimum level; at very high output, the plant will be operating beyond its optimum, with inadequate maintenance, with direct workers on overtime, with lower quality and more rejections, etc.

Exercise 20.4
Discuss the factors which contribute to the total cost of manufacturing a number

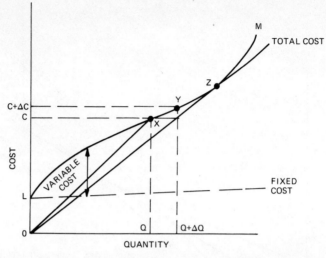

Fig. 20.4

of products and which are likely to give rise to a graph of total cost versus quantity, which is not linear.

(Overtime, the introduction of shift working, the reduction of maintenance to give continuous working, the increase in the number of indirect workers, . . .)

The economist derives several useful concepts from the curve of total cost versus quantity.

Consider the point X on Fig. 20.4. Here Q units have been made at a total cost of C.

The **average cost** of a unit if Q are manufactured is $AC = C/Q$.

Note that the average cost if Q units are made is given by the slope of the line OX.

As we move X along the curve from L to M, i.e. as Q increases from O to some maximum figure, $AC = C/Q$ starts by being infinity (OX is vertical), reduces until well up the curve, and finally starts increasing again as Q, the quantity produced, nears the capacity of the plant.

The **marginal cost**, MC, of the Qth unit is the increase in total cost when we make the Qth unit. In Fig. 20.4, when we increase Q to $Q + \Delta Q$ we increase C to $C + \Delta C$ so that

$$MC = \Delta C / \Delta Q$$

provided ΔQ is small or one.[†]

[†]Those familiar with calculus will have recognised that, in the limit

    Marginal cost $= MC = \Delta C/\Delta Q \rightarrow dC/dQ$ or

        $MC =$ the gradient of the curve at the point (Q, C).

If we were to plot the marginal cost and the average cost of a product versus quantity made, we would obtain graphs of the shape shown in Fig. 20.5.

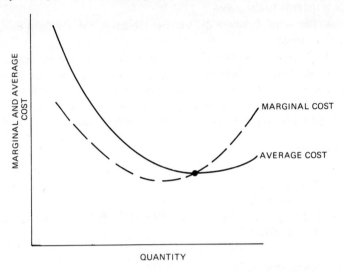

Fig. 20.5

Exercise 20.5

The production manager of XY Ltd has determined the cost of producing grommets and listed the results in the following table:

Total production (1000's of grommets)	0	1	2	3	4	5	6	7	8	9	10
Total cost (£1000's)	5.0	8.0	9.5	10.3	11.0	11.5	12.3	13.0	14.5	19.0	30.0

(i)   *Plot the curve of total cost versus total production.*
(ii)   *Determine the average cost of producing a grommet when total production is (a) zero, (b) 1000, (c) 2000, (d) 3000, (e) 4000, (f) 5000, (g) 6000, (h) 7000, (j) 8000, (k) 9000, and (l) 9500 grommets.*
(iii) *Plot the average cost of producing a grommet versus total production.*
(iv)   *Determine the marginal cost of producing a grommet when total production is (a) zero, (b) 1000, (c) 2000, (d) 3000, (e) 4000, (f) 5000, (g) 6000, (h) 7000, (j) 8000, (k) 9000, and (l) 9500 grommets.*
(v)   *Plot the marginal cost of a grommet versus quantity produced.*

On Fig. 20.4 observe again that, at the point X,

AC is the slope of the line OX
MC is the slope of a line joining X & Y

Now use a straight edge from O to any point on the curve to show that at the point on the curve where the average cost starts to increase, the straight edge is tangent to the curve.

At the point Z, where OZ touches the curve, the line from the origin has its minimum slope.

At the point Z, where OZ is tangent to the curve, average cost is a minimum.

At the point Z, where OZ is tangent to the curve, the slope of OZ represents both the average cost of the product and the marginal cost of the product.

At the quantity of production which gives the minimum average cost of making the product, average cost (AC) is equal to marginal cost (MC).

Exercise 20.6

(i)   *Use the graphs of Exercise 20.5 and a straight edge to convince yourself that at the production level at which the average cost of producing a grommet is minimum, $AC = MC$*

(ii) *Formalise the argument that when $AC = MC$ the average cost of production is a minimum.* [†]

PRICE AND REVENUE

We have seen that costs are related to the quantity of goods produced. It is worth asking whether we can investigate prices in the same way.

Let us assume that our management is so good that we sell all the goods we produce (or that we produce exactly the number of goods that we are able to sell). This will be discussed more fully in Chapter 21 but commonsense tells us, at least, that to make what we expect to sell is one reasonable objective of management.

How would we expect the quantity of products we sell to be related to the price that we charge for each product? Again, commonsense suggests that, at least approximately, we would expect that the more we charge for each product, the fewer we would expect to sell.

[†]A simple procedure for those familiar with calculus is:

Average cost $= AC = C/Q$

$$\frac{d(AC)}{dQ} = \frac{1}{Q} \cdot \frac{dC}{dQ} - \frac{C}{Q^2}$$

$$= 0 \text{ if } AC \text{ is extreme}$$

i.e. $\dfrac{dC}{dQ} = \dfrac{C}{Q}$

or $MC = AC$.

Exercise 20.7
Discuss

(i)   *the probability that the less we charge for a product, the more we will sell. Use examples to strengthen your argument.*
(Is this the idea behind sales? Is more (less) oil bought when the price goes down (up)? Do more people buy houses when the price goes down? What do we mean by the price of a house and how is it related to what the customer actually pays? ...)

(ii) *counter examples to the idea that the less a product costs the more will be sold.*
(Rolls-Royce are alleged to sell some cars because their price is high; the market for some named brands of ladies' wear and perfume is said to be maintained by charging high prices. Does 'snob appeal' really counter the argument that the lower the price of the product, the more products will be sold?)

Let us assume that Fig. 20.6 gives an approximation to the way the number of units of a product sold varies with the price of the product. This suggests that if we charge a sufficiently high price we will sell none of our products and if we charge nothing the market will be very large indeed (although unlikely to be profitable). If the curve of Fig. 20.6 is reasonably smooth between these two extremes we may discuss the revenue that any particular price will bring us.

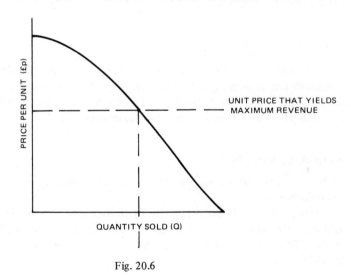

Fig. 20.6

Clearly the revenue $R = P \times Q$. That is, the total amount of money that we take off the customers will be equal to the price of each article multiplied by the number of articles sold.

If we were to plot the curve of revenue versus quantity sold then we would obtain a curve, roughly of the shape shown in Fig. 20.7. Obviously, this curve will start at the origin with revenue equal to zero because, from Fig. 20.6, we see that Q is equal to zero and so $R = P \times Q = 0$. Again the revenue curve will end at zero revenue because, when the price, $P = O$, $R = P \times Q = 0$.

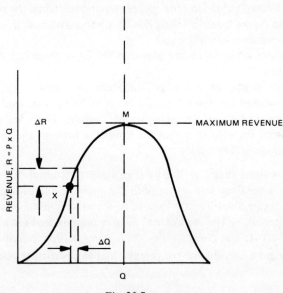

Fig. 20.7

The maximum revenue will not be achieved when the selling price is a maximum but at some point, shown on Fig. 20.7. At this point, we can read, not only the maximum revenue and the quantity sold but by projection on to Fig. 20.6, the price which will give the maximum revenue.

MARGINAL REVENUE

We have already introduced the idea of marginal cost. Can we give a meaning to marginal revenue?

At any point (for example, point X) on the curve of revenue versus quantity sold we can determine how the revenue will change as the quantity sold increases by one. This is the marginal revenue, MR, and at the point X we see that, as long as ΔQ is small

Marginal revenue $= MR = \Delta R/\Delta Q^{\dagger}$.

---

†Again, readers with a knowledge of calculus will have realised that the limiting value of MR as $\Delta Q \to 0$ is dR/dQ, and this is really a more useful definition of MR.

Obviously, if we move the point X along the curve of Fig. 20.7 we will get different values of MR.

However, when we reach the point on the revenue curve where revenue is a maximum

$MR = \Delta R / \Delta Q = 0$ because, for a very short length of the curve, R does not change (i.e. $\Delta R = 0$) for a very small change in Q (i.e. for a small ΔQ).

Exercise 20.8

If the sales director estimates that the sales of widgets will be related to the price of a widget in the way shown by the following table

(i)   *plot the curve of price versus quantity sold,*
(ii) *plot the curve of revenue versus quantity sold,*
(iii) *plot the curve of marginal revenue versus quantity sold and*
(iv) *determine the maximum revenue and the price at which maximum revenue will be obtained.*

Price (£)	80	76	70	65	58	50	42	32	22	12	0
Sales	0	10	20	30	40	50	60	70	80	90	100

Maximum revenue occurs where the quantity sold $\doteqdot 55$ at a unit price of £46.

MAXIMISING PROFIT

We have seen that marginal cost is related to minimum average cost and marginal revenue is related to maximum revenue, but we do not necessarily wish to minimise the one or maximise the other.

We wish to maximise the total profit, *TP*, where

$$TP = R - C \qquad \text{where} \qquad R = \text{revenue and}$$
$$C = \text{total cost} \ .$$

The student familiar with calculus will be able to find the maximum total profit where

$$\frac{d(TP)}{dQ} = \frac{dR}{dQ} - \frac{dC}{dQ} = 0$$

or where $\quad \dfrac{dR}{dQ} = \dfrac{dC}{dQ}$

or where $MR = MC$, i.e. where

Marginal revenue = Marginal cost

Exercise 20.9

Sketch a curve of cost versus quantity made on the same axes as a curve of revenue versus quantity sold. Assume that what is made is sold and argue from the shapes of your curves that we would expect the maximum profit to occur where the slope of the cost curve equals the slope of the revenue curve.

(Argue from Fig. 20.8).

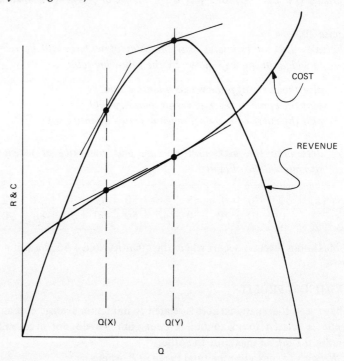

Fig. 20.8 – At $Q = Q(X)$ the slope of the revenue curve is greater than the slope of the cost curve (or the marginal revenue is greater than the marginal cost).

Increasing Q by one will create an increase in revenue that is greater than the increase in cost.

We are therefore searching for a quantity greater than $Q(X)$.

At $Q = Q(Y)$, increasing Q by one will create an increase in revenue that is less than the increase in cost.

We are therefore searching for a quantity less than $Q(Y)$.

We will find the optimum quantity where the two curves have the same slope.

Exercise 20.10

The price versus sales curve is given in Table 1 and the cost versus quantity made is given in Table 2.

(i)   *Plot the cost and revenue curves on the same axes and determine the quantity at which maximum profit occurs.*

(ii)   *Plot the profit curve and confirm that the maximum profit occurs at the quantity determined in (i).*

Table 1

Price (£)	80	76	70	65	58	50	42	32	22	12	0
Sales	0	10	20	30	40	50	60	70	80	90	100

Table 2

Cost (£)	740	950	1100	1250	1400	1500	1650	1800	2050	2400	2900
Quantity	0	10	20	30	40	50	60	70	80	90	100

Assume that quantity produced = sales

21

Supply and demand

THE DEMAND CURVE

It is a matter of common observation that, with most goods, the cheaper they are, the more will be bought. Graphically this is expressed on Fig. 21.1 which shows the number of goods sold (Q) increasing as the price (P) is reduced.

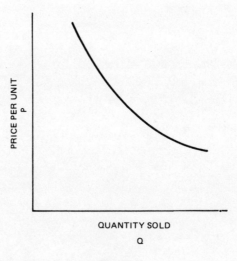

Fig. 21.1

If the price of motor cars falls, more people buy motor cars and, also, the family with one motor car may buy a second or replace its cars more often.

We would expect the curve of Fig. 21.1 to eventually drop steeply as price is reduced because we might approach the point at which demand is satisfied. When every family that wants to can have two cars and replace them at two-yearly intervals, it will be very difficult to increase the sale of cars.

THE SUPPLY CURVE

The demand curve (if we know it) does not, by itself, tell us how many products will be sold. We must relate the demand to the price at which producers are prepared to supply. Again it is a matter both of common sense and of observation that the more the producer can get for his product, the more he will attempt to supply. This is demonstrated in the supply curve of Fig. 21.2. This curve may be exemplified by suggesting that if Pembrokeshire farmers expect to get high prices for potatoes they will plant more acres with potatoes. If cars are fetching high prices the suppliers will attempt to produce more; if washing machines are fetching low prices the producers will produce fewer, etc.

Fig. 21.2

Other things being equal, it will cost the farmer more money per hundred-weight of potatoes produced as he increases production. He will use less suitable land, he will plough up to the hedges (taking more time per acre to plough). Again, other things being equal, the car manufacturer who can get a high price for his cars will push up his supply by increasing the cost per car. He will allow more overtime working at higher wages per hour, he will permit more bonus to be earned in order to increase output, etc.

EQUILIBRIUM, SUPPLY AND DEMAND

If we superimpose the supply curve on to the demand curve, we find the equilibrium point at which the goods will be sold. This is shown in Fig. 21.3. At the intersection of the supply curve and the demand curve, (A), the quantity bought is equal to the quantity sold and the price the customer is prepared to pay is the price at which the supplier is prepared to sell. If the negotiation between buyers and sellers started with the suppliers asking the price at B, the customers would demand much less than the number of products available and so the suppliers would have to reduce the product price to sell their stocks. The price and quantities would be driven towards those at A. Similarly, if negotiations started at a lower price than that at A, the quantity demanded would be driven up and the quantity offered driven down. A is an equilibrium point.

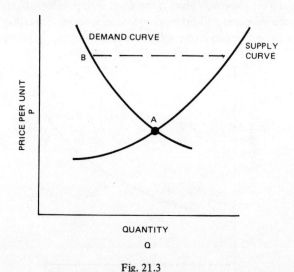

Fig. 21.3

In real life, the situation is, of course, complicated by the time at which events take place. The Pembrokeshire farmer who realises that he can get a high price for his potatoes will have to wait a year before making more available and, in any case, God will take a hand.

The equilibrium point on the curves of supply and demand will be defined

(i)   only with time, i.e. when the customer is willing to go on buying that quantity at that price and the supplier is willing to go on selling that quantity at that price, and

(ii)   only if every thing else remains unchanged.

If as we suggested in the example of potatoes, God intervenes to produce a bad harvest, the farmer will want more per pound for his crop. That has the effect of shifting the supply curve to the left, giving the situation of Fig. 21.4. Here, the expected supply curve was (a) but because of poor yields the farmer offered less for the same price and the supply curve became (b). The equilibrium point moved from A to C and the buyer eventually bought fewer potatoes at a higher price. The supply curve could be moved to the right, for suppose a manufacturer of aircraft equipment discovered that a newly available, numerically controlled mill reduced his manufacturing costs, he could afford to supply more goods at the same price. This would move his supply curve to the right and eventually mean an equilibrium at which more goods were sold at a lower price.

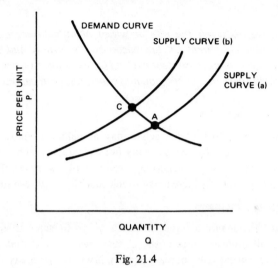

Fig. 21.4

The demand curve could also be displaced to the right or left by changes in the environment. A general increase in the wealth of a country would mean that customers would be prepared to spend more on cars, washing machines, etc., shifting the demand curve to the right to move the equilibrium point to one at which more goods are sold at a higher price.

Exercise 21.1
Give examples of transactions for which supply and demand curves might be drawn and equilibrium points found.

(The price of jeans and the numbers of pairs bought;
the cost of aircraft seats and the number of people flying;
the wages of engineers and the number of engineers produced each year;
the cost of houses and the number built;
. . . .
. . . .)

Exercise 21.2
In the cases that you have listed in answer to Exercise 21.1, suggest some environmental changes which could move the demand curve to the right or left and some environmental changes which could move the supply curve to the right or left.

(The production of wide-bodied jet aircraft enabled operators to offer more seats at lower prices (shifting the supply curve to the right); the reduction of interest rates makes it possible for more people to buy houses (shifting the demand curve to the right.)

Exercise 21.3
In Chapter 5, we discussed the rate at which manufacturers are permitted to write down capital equipment for tax purposes. Use supply and demand curves to discuss the effect that government action (for example, in permittting quicker write down) might have in encouraging more investment in capital equipment.

ELASTICITY OF DEMAND

We have seen in Fig. 20.1 that a seller may actually be prepared to sell at a lower price if by doing so he sells so many more products that his profit increases.

A related idea is that the seller may wish to know whether, if he reduces his price, the quantity sold will increase so much that the total revenue,

$$P \times Q \quad \text{increases.}$$

Although this is not a direct measure of profit since it is probable that increasing Q will increase total costs, at least we can say that if we reduce P to increase Q, and eventually increase profits, it will be necessary that

$$P \times Q \quad \text{increases.}$$

Consider the situation in which the demand curve is as shown in Fig. 21.1. The supplier sells at some point on this curve, where the price is P and the quantity of goods sold is Q. He wants to know if and when he reduces P by a small amount, Q will rise sufficiently to increase the total revenue.

The supplier reduces the price from P to $P-\Delta P$ where ΔP is positive, and observes that the number sold is now $Q + \Delta Q$, where ΔQ is positive.

The new total revenue is $(P-\Delta P) (Q + \Delta Q)$ where the old total revenue was $P Q$.

Is the new revenue greater than the old, i.e. is

$$(P - \Delta P) (Q + \Delta Q) > PQ \, ?$$

i.e. is $\quad -Q\Delta P + P\Delta Q - \Delta P . \Delta Q > 0 \, ?$

i.e. is $\quad \dfrac{P\Delta Q}{Q\Delta P} \quad > 1 + \dfrac{\Delta Q}{Q} \, ?$

If we are making very small changes, ΔQ will be very small and we are concerned whether

$$\frac{P}{Q} \cdot \frac{\Delta Q}{\Delta P} > 1 \, . \tag{21.1}$$

For readers with a knowledge of calculus, this reduces to $-P/Q \; dQ/dP > 1$ in the limiting case where $\Delta P, \; \Delta Q \to 0$; note that $\Delta Q/\Delta P \to - dQ/dP$ because we have said the ΔP is the positive reduction in price.

Note that, if we re-write equation (21.1) in the form $\Delta Q/Q > \Delta P/P$ we can see immediately that it implies that the percentage change in Q is greater than the percentage reduction in P. That is, the reduction in price is more than accounted for by the increase in sales.[†]

$-P/Q \; . \; dQ/dP$ is called the demand elasticity, E_d, and if ΔP and ΔQ are small we have a good estimate of E_d in $P/Q \; . \; \Delta P/\Delta Q$.

When $E_d > 1$, that is when cutting P slightly raises Q so that PQ increases, we say that the demand is elastic.

When $E_d = 1$, a small cut in P raises Q exactly to the point where PQ remains unaltered.

When $E_d < 1$, that is when a small cut in P raises Q but by so little that PQ falls, we say that demand is inelastic.

ELASTICITY AND SUPPLY

If we look at the supply curve we can derive a similar concept of elasticity to that already derived from the demand curve. If we look at Fig. 21.2 it is natural to ask how our quantity supplied will respond to an increase in the price that is offered.

As before, we define

$$\text{Elasticity of supply} = E_s = \frac{P}{Q} \cdot \frac{dQ}{dP} \quad \text{or} \quad \frac{P}{Q} \cdot \frac{\Delta Q}{\Delta P} \text{ if } \Delta P \text{ and } \Delta Q \text{ are small} \;.$$

There is a difference of sign because we are talking about the increase that the suppliers will make available in response to an *increase* in price offered. In the case of demand we were talking about the increase in the quantity that will be bought in response to a *reduction* in price.

[†]For those with a knowledge of calculus it might be simpler to argue that we are interested in how PQ changes as we reduce P, and we require

$$-\frac{d(PQ)}{dP} > 0$$

or $\qquad -Q - \dfrac{PdQ}{dP} > 0$

or $\qquad -\dfrac{P}{Q} \dfrac{dQ}{dP} > 1 \;.$

THE LONG RUN AND THE SHORT RUN

As we have already remarked, time plays an important role in supply and demand. If the demand for a product increases — if, for example, wages generally have increased and people can afford to buy more meat — we have a shift upwards in the demand curve. Immediately, the butchers can do nothing about meeting the increased demand and so the supply curve will be vertical — that is, the butcher can only sell the meat that he has. We have the situation of Fig. 21.5 The supply curve is vertical because the butchers are not able to increase the supply of meat instantaneously. The demand curve is shifted up by external changes (wages have risen), and so the price paid will be higher although no more meat is bought (point A).

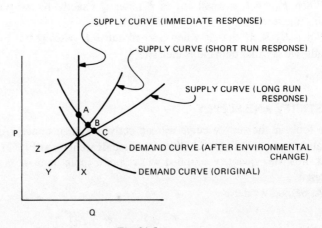

Fig. 21.5

In the short run, the butcher will be able to increase the supply of meat by negotiating with his suppliers to kill animals younger, perhaps to kill off stock intended for other roles (milking?). Such policies will be expensive and hence, although supply is increased, prices are also increased. The new price and quantity sold will be at point B.

In the long run, the butcher's suppliers will be able to make a better response to his increased demand. They will breed more stock for fattening, allocate more resources to fatstock, etc., and so, while this will increase supply and prices, the more ordered response by the suppliers will give lower prices than the short run responses. Equilibrium will be achieved at point C of Fig. 21.5.

The supply curve XA is completely inelastic in that

$$E_s = \frac{P}{Q} \cdot \frac{dQ}{dP} = 0 \text{ because } dQ = 0 \text{ whatever the change in } P.$$

The supply curve YB is more elastic, and ZC more elastic still.

CURVE SHIFT AND SHIFT ALONG A CURVE

A serious difficulty arises in using demand and supply curves. Each curve gives the relationship between price and quantity (demanded or supplied) provided that everything else remains unchanged. Thus we argue that if the Pembrokeshire farmer wishes to increase his supply, he will move *along* the curve, increasing the price at which he is prepared to sell, by using methods which have always been available to him.

If the weather changes, if new strains of potato are discovered, if new methods of cultivation are developed, or if new machinery is developed, then we cannot say that 'everything else remains unchanged', and we have a curve shift.

The problem is even more difficult if we consider manufactured articles. We are being much too glib if we talk of the supply of cars, for example, without differentiating between one car and another. The mass produced, small family saloon car must be regarded as a different product from the large, luxury, craftsman made product. The methods appropriate to the manufacture of the one would give a quite different supply curve from those appropriate to the other.

In both cases, the supply curve might be almost flat because if the quantity to be supplied increases, it is possible to increase the number of plants making cars and the unit price will not be changed until so many resources are diverted to the new plants that the resources themselves go up in price. To some extent we see the industry fighting this by, for example, setting their new plants up in countries where labour is cheaper, and this is really a curve shift as we can see in Fig. 21.6. Supply curve (ii) is the case for cars made by exactly the same engineering process as for supply curve (i) but in a country where labour is cheaper.

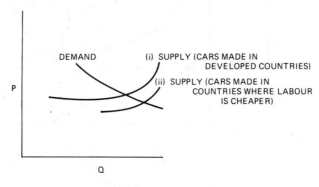

Fig. 21.6

PROBLEMS OF SCALE

We might argue from Fig. 20.1 that the supply curve should, in fact, slope downwards from left to right because the more products we offer for sale, the less contribution will each be required to make to the fixed cost. Indeed, if we plot the effect of fixed cost on unit cost we have the total cost of a unit

$$= TC \quad = F/Q + V$$

where F = fixed costs

   V = variable cost

and Q = number made .

If the manufacturer wishes to add a fixed profit, p, to the manufacturing cost of each product we have

$$P = \frac{F}{Q} + V + p \quad \text{where } P \text{ is the selling price.}$$

Plotting P against Q we obtain Fig. 21.7 in which P reduces with increasing Q, gradually approaching, but never reaching, a price which is the variable cost plus the profit per unit. In fact, at some point the capacity of the plant will be approached, when more products can be produced only with overtime and other expensive procedures. Later, the absolute capacity of the plant will be reached. The effect of plant capacity will mean that the curve of P versus Q will become the broken line of Fig. 21.7.

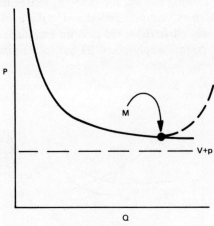

FIXED AND VARIABLE COSTS
RELATED TO UNIT COSTS

Fig. 21.7

But Fig. 21.7 is not the supply curve as we have been discussing it. Fig. 21.7 shows the price for which one manufacturer will be able to sell his product, but if we assume that there is competition to produce and sell the product, some other manufacturer will be operating nearer the optimum point, M. The market price for the product will not be determined by a point on any one manufacturer's *PQ* curve but by the best point on the curves of all competing manufacturers.

The director making decisions within a company must distinguish between the behaviour of his company and the general picture which is the sum of the performances of all the companies which are in competition to produce the product.

Usually global demand and supply curves cannot be predicted with any accuracy, and so they will not be immediately useful in telling the marketing director how to determine the price that he should fix for the product that he has to sell. An understanding of demand and supply curves will give him a qualitative idea of what might happen to demand and supply in response to certain changes.

RESPONSE TO SOME CHANGES

We have already discussed the way in which the demand curve would be shifted by the customer's increased affluence.

What happens if a product is taxed? The customer's demand curve is not changed at all, because it simply states the relationship between what the customer will buy and the price he has to pay. The producer, however, will have to increase the price of the product in order to pay for the tax as well as his own manufacturing cost and profit. The supply curve is therefore shifted upwards by the amount of the tax. The effect is therefore that shown in Fig. 21.8. The result is that fewer goods will be sold and the new equilibrium price will be higher than the old but by less than the tax increase.

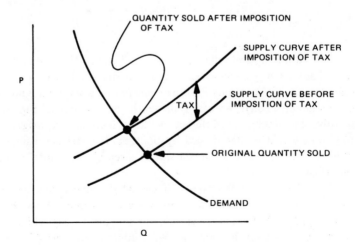

Fig. 21.8

What happens if prices are fixed? Consider the situation in the European Community's Common Agriculture Policy in which high prices paid to farmers are maintained. Fig. 21.9 shows what will happen. The demand curve (DD) and the supply curve (SS) meet at point A, and without intervention this gives the price the customer will pay and the quantity that he will buy. If, however, the community intervenes to insist that price X will be paid, the supplier will produce the quantity of goods given by point B, and the customer, at that price will buy the quantity of goods given by point C. The community will buy the quantity of goods necessary to bring the number sold from the quantity at C to the quantity at B. These goods will be stored in the butter mountain, wine lake, or wherever can be found.

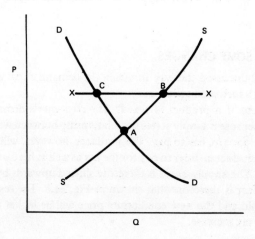

Fig. 21.9

Not all buying and selling is of material goods. Many men sell their labour. What happens when employers are not permitted to pay wages below some stated minimum (as occurs in some countries or when trade unions are able to fix minimum wages)? We can again reach the situation of Fig. 21.9 although, socially, the results are different. Without intervention, wages and numbers employed would be determined by point A. If wages are maintained by edict to level X, the number employed will be given by the point C and fewer people will be employed.

What happens to the supply of capital if interest rates are fixed by law? Lately we have seen attempts to raise the cost of capital. Again, Fig. 21.9 shows what happens. Without intervention, the amount of capital borrowed and the interest paid is given by point A. With interest rates raised by law to level X, the amount of capital borrowed (and invested) is that given by point C.

Exercise 21.4

(i) *Explain, with examples, why a demand curve (P, price plotted vertically and Q, quantity plotted horizontally) might be expected to slope downwards to the right.*

(ii) *Explain, with examples, why a supply curve might be expected to slope upwards to the right.*

(iii) *Give an example of a demand curve that is displaced by a change in external circumstances.*

(iv) *Give an example of a supply curve that is displaced by a change in external circumstances.*

Exercise 21.5

Use demand and price curves to discuss what happens if a product is in short supply (say petrol is scarce during a war in the middle east) and the government

(i) *dictates a ceiling price per gallon of petrol above which it may not be sold and then, in addition*

(ii) *rations petrol to x gallons a month per car owner.*

(On Fig. 21.10 is sketched the original demand and supply curves, with equilibrium price and quantity sold at *A*. If the supply of petrol is curtailed, the supply curve changes to a largely vertical line (or fixed quantity). This leads to a new equilibrium price and quantity at *B*. If the government believe that the price charged at *B* is too high because poor voters can no longer afford to motor, then it restricts the price to *X* at which the customers would be prepared to buy the quantity at *C* but this quantity is not available. But since some customers, at least, are prepared to spend *B* on a gallon of petrol, it is probable that a black market will develop. If the government attempts to restrict demand by rationing then it must set the ration so that the demand will be reduced to equilibrium at *D*.)

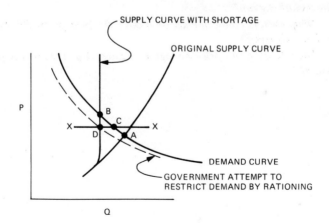

Fig. 21.10

Exercise 21.6

(i)   *Give and justify examples of products for which demand could be relatively elastic.*   (Holidays in Spain, cars, freezers, . . .)

(ii) *Give and justify examples of products for which demand could be relatively inelastic.*   (Insulin, schoolmasters, professional cricketers, . . .)

Exercise 21.7

10 000 cars of a particular type are sold each month at £5000 each.
   If the price is reduced by £100, 10 500 cars are sold.
   What is the elasticity of demand, E_d?
   Would you describe the demand for these cars as elastic?
   What do you mean by elastic, in this example?

(2.5, yes, total revenue increases when price is reduced.)

Exercise 21.8

Twenty-five million gallons of petrol are sold every week at a price of £1.60 a gallon. The suppliers raise their price by 5p a gallon and observe that sales have fallen by half a million gallons a week.
   What is the elasticity of demand?
   Would you describe the demand for petrol as elastic or inelastic?

(0.64; inelastic)

Exercise 21.9

In a certain country the railways are closed and this increases the demand for motor cars. Explain what happens in terms of the demand curve.

(There is a shift upwards in the demand curve because of an external change.)

What will this do to the price of cars (i) immediately, (ii) in the short run, and (iii) in the long run?

What factors could operate to reduce the price from the short run price to the long run price?

Will the long run price be higher or lower than the price before the railways closed?

22

Utility

UTILITY OR MONEY?

A thirsty student would put a great value on his first pint of beer of the evening. He would probably place much less value on his sixth or seventh.

If a tramp with only a few coppers in his pocket finds a pound note he will value it very highly. If a millionaire sees a pound note in the gutter, he will value it so little that he might not even bother to pick it up.

We clearly cannot measure the satisfication or pleasure that a customer gets from the nth unit of a good that he acquires in money. We have seen that the millionth pound acquired gives far less satisfaction than the first. The seventh pint of beer gives less satisfaction than the first although it costs the same.

The satisfaction that you get from acquiring the first unit is said to give more 'utility' (or more 'utiles') than the nth. Usually, the way that the utility of possessing a quantity of a product increases with quantity is as shown in Fig. 22.1. Here the first unit is valued at 2 utiles, the second at 1.8 utiles, the third at 1.6 utiles, ..., the ninth at 0.4 utiles, and the tenth at 0.2 utiles. We do not need to know what we mean by a utile in absolute terms as long as we understand that the measurement is relative. Thus in Fig. 22.1, the value that the customer puts on possession of the tenth unit is one tenth of the value that he puts on possession of the first.

Suppose the good that we are discussing in Fig. 22.1 is beer at 50p a pint, then we can replace the horizontal scale by a money scale. This is shown beneath the quantity scale, and from it we may say that, when buying beer, the customer gets one tenth the value from the tenth 50p spent that he gets from the first.

Generally as quantity increases, total utility increases but at a rate which decreases.

MARGINAL UTILITY

Because we are more interested in changes in utility than in its absolute value it is useful to introduce the idea of marginal utility.

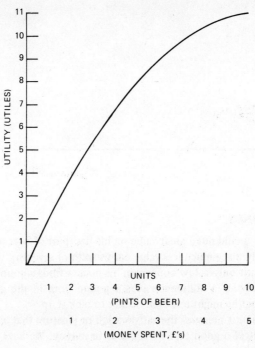

Fig. 22.1

Marginal utility is defined as the increase in total utility when one more unit of the good is bought.

In the situation illustrated in Fig. 22.1 we have already seen that the marginal utility of the first pint of beer is 2 utiles, the marginal utility of the second is 1.8 utiles, . . . , the marginal utility of the 10th pint is 0.2 utiles.

With the money scale, we can also argue that, when buying beer, the marginal utility of the 10th 50 pence spent is 0.2 utiles.

If we approximate the utility graph to a continuous curve we may define the marginal utility symbolically as $\Delta U/\Delta Q$ for the Qth good bought

$$\Delta U/\Delta C \text{ for the } C\text{th unit of money spent.}^\dagger$$

MIX OF GOODS BOUGHT AND EQUAL MARGINAL UTILITIES

Now consider a customer who spends a total of $£C(T)$ on a mixture of the goods he needs. He spends $C(1)$ on the first, $C(2)$ on the second, $C(3)$ on the third, etc., so that $C(T) = C(1) + C(2) + C(3) + \ldots$

---

†Students with a knowledge of the calculus will have already realised that marginal utility is dU/dC where U is the vertical scale in utiles and C is the horizontal scale in some money unit, pounds or pence, say.

If the customer has spent wisely then the marginal utility of the last penny he spent on good (1) will be equal to the marginal utility of the last penny he spent on good (2), and the marginal utility of the last penny he spent on good (3), etc. Suppose this were not the case. Suppose, for example, that the marginal utility of the last penny that he spent on good (1) was greater than the marginal utility of the last penny that he spent on good (2). Then he whould have gained more satisfaction if he had spent a penny more on good (1) and a penny less on good (2).

Only if the marginal utility of the last penny spent on good (1) was the same as the marginal utility of the last penny spent on every other good will he not have been able to change his mix of purchases with advantage[†].

The careful reader will have noticed that we have assumed that there is some meaning to the last penny spent on a good. This means that we have assumed that if we plot the utility versus money spent for each good we will obtain a smooth curve, as in Fig. 22.2. With many goods this is not so. If, for example, we spend £5000 on our first car, we cannot spend less than £5000 on our second. We then have to resort to step by step procedures or we have to convert large expenditure into equivalent annual or monthly expenditures.

Exercise 22.1

(i)   *Explain the difference between the utility of a good and the price you pay for it*

(ii) *Sketch a graph of utility versus quantity for some product such as beer, suits of clothes, holidays in Spain, motor cars, . . .*

[†]A more formal explanation for those familiar with calculus is as follows.
If $U(1)$ is the utility of good (1) when $C(1)$ is spent on it;
  $U(2)$ is the utility of good (2) when $C(2)$ is spent on it;
  etc.,
    U is the total utility obtained and
    C is the total money available then

$$U = U(1) + U(2) + U(3) + \ldots$$
and $C = C(1) + C(2) + C(3) + \ldots$
Form the Lagrangian
$$L = U(1) + U(2) + U(3) + \ldots + \lambda(C(1) + C(2) + C(3) +)$$

then a necessary condition for U to be a maximum

is $\dfrac{\partial L}{\partial C(1)} = \dfrac{\partial U(1)}{\partial C(1)} + \lambda = 0$ or $\dfrac{\partial U(1)}{\partial C(1)} = -\lambda$

Similarly $\dfrac{\partial U(2)}{\partial C(2)} = \dfrac{\partial U(3)}{\partial C(3)} = \text{ètc.} = -\lambda$.

That is, a necessary condition for a maximum U is that all marginal utilities are equal.

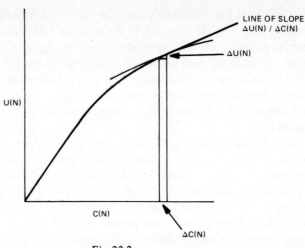

Fig. 22.2

(iii)   *Use your graph to explain what is meant by marginal utility.*
(iv)   *Why would you expect the marginal utility of a good to diminish as more of the good is bought?*
        Describe diminishing marginal utility by referring to the graph you have drawn.

Exercise 22.2
  (i)   *Out of your monthly salary you buy a mixture of goods – food, clothes, coal, wine, petrol, visits to the pictures, ...*
        Explain why you would expect the marginal utility of the last pound spent on each of these goods to be approximately the same.
 (ii)   *How is your reasoning distorted by the fact that in one month you buy potatoes at 5p a pound and a ton of coal for £100?*

INDIFFERENCE CURVES

Suppose Charlie Brown is in a pub and has consumed seven pints of beer. He is feeling rather full and when offered another drink he decides to have a tot of whisky.

Charlie is, in fact, substituting whisky for beer because, after seven pints, he finds the marginal utility of the next (eighth) pint less then the marginal utility of his first tot of whisky.

No doubt Charlie has gained some satisfaction from 7 pints of beer and 1 tot of whisky.

He might have spent the evening consuming a different mix of beer and whisky for the same amount of money spent. For simplicity, let us assume that a tot of whisky costs the same as a pint of beer (60p). Charlie has spent £4.80 and might ask himself the question 'Could I have spent my £4.80 in a different manner and have obtained more satisfaction?'

As Charlie never drinks half pints his choice would have been narrowed to

    8 whiskies
    7 whiskies and 1 pint of beer,
    6 whiskies and 2 pints of beer,
    5 whiskies and 3 pints of beer,
    4 whiskies and 4 pints of beer,
    3 whiskies and 5 pints of beer,
    2 whiskies and 6 pints of beer,
    1 whisky and 7 pints of beer, or
    0 whiskies and 8 pints of beer

We can plot Charlie's available choices on Fig. 22.3.

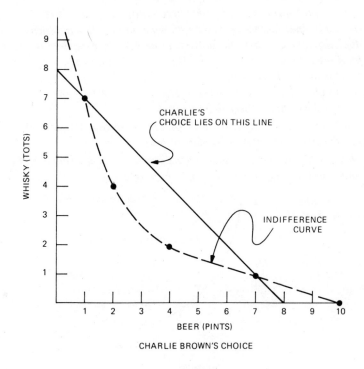

Fig. 22.3

Another question Charlie might ask himself is 'Would I have got the same satisfaction from a different combination of beer and whisky?'

Let us assume that in answer to this question, Charlie decided that he would have gained equal satisfication from

> 10 pints of beer and no whisky,
> 7 pints of beer and one whisky,
> 4 pints of beer and two whiskies,
> 2 pints of beer and four whiskies,
> 1 pint of beer and seven whiskies, and
> No beer and ten whiskies.

The economist would say that Charlie is indifferent between these six choices. The choices are plotted on Fig. 22.3 and the curve joining these choices is called an 'indifference curve'. Charlie is indifferent between the combinations on this curve, or the utilities of all combinations on this curve are the same.

Exercise 22.3

(i) *Fig. 22.4 is a sketch of an indifference curve.*
   Explain the meaning of this curve in terms of any point on it.

(ii) *Generally, indifference curves are shown as in Fig. 22.4 in which the curve does not reach either the horizontal or vertical axis. In Fig. 22.3 the indifference curve actually meets the horizontal axis at the point (10,0). What is the significance of this?*

(The eleventh pint of beer would give no satisfaction at all)
   Sketch the utility of beer only.

(Note that because the marginal utility of beer is zero at 10 pints, the utility curve must become horizontal at 10 pints of beer.)

(iii) *Why would you expect an indifference curve to be shaped approximately as shown in Fig. 22.4 (i.e. roughly the shape of a hyperbola)?*

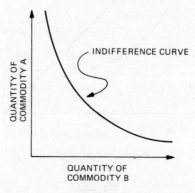

Fig. 22.4

Let us assume that the customer is not forced to make discrete choices and that both his curve of constant cost and his indifference curve are continuous.

This is similar to suggesting that Charlie could have chosen a combination of five pints of beer and 1.55 tots of whisky.

This assumption that the curves are continuous would be acceptable if we were dealing with large numbers of products or if we really could buy fractional parts of any product (we could, for example, with petrol or pounds of sugar).

We will generalise by considering a customer who is asked to list combinations of quantities of goods A and B which will give him equal satisfaction. From the customer's lists we can draw families of indifference curves as shown in Fig. 22.5. In this figure, all the combinations on curve (a) have the same utility U(a), all the combinations on curve (b) have the same utility U(b), and so on. Although only four curves are shown there are, of course, an infinity of such curves, each of which represents a constant utility.

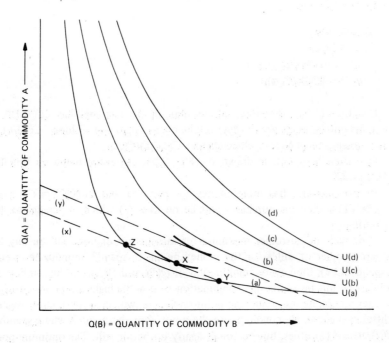

Fig. 22.5

Points on curve (d) all give the satisfaction (U(d) utiles) which is greater than the satisfaction offered by points on curve (c), (U(c) utiles). Points on curve (c) offer more satisfaction than points on curve (b) which offer U(b) utiles, etc.

$$U(\text{d}) > U(\text{c}) > U(\text{b}) > U(\text{a}) \ .$$

Now consider the amount that the customer has to spend and how he can spent it.

Let us assume that each unit of B costs £C(B) and each unit of A costs £C(A).

If the customer buys Q(B) of B and Q(A) of A he will spend

$$£C(\text{TOT}) = £[C(B) \times Q(B)] + £[C(A) \times Q(A)] \qquad (22.1)$$

If £C(TOT) is a fixed, budgeted sum then equation (22.1) is represented by a straight line $C(\text{TOT}) = C(B) . Q(B) + C(A) . Q(A)$ which may be re-written as

$$Q(A) = - [C(B)/C(A)] . Q(B) + [C(\text{TOT})/C(A)] \qquad (22.2)$$

where Q(A) and Q(B) are the variables. Equation (22.2) may be compared with the line $y = mx + C$

if $x \equiv Q(B)$
   $y \equiv Q(A)$
   $C \equiv C(\text{TOT})/C(A)$ and
   $m \equiv - [C(B)/C(A)]$

Equation (22.1) therefore tells us that, if the customer has £C(TOT) to spend, his purchases Q(B) and Q(A) will lie on a straight line of slope $-C(B)/C(A)$ which crosses the Q(A) axis where $Q(A) = C(\text{TOT})/C(A)$.

One such line, (x), is drawn on Fig. 22.5. At every point on this line $C(\text{TOT}) = C(x)$.

If the customer has more money to spend so that $C(\text{TOT}) = C(y)$ and $C(y) > C(x)$, then his purchases will lie on line (y) which is parallel to line (x) but higher.

How will the customer maximise his satisfaction or how will he buy the greatest number of utiles for the money he has to spend? Suppose he intends to spend £$C(x)$, then every combination of Q(B) and Q(A) that he can buy lies on line (x). But he wants this combination to give the highest number of utiles. In other words, he must find the point on line (x) which also lies on the highest indifference curve. He could choose the point Z or the point Y where spending £$C(x)$ gives U(a) utiles, but he could clearly do better still. The optimum point is X where the line (x) touches an indifference curve. He cannot buy more utiles than at X because no point on (x) reaches a higher indifference curve. He would be silly to buy fewer utiles than are obtained at X.

Exercise 22.4
Construct an argument that will satisfy you that the customer's optimum purchase lies   (i) on a straight line representing a constant expenditure and
*   (ii) lies on an indifference curve*
where (iii) the line touches the curve.

Exercise 22.5

(i)   *Sketch a graph, similar to that of Fig. 22.5, to show a family of indifference curves and a line showing what the customer can buy with a fixed sum of money.*

(ii) *What happens to the line of constant expenditure if the customer finds that he has more money available than he originally budgeted?*

(iii) *If the customer has more money available than he originally budgeted, use your sketch to show how his mix of purchases will change.*

(iv) *What happens to the line of constant expenditure if the price of one of the products is increased?*

(v)   *If the price of one of the products is increased, use your sketch to show how the customers' mix of purchases will change.*

23

Opportunity costs and resources

RESOURCES

We often assume that good management will ensure that our resources will be used to the full but this is not necessarily the case.

Exercise 23.1

PQ Ltd. is a jobbing company with three machines, A, B, and C.

The company is offered four jobs W, X, Y, and Z.

Job W takes 10 hours on machine A

5 hours on machine B

and   5 hours on machine C

and the operations on the machines will be done in the order A, B, C.

Job X takes   6 hours on machine A

5 hours on machine B

and   4 hours on machine C

and again the operations order is A, B, C.

Job Y takes   9 hours on machine A

5 hours on machine B

and   10 hours on machine C

here again, the operations order is A, B, C.

Job Z takes   4 hours on machine A

4 hours on machine B

and   10 hours on machine C

here again, the operations order is A, B, C.

How will the machines be used if we do the jobs in the order W, X, Y, Z?

Note that a job cannot go on to B machine until it is finished on A or on to C until it is finished on B.

Draw a chart with time extending from left to right horizontally, to show the use of each machine by each job.

[The solution is shown on Fig. 23.1

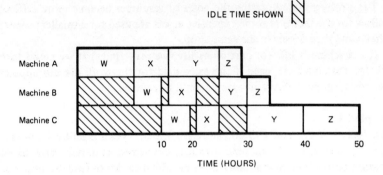

Fig. 23.1

Notice that in the solution, machines are idle.

Can you think of a better order of doing the jobs?

Although Example 23.1 is very much simpler than would arise in a real jobbing shop where, at any one time there could be several hundred jobs going through the shop and thirty or forty machine sections (or other work stations), it does demonstrate that it is not usually possible to use every resource for the whole of its available time.

Queueing theory and simulation methods also demonstrate that we would be very lucky to be able to use a machine or other resource for more than about 80% of the time that it is available. It is interesting to note, from Fig. 23.1, that even though machines are idle from time to time, jobs are also idle in the sense that when a job comes off one machine it may well have to wait before it can get on to the next.

We have already seen that, if we are to allocate the cost of a machine to the work it does, we can find the annual equivalent (or hourly equivalent) cost of the machine, but we must be careful that, when we distribute the hourly cost of the machine to the number of jobs done by the machine in an hour, we do not assume that every available machine hour will be usefully employed.

The interruptions to the use of any asset will depend on the type of work being done. A machine used within a specially designed plant producing motor cars, washing machines, or some other consumer product by mass production will be used only for the one product, and its cost can be divided easily among the products made. A machine being used within a factory making batches of different products must clearly have its costs shared among the products that it helps to make. We may be able to distribute machine costs in some equitable way between the products, but we have to be careful how we distribute idle time costs. In some cases, where machine costs are lumped into a shop overhead, we may even find that the machine's capital costs are paid for, in part, by products which it does not help to make.

The problems of allocating the costs of resources become more difficult if we allow for the fact that some expensive assets are used for a smaller proportion of their time than others in the same shop.

If a machine is idle for part of its life, we may find that we could take on work for that machine, even if the price paid for the work did not apparently cover costs, simply because idle time would be reduced.

Example 23.1

A test facility which cost £75 000 and has a life of 5 years is let by the hour.
Running costs are £30 an hour (labour, consumed materials, and all other operating costs), and capital costs must be added to this to find the total hourly cost. Interest is 15% and the facility is let for 24 hours a week for 50 weeks a year. What are the total costs per hour?

$$\text{(Capital costs/hour} = £75\ 000 \div (P/A)_5^{0.15} \div 50 \div 24$$
$$= £18.64 \text{ per hour}$$
$$\text{therefore total costs} = £48.64 \text{ per hour.)}$$

The opportunity arises to let the facility for 4 more hours a week at £45/hour. Should the opportunity be realised?

(The immediate answer is yes because the 24 hours a week already let pay for the operation of the machine and for the capital required to purchase it. The extra 4 hours a week bring in £15 × 4 × 50 = £3000 a year after paying for the machine and for the running costs.)

This example illustrates the fact that we can apparently determine the cost per hour of a facility and then show a profit if we sell time on the facility at less than the calculated cost.

Exercise 23.2

Use the arguments of Example 23.1 to explain how a foreign country might 'dump' textiles on to the UK market quite profitably, even though they are charging a price that is alleged to be below the cost of production.

One argument we can use for taking on jobs at an apparent loss comes from the consideration of opportunity cost.

The opportunity cost of a project is the saving that will accrue if the project is not implemented.

This leads us to consider what we will do if a project is not implemented, i.e. what is the alternative project?

Consider the extra letting of the test facility discussed in Example 23.1.

The project under consideration is to let the facility for 4 hours a week at £45 per hour.

£30 of this will be required to pay the running costs — direct labour, materials, etc.

The alternative project is to do nothing.

What do we save if we take the 'do nothing' alternative?

(i)   Assuming that the labour and raw materials can be used elsewhere in the factory, we save £30; and

(ii) because the facility has already been paid for by other work, doing nothing saves nothing of the capital costs.

The opportunity costs of the extra letting are therefore £30 an hour, and any job which brings in more than this is profitable.

Now suppose that the running costs of the facility are £30 per hour and of this £12 per hour is used to pay operators who are idle for 7 hours a week.

Now we must argue that if we take the 'do nothing' alternative, we must still pay the idle operators. We then save

(i)   not £30 per hour running costs but £18 per hour because we still pay the operators, and

(ii) there is no capital saving in not using the facility.

The opportunity costs of the extra letting are now only £18 an hour and we could profitably charge any figure greater than this for the extra four hours a week.

We have used the idea of opportunity cost before although we did not give it a name. When we calculated the rate of return of a project we argued that for the project to be acceptable, its rate of return must be greater than that of any readily available, risk free, external investment.

If any money could be invested externally at $I(EXT)\%$ and if the Rate of Return on an internal project is $I(INT)\%$, then we must have $I(INT) > I(EXT)$ for the internal project to be justified.

We are merely saying that, for an internal project costing £100, the opportunity cost is £$I(EXT)$ because that would be the saving if we did not take on the internal project.

Opportunity costs are an important idea in assessing any project because they force us to look at the alternative projects. Even if there is only one alternative — to do nothing — we must still consider the differences between alternatives rather than the absolute returns from projects under consideration.

If we are using discounted cash flow methods to determine the present value of a number of projects we may have to consider capital budgets to determine which among a number of alternatives we will accept. We may, of course, have other resource limits (such as skilled labour, floor space, or computer time), and again we would have to consider all the alternatives to decide which among the projects we wish to accept and will come within resource limits. We would not necessarily be calling on the concept of opportunity costs, but we would be considering all alternatives, and this leads to the same results.

If we are using rates of return and a cut-off rate of return to select projects within a capital budget we are effectively using the concept of opportunity cost because we are treating the pay-off from an external project as an opportunity cost.

Opportunity cost, used in the simple way of Example 23.1 is really a simplified concept which enables a rough but immediate comparison to be made between alternatives.

Exercise 23.3

(i) *How can we ignore opportunity costs when selecting projects with positive present value?*

(ii) *Give an example of the need to determine the idle time cost of a resource which may be used for one or other of two projects which are being assessed for present value.*

Exercise 23.4

(i) *How can we ignore opportunity costs when we are ranking projects by rate of return?*

(ii) *Give an example of the need to determine the idle time costs of a resource which may be used for one or other of two projects which are being assessed for rates of return.*

Exercise 23.5

Give examples of the costs involved in two alternative projects A and B and say which costs of project A must be taken into account when assessing project B.

    (For example, consider using a lorry to carry goods from Swansea to London (project A) or from Swansea to Birmingham (project B). Both jobs are required to be done on the same day, and so one will be rejected.

    Do the costs of the driver,

       the costs of the fuel,

       the cost of the licence,

       . . . . ,

       . . . . , for job A need

    to be considered in assessing job B?)

Appendices

APPENDIX 1 — Present worth of a future payment (P/F)I, N

YEARS	0.5%	1.0%	1.5%	2.0%	2.5%	3.0%	4.0%	5.0%	6.0%	8.0%	10.0%	12.0%	14.0%	15.0%	16.0%	18.0%
1	0.995	0.990	0.985	0.980	0.976	0.971	0.962	0.952	0.943	0.926	0.909	0.893	0.877	0.870	0.862	0.847
2	0.990	0.980	0.971	0.961	0.952	0.943	0.925	0.907	0.890	0.857	0.826	0.797	0.769	0.756	0.743	0.718
3	0.985	0.971	0.956	0.942	0.929	0.915	0.889	0.864	0.840	0.794	0.751	0.712	0.675	0.658	0.641	0.609
4	0.980	0.961	0.942	0.924	0.906	0.888	0.855	0.823	0.792	0.735	0.683	0.636	0.592	0.572	0.552	0.516
5	0.975	0.951	0.928	0.906	0.884	0.863	0.822	0.784	0.747	0.681	0.621	0.567	0.519	0.497	0.476	0.437
6	0.971	0.942	0.915	0.888	0.862	0.837	0.790	0.746	0.705	0.630	0.564	0.507	0.456	0.432	0.410	0.370
7	0.966	0.933	0.901	0.871	0.841	0.813	0.760	0.711	0.665	0.583	0.513	0.452	0.400	0.376	0.354	0.314
8	0.961	0.923	0.888	0.853	0.821	0.789	0.731	0.677	0.627	0.540	0.467	0.404	0.351	0.327	0.305	0.266
9	0.956	0.914	0.875	0.837	0.801	0.766	0.703	0.645	0.592	0.500	0.424	0.361	0.308	0.284	0.263	0.225
10	0.951	0.905	0.862	0.820	0.781	0.744	0.676	0.614	0.558	0.463	0.386	0.322	0.270	0.247	0.227	0.191
11	0.947	0.896	0.849	0.804	0.762	0.722	0.650	0.585	0.527	0.429	0.350	0.287	0.237	0.215	0.195	0.162
12	0.942	0.887	0.836	0.788	0.744	0.701	0.625	0.557	0.497	0.397	0.319	0.257	0.208	0.187	0.168	0.137
13	0.937	0.879	0.824	0.773	0.725	0.681	0.601	0.530	0.469	0.368	0.290	0.229	0.182	0.163	0.145	0.116
14	0.933	0.870	0.812	0.758	0.708	0.661	0.577	0.505	0.442	0.340	0.263	0.205	0.160	0.141	0.125	0.099
15	0.928	0.861	0.800	0.743	0.690	0.642	0.555	0.481	0.417	0.315	0.239	0.183	0.140	0.123	0.108	0.084
16	0.923	0.853	0.788	0.728	0.674	0.623	0.534	0.458	0.394	0.292	0.218	0.163	0.123	0.107	0.093	0.071
17	0.919	0.844	0.776	0.714	0.657	0.605	0.513	0.436	0.371	0.270	0.198	0.146	0.108	0.093	0.080	0.060
18	0.914	0.836	0.765	0.700	0.641	0.587	0.494	0.416	0.350	0.250	0.180	0.130	0.095	0.081	0.069	0.051
19	0.910	0.828	0.754	0.686	0.626	0.570	0.475	0.396	0.331	0.232	0.164	0.116	0.083	0.070	0.060	0.043
20	0.905	0.820	0.742	0.673	0.610	0.554	0.456	0.377	0.312	0.215	0.149	0.104	0.073	0.061	0.051	0.037
21	0.901	0.811	0.731	0.660	0.595	0.538	0.439	0.359	0.294	0.199	0.135	0.093	0.064	0.053	0.044	0.031
22	0.896	0.803	0.721	0.647	0.581	0.522	0.422	0.342	0.278	0.184	0.123	0.083	0.056	0.046	0.038	0.026
23	0.892	0.795	0.710	0.634	0.567	0.507	0.406	0.326	0.262	0.170	0.112	0.074	0.049	0.040	0.033	0.022
24	0.887	0.788	0.700	0.622	0.553	0.492	0.390	0.310	0.247	0.158	0.102	0.066	0.043	0.035	0.028	0.019
25	0.883	0.780	0.689	0.610	0.539	0.478	0.375	0.295	0.233	0.146	0.092	0.059	0.038	0.030	0.024	0.016
26	0.878	0.772	0.679	0.598	0.526	0.464	0.361	0.281	0.220	0.135	0.084	0.053	0.033	0.026	0.021	0.014
27	0.874	0.764	0.669	0.586	0.513	0.450	0.347	0.268	0.207	0.125	0.076	0.047	0.029	0.023	0.018	0.011
28	0.870	0.757	0.659	0.574	0.501	0.437	0.333	0.255	0.196	0.116	0.069	0.042	0.026	0.020	0.016	0.010
29	0.865	0.749	0.649	0.563	0.489	0.424	0.321	0.243	0.185	0.107	0.063	0.037	0.022	0.017	0.014	0.008
30	0.861	0.742	0.640	0.552	0.477	0.412	0.308	0.231	0.174	0.099	0.057	0.033	0.020	0.015	0.012	0.007
31	0.857	0.735	0.630	0.541	0.465	0.400	0.296	0.220	0.164	0.092	0.052	0.030	0.017	0.013	0.010	0.006
32	0.852	0.727	0.621	0.531	0.454	0.388	0.285	0.210	0.155	0.085	0.047	0.027	0.015	0.011	0.009	0.005
33	0.848	0.720	0.612	0.520	0.443	0.377	0.274	0.200	0.146	0.079	0.043	0.024	0.013	0.010	0.007	0.004
34	0.844	0.713	0.603	0.510	0.432	0.366	0.264	0.190	0.138	0.073	0.039	0.021	0.012	0.009	0.006	0.004
35	0.840	0.706	0.594	0.500	0.421	0.355	0.253	0.181	0.130	0.068	0.036	0.019	0.010	0.008	0.006	0.003
36	0.836	0.699	0.585	0.490	0.411	0.345	0.244	0.173	0.123	0.063	0.032	0.017	0.009	0.007	0.005	0.003
37	0.831	0.692	0.576	0.481	0.401	0.335	0.234	0.164	0.116	0.058	0.029	0.015	0.008	0.006	0.004	0.002
38	0.827	0.685	0.568	0.471	0.391	0.325	0.225	0.157	0.109	0.054	0.027	0.013	0.007	0.005	0.004	0.002
39	0.823	0.678	0.560	0.462	0.382	0.316	0.217	0.149	0.103	0.050	0.024	0.012	0.006	0.004	0.003	0.002
40	0.819	0.672	0.551	0.453	0.372	0.307	0.208	0.142	0.097	0.046	0.022	0.011	0.005	0.004	0.003	0.001
41	0.815	0.665	0.543	0.444	0.363	0.289	0.200	0.135	0.092	0.043	0.020	0.010	0.005	0.003	0.002	0.001
42	0.811	0.658	0.535	0.435	0.354	0.281	0.193	0.129	0.087	0.039	0.018	0.009	0.004	0.003	0.002	0.001
43	0.807	0.645	0.527	0.427	0.346	0.272	0.185	0.123	0.082	0.037	0.017	0.008	0.003	0.002	0.002	0.001
44	0.803	0.645	0.519	0.418	0.337	0.264	0.178	0.117	0.077	0.034	0.015	0.007	0.003	0.002	0.001	0.001
45	0.799	0.639	0.512	0.410	0.329	0.257	0.171	0.111	0.073	0.031	0.014	0.006	0.003	0.002	0.001	0.001
46	0.795	0.633	0.504	0.402	0.321	0.249	0.165	0.106	0.069	0.029	0.012	0.005	0.002	0.001	0.001	0.000
47	0.791	0.626	0.497	0.394	0.313	0.242	0.158	0.101	0.065	0.027	0.011	0.005	0.002	0.001	0.001	0.000
48	0.787	0.620	0.489	0.387	0.306	0.235	0.152	0.096	0.061	0.025	0.010	0.004	0.002	0.001	0.001	0.000
49	0.783	0.614	0.482	0.379	0.298	0.228	0.146	0.092	0.058	0.023	0.009	0.003	0.001	0.001	0.001	0.000
50	0.779	0.608	0.475	0.372	0.291	0.228	0.141	0.087	0.054	0.021	0.009	0.003	0.001	0.001	0.001	0.000

APPENDIX 1 – continued

YEARS	20.0%	25.0%	30.0%	35.0%	40.0%	50.0%
1	0.833	0.800	0.769	0.741	0.714	0.667
2	0.694	0.640	0.592	0.549	0.510	0.444
3	0.579	0.512	0.455	0.406	0.364	0.296
4	0.482	0.410	0.350	0.301	0.260	0.198
5	0.402	0.328	0.269	0.223	0.186	0.132
6	0.335	0.262	0.207	0.165	0.133	0.088
7	0.279	0.210	0.159	0.122	0.095	0.059
8	0.233	0.168	0.123	0.091	0.068	0.039
9	0.194	0.134	0.094	0.067	0.048	0.026
10	0.162	0.107	0.073	0.050	0.035	0.017
11	0.135	0.086	0.056	0.037	0.025	0.012
12	0.112	0.069	0.043	0.027	0.018	0.008
13	0.093	0.055	0.033	0.020	0.013	0.005
14	0.078	0.044	0.025	0.015	0.009	0.003
15	0.065	0.035	0.020	0.011	0.006	0.002
16	0.054	0.028	0.015	0.008	0.005	0.002
17	0.045	0.023	0.012	0.006	0.003	0.001
18	0.038	0.018	0.009	0.005	0.002	0.001
19	0.031	0.014	0.007	0.003	0.002	0.001
20	0.026	0.012	0.005	0.002	0.001	0.000
21	0.022	0.009	0.004	0.002	0.001	0.000
22	0.018	0.007	0.003	0.001	0.001	0.000
23	0.015	0.006	0.002	0.001	0.000	0.000
24	0.013	0.005	0.002	0.001	0.000	0.000
25	0.010	0.004	0.001	0.001	0.000	0.000

APPENDIX 2 — Present worth of a uniform series (Annuities) (P/A)I, N

YEARS	0.5%	1.0%	1.5%	2.0%	2.5%	3.0%	4.0%	5.0%	6.0%	8.0%	10.0%	12.0%	14.0%	15.0%	16.0%	18.0%
1	0.995	0.990	0.985	0.980	0.976	0.971	0.962	0.952	0.943	0.926	0.909	0.893	0.877	0.870	0.862	0.847
2	1.985	1.970	1.956	1.942	1.927	1.913	1.886	1.859	1.833	1.783	1.736	1.690	1.647	1.626	1.605	1.566
3	2.970	2.941	2.912	2.884	2.856	2.829	2.775	2.723	2.673	2.577	2.487	2.402	2.322	2.283	2.246	2.174
4	3.950	3.902	3.854	3.808	3.762	3.717	3.630	3.546	3.465	3.312	3.170	3.037	2.914	2.855	2.798	2.690
5	4.926	4.853	4.783	4.713	4.646	4.580	4.452	4.329	4.212	3.993	3.791	3.605	3.433	3.352	3.274	3.127
6	5.896	5.795	5.697	5.601	5.508	5.417	5.242	5.076	4.917	4.623	4.355	4.111	3.889	3.784	3.685	3.498
7	6.862	6.728	6.598	6.472	6.349	6.230	6.002	5.786	5.582	5.206	4.868	4.564	4.288	4.160	4.039	3.812
8	7.823	7.652	7.486	7.325	7.170	7.020	6.733	6.463	6.210	5.747	5.335	4.968	4.639	4.487	4.344	4.078
9	8.779	8.566	8.361	8.162	7.971	7.786	7.435	7.108	6.802	6.247	5.759	5.328	4.946	4.772	4.607	4.303
10	9.730	9.471	9.222	8.983	8.752	8.530	8.111	7.722	7.360	6.710	6.145	5.650	5.216	5.019	4.833	4.494
11	10.677	10.368	10.071	9.787	9.514	9.253	8.760	8.306	7.887	7.139	6.495	5.938	5.453	5.234	5.029	4.656
12	11.619	11.255	10.908	10.575	10.258	9.954	9.385	8.863	8.384	7.536	6.814	6.194	5.660	5.421	5.197	4.793
13	12.556	12.134	11.732	11.348	10.983	10.635	9.986	9.394	8.853	7.904	7.103	6.424	5.842	5.583	5.342	4.910
14	13.489	13.004	12.543	12.106	11.691	11.296	10.563	9.899	9.295	8.244	7.367	6.628	6.002	5.724	5.468	5.008
15	14.417	13.865	13.343	12.849	12.381	11.938	11.118	10.380	9.712	8.559	7.606	6.811	6.142	5.847	5.575	5.092
16	15.340	14.718	14.131	13.578	13.055	12.561	11.652	10.838	10.106	8.851	7.824	6.974	6.265	5.954	5.668	5.162
17	16.259	15.562	14.908	14.292	13.712	13.166	12.166	11.274	10.477	9.122	8.022	7.120	6.373	6.047	5.749	5.222
18	17.173	16.398	15.673	14.992	14.353	13.754	12.659	11.690	10.828	9.372	8.201	7.250	6.467	6.128	5.818	5.273
19	18.082	17.226	16.426	15.678	14.979	14.324	13.134	12.085	11.158	9.604	8.365	7.366	6.550	6.198	5.877	5.316
20	18.987	18.046	17.169	16.351	15.589	14.877	13.590	12.462	11.470	9.818	8.514	7.469	6.623	6.259	5.929	5.353
21	19.888	18.857	17.900	17.011	16.185	15.415	14.029	12.821	11.764	10.017	8.649	7.562	6.687	6.312	5.973	5.384
22	20.784	19.660	18.621	17.658	16.765	15.937	14.451	13.163	12.042	10.201	8.772	7.645	6.743	6.359	6.011	5.410
23	21.676	20.456	19.331	18.292	17.332	16.444	14.857	13.489	12.303	10.371	8.883	7.718	6.792	6.399	6.044	5.432
24	22.563	21.243	20.030	18.914	17.885	16.936	15.247	13.799	12.550	10.529	8.985	7.784	6.835	6.434	6.073	5.451
25	23.446	22.023	20.720	19.523	18.424	17.413	15.622	14.094	12.783	10.675	9.077	7.843	6.873	6.464	6.097	5.467
26	24.324	22.795	21.399	20.121	18.951	17.877	15.983	14.375	13.003	10.810	9.161	7.896	6.906	6.491	6.118	5.480
27	25.198	23.560	22.068	20.707	19.464	18.327	16.330	14.643	13.211	10.935	9.237	7.943	6.935	6.514	6.136	5.492
28	26.068	24.316	22.727	21.281	19.965	18.764	16.663	14.898	13.406	11.051	9.307	7.984	6.961	6.534	6.152	5.502
29	26.933	25.066	23.376	21.844	20.454	19.188	16.984	15.141	13.591	11.158	9.370	8.022	6.983	6.551	6.166	5.510
30	27.794	25.808	24.016	22.396	20.930	19.600	17.292	15.372	13.765	11.258	9.427	8.055	7.003	6.566	6.177	5.517
31	28.651	26.542	24.646	22.938	21.395	20.000	17.588	15.593	13.929	11.350	9.479	8.085	7.020	6.579	6.187	5.523
32	29.503	27.270	25.267	23.468	21.849	20.389	17.874	15.803	14.084	11.435	9.526	8.112	7.035	6.591	6.196	5.528
33	30.352	27.990	25.879	23.989	22.292	20.766	18.148	16.003	14.230	11.514	9.569	8.135	7.048	6.600	6.203	5.532
34	31.196	28.703	26.482	24.499	22.724	21.132	18.411	16.193	14.368	11.587	9.609	8.157	7.060	6.609	6.210	5.536
35	32.035	29.409	27.076	24.999	23.145	21.487	18.665	16.374	14.498	11.655	9.644	8.176	7.070	6.617	6.215	5.539
36	32.871	30.108	27.661	25.489	23.556	21.832	18.908	16.547	14.621	11.717	9.677	8.192	7.079	6.623	6.220	5.541
37	33.703	30.800	28.237	25.969	23.957	22.167	19.143	16.711	14.737	11.775	9.706	8.208	7.087	6.629	6.224	5.543
38	34.530	31.485	28.805	26.441	24.349	22.492	19.368	16.868	14.846	11.829	9.733	8.221	7.094	6.634	6.228	5.545
39	35.353	32.163	29.365	26.903	24.730	22.808	19.584	17.017	14.949	11.879	9.757	8.233	7.100	6.638	6.231	5.547
40	36.172	32.835	29.916	27.355	25.103	23.115	19.793	17.159	15.046	11.925	9.779	8.244	7.105	6.642	6.233	5.548
41	36.987	33.500	30.459	27.799	25.466	23.412	19.993	17.294	15.138	11.967	9.799	8.253	7.110	6.645	6.236	5.549
42	37.798	34.158	30.994	28.235	25.821	23.701	20.186	17.423	15.225	12.007	9.817	8.262	7.114	6.648	6.238	5.550
43	38.605	34.810	31.521	28.662	26.166	23.982	20.371	17.546	15.306	12.043	9.834	8.270	7.117	6.650	6.239	5.551
44	39.408	35.455	32.041	29.080	26.504	24.254	20.549	17.663	15.383	12.077	9.849	8.276	7.120	6.652	6.241	5.551
45	40.207	36.095	32.552	29.490	26.833	24.519	20.720	17.774	15.456	12.108	9.863	8.283	7.123	6.654	6.242	5.552
46	41.002	36.727	33.056	29.892	27.154	24.775	20.885	17.880	15.524	12.137	9.875	8.288	7.126	6.656	6.243	5.552
47	41.793	37.354	33.553	30.287	27.467	25.025	21.043	17.981	15.589	12.164	9.887	8.293	7.128	6.657	6.244	5.553
48	42.580	37.974	34.043	30.673	27.773	25.267	21.195	18.077	15.650	12.189	9.897	8.297	7.130	6.659	6.245	5.553
49	43.364	38.588	34.525	31.052	28.071	25.502	21.341	18.169	15.708	12.212	9.906	8.301	7.131	6.660	6.246	5.554
50	44.143	39.196	35.000	31.424	28.362	25.730	21.482	18.256	15.762	12.233	9.915	8.304	7.133	6.661	6.246	5.554

APPENDIX 2 – continued

YEARS	20.0%	25.0%	30.0%	35.0%	40.0%	50.0%
1	0.833	0.800	0.769	0.741	0.714	0.667
2	1.528	1.440	1.361	1.289	1.224	1.111
3	2.106	1.952	1.816	1.696	1.589	1.407
4	2.589	2.362	2.166	1.997	1.849	1.605
5	2.991	2.689	2.436	2.220	2.035	1.737
6	3.326	2.951	2.643	2.385	2.168	1.824
7	3.605	3.161	2.802	2.508	2.263	1.883
8	3.837	3.329	2.925	2.598	2.331	1.922
9	4.031	3.463	3.019	2.665	2.379	1.948
10	4.192	3.571	3.092	2.715	2.414	1.965
11	4.327	3.656	3.147	2.752	2.438	1.977
12	4.439	3.725	3.190	2.779	2.456	1.985
13	4.533	3.780	3.223	2.799	2.469	1.990
14	4.611	3.824	3.249	2.814	2.478	1.993
15	4.675	3.859	3.268	2.825	2.484	1.995
16	4.730	3.887	3.283	2.834	2.489	1.997
17	4.775	3.910	3.295	2.840	2.492	1.998
18	4.812	3.928	3.304	2.844	2.494	1.999
19	4.843	3.942	3.311	2.848	2.496	1.999
20	4.870	3.954	3.316	2.850	2.497	1.999
21	4.891	3.963	3.320	2.852	2.498	2.000
22	4.909	3.970	3.323	2.853	2.498	2.000
23	4.925	3.976	3.325	2.854	2.499	2.000
24	4.937	3.981	3.327	2.855	2.499	2.000
25	4.948	3.985	3.329	2.856	2.499	2.000

APPENDIX 3

INTERACTIVE COMPUTER PROGRAMMING IN BASIC V

A. 3.1 Acknowledgement

For the program and examples of their use, I am indebted to Mr Farhad Etemad, a post graduate student in the department of Management Science at the University College of Swansea.

A. 3.2 Introduction

An interactive computer program, written in BASIC V language is presented in this appendix. Program listings and examples of their use are included.

The program yields four pieces of information for any cash flow stream for up to fifty periods. This information is listed below.

(i) Net present worth.

   The net present worth can be calculated for different interest rates. The interest rates are specified by the program user.

(ii) Rate of return.

   The rate of return can be calculated if it is between 0% and 200%. Two rates of return will be calculated for cash flow streams which have more than one rate of return in the range.

(iii) Annual equivalent cash flow.

   The annual equivalent cash flow can be calculated for different interest rates. The interest rates are specified by the program user.

(iv) Graph of present worth against interest rate.

   Graphs will be plotted on the terminal for one or two cash flow streams. The program calculates twenty-one present worths for each cash flow stream using interest rates from 0% to 100% in steps of 5%. The greater absolute value of present worth is divided by 30 to give a first assessment of scale. This scale is then compared with 5, 10, 20, 50, 100, 200, ... The first greater round figure will be chosen as the scale in which the graph is actually plotted.

   Because the graphs have been designed to use only a simple alphanumeric output, they will be useful more for demonstration of curve shape than for accurate determination of either present worth or rate of return.

A. 3.3 Discounted Cash Flow Program Listing

```
1000 F=1
1005 PRINT"THIS PROGRAM PRODUCES FOUR DIFFERENT PIECES OF INFORMATION ABOUT"
1010 PRINT"ANY CASH FLOW STREAM FOR UP TO 50 YEARS ."
1015 PRINT
1020 PRINT"THIS INFORMATION IS LISTED BELOW ."
1025 PRINT
1030 PRINT"1- NET PRESENT WORTH .                   ( NPW )"
1035 PRINT
1040 PRINT"2- RATE OF RETURN .                      ( ROR )"
1045 PRINT
1050 PRINT"3- ANNUAL EQUIVALENT CASH FLOW .         ( AE )"
1055 PRINT
1060 PRINT"4- GRAPH ,i AGAINST  NPW .               ( GR )"
1065 PRINT"   NOTE: WHEN GRAPH IS PLOTTED ,TO CONTINUE THE PROGRAM ,"
1070 PRINT"   ENTER  O.K  ."
1072 PRINT
1075 PRINT"IF YOU WANT TO RUN THIS PROGRAM , SELECT YOUR OPTION AND ENTER"
1080 PRINT"ONE OF THE IDENTIFIERS , WHICH ARE SHOWN BETWEEN THE BRACKETS "
1085 PRINT"ABOVE ."
1090 PRINT"IF NO MORE CALCULATIONS ARE REQUIRED ,ENTER    END ."
1100 PRINT
1105 PRINT
1110 INPUT I$
1115 IF I$="NPW" THEN 2000
1120 IF I$="ROR" THEN 3000
1125 IF I$="AE"  THEN 5000
1130 IF I$="GR"  THEN 6000
1135 IF I$="END" THEN 1180
1140 IF  F=2     THEN 1180
1145 PRINT"IDENTIFIER IS NOT RECOGNISED . IF YOU WANT TO TRY AGAIN , ENTER"
1150 PRINT"YES , OTHERWISE ENTER  NO . IF THE ANSWER IS NO , PROGRAM WILL"
1155 PRINT"GO TO THE END ."
1160 PRINT
1165 PRINT
1170 INPUT W$
1175 IF W$="YES" THEN 1000
1180 END




1195 REM
1196 REM
1197 REM                  (ENTRY OF CASH FLOW STREAM)
1198 REM
1199 REM
1200 PRINT"ENTER THE VALUE FOR N ,WHICH IS THE NUMBER OF YEARS ."
1205 PRINT"( DURATION OF CASH FLOW STREAM )"
1210 PRINT"EXAMPLE;"
1215 PRINT"CASH FLOW,     YEAR 0     YEAR 1     YEAR 2     YEAR 3"
1220 PRINT"              -500        300        400        600"
1225 PRINT"THE VALUE OF N IS EQUAL TO 3 ,THEREFORE ENTER   3 ."
1230 PRINT
1235 PRINT"     N=?    (N <= 50)"
1240 PRINT
1245 INPUT N
1246 IF N<0 OR N>50 THEN 1277
1250 DIM X(51)
1255 FOR I=1 TO N+1
1260 K=I-1
1265 PRINT"ENTER THE AMOUNT FOR YEAR    [ ";K;" ] ."
1270 INPUT X(I)
1275 NEXT I
1276 GOTO 1280
1277 PRINT"INPUT DATA ERROR.PLEASE TRY AGAIN ( 0 < N <= 50 ) ."
1278 PRINT
1279 GOTO 1230
1280 RETURN
```

```
1295 REM
1296 REM
1297 REM                    (CASH FLOW STREAM ON LINE PRINTER)
1298 REM
1299 REM
1300 F=2
1305 PRINT"                           CASH FLOW"
1310 FOR J=1 TO N+1
1315 L=J-1
1320 PRINT"YEAR    [ ";L;" ]";TAB(44);X(J)
1325 NEXT J
1330 PRINT
1335 PRINT
1340 RETURN
1395 REM
1396 REM
1397 REM                    (CALCULATION OF NET PRESENT WORTH)
1398 REM
1399 REM
1400 B=0.0
1405 FOR K=1 TO N+1
1410 B=B+(X(K)/((1+A)**(K-1)))
1415 NEXT K
1420 RETURN




1495 REM
1496 REM
1497 REM                    (QUESTION ABOUT ENTRY OF CASH FLOW)
1498 REM
1499 REM
1500 PRINT"ENTRY OF CASH FLOW STREAM"
1505 PRINT
1510 PRINT
1515 PRINT"IF CASH FLOW STREAM IS ALREADY ENTERED AND YOU WANT IT TO BE USED"
1520 PRINT"AGAIN , ENTER  OLD , OTHERWISE ENTER  NEW ."
1525 PRINT
1530 PRINT
1535 INPUT C$
1540 IF C$="NEW" THEN 1200
1541 IF C$="NEW" OR C$="OLD" THEN 1545
1542 PRINT"IDENTIFIER IS NOT RECOGNISED.PLEASE TRY AGAIN."
1543 PRINT
1544 GOTO 1500
1545 RETURN
1595 REM
1596 REM
1597 REM                    (START ,NEW CASH FLOW STREAM OR END)
1598 REM
1599 REM
1600 F=1
1605 PRINT"IF YOU WANT TO TRY ANOTHER CASH FLOW STREAM , ENTER  NEW ."
1610 PRINT"TO USE THE OTHER AVAILABLE INFORMATION , ENTER  START ."
1615 PRINT"IF NO MORE CALCULATIONS ARE REQUIRED , ENTER  END ."
1620 PRINT
1625 PRINT
1630 INPUT D$
1635 IF D$="START" THEN 1000
1640 IF D$="NEW"    THEN 1200
1645 IF D$="END"    THEN 1180
1646 IF D$="START" OR D$="NEW" OR D$="END" THEN 1650
1647 PRINT"IDENTIFIER IS NOT RECOGNISED.PLEASE TRY AGAIN."
1648 PRINT
1649 GOTO 1600
1650 RETURN
```

```
1995 REM
1996 REM
1997 REM                    (SUBROUTINE              NPW)
1998 REM
1999 REM
2000 PRINT"NET PRESENT WORTH"
2005 PRINT
2010 PRINT
2015 PRINT"TO FIND PW , GIVEN CASH FLOW STREAM  Fj: j=0,N (N LESS THAN OR-"
2020 PRINT"EQUAL TO 50) ; AND i ."
2022 PRINT
2025 GOSUB 1500
2027 PRINT
2030 PRINT"ENTER THE VALUE FOR i, WHICH IS THE ANNUAL INTEREST RATE ."
2035 PRINT"EXAMPLE ;"
2040 PRINT"FOR i=26% , ENTER    0.26  ."
2045 F=1
2050 PRINT
2055 PRINT"        i=?"
2060 PRINT
2065 INPUT A
2070 PRINT
2075 GOSUB 1400
2080 IF F<>1 THEN 2090
2085 GOSUB 1300
2090 PRINT
2095 PRINT"THE INTEREST RATE                                      i=";A
2100 PRINT
2105 PRINT"THE NET PRESENT WORTH FOR THE GIVEN CASH FLOW STREAM     PW=";B
2110 PRINT
2115 PRINT"IF YOU WANT TO TRY ANOTHER INTEREST RATE ,"
2120 PRINT"ENTER   YES , OTHERWISE ENTER   NO ."
2125 PRINT
2130 INPUT E$
2135 IF E$="YES" THEN 2050
2136 IF E$="YES" OR E$="NO" THEN 2140
2137 PRINT"IDENTIFIER IS NOT RECOGNISED.PLEASE TRY AGAIN."
2138 PRINT
2139 GOTO 2110
2140 PRINT
2141 GOSUB 1600
2145 GOTO   2045
2150 RETURN


2995 REM
2996 REM
2997 REM                    (SUBROUTINE              ROR)
2998 REM
2999 REM
3000 PRINT"RATE OF RETURN"
3005 PRINT
3010 PRINT
3015 PRINT"TO FIND ROR , GIVEN CASH FLOW STREAM  Fj: j=0,N (N LESS THAN OR-"
3020 PRINT"EQUAL TO 50) ."
3022 PRINT
3025 GOSUB 1500
3030 GOSUB 1300
3035 P=1
3037 R1=0.0
3038 R2=0.0
3040 A=0.0
3045 GOSUB 1400
3047 IF B=0.0 THEN 3320
3050 IF B<0.0 THEN 3060
3055 GOTO   3070
3060 P=2
3065 GOTO   3150
3070 A=A+0.05
3072 R1=A
3075 IF A>2.0 THEN 3230
```

```
3080 GOSUB 1400
3085 IF B>0.0 THEN 3070
3095 A1=A-0.05
3100 D=(A-A1)/2.0
3105 A=A-D
3110 GOSUB 1400
3115 IF (A-A1)<0.0005 THEN 3145
3120 IF B>0.0          THEN 3130
3125 GOTO 3100
3130 A1=A
3135 A=A+D
3140 GOTO 3100
3145 R1=A
3147 IF P=2 THEN 3230
3150 A=A+0.05
3152 R2=A
3155 IF A>2.0 THEN 3230
3160 GOSUB 1400
3165 IF B<0.0 THEN 3150
3170 A1=A-0.05
3175 D=(A-A1)/2.0
3180 A=A-D
3185 GOSUB 1400
3190 IF (A-A1)<0.0005 THEN 3220
3195 IF B<0.0          THEN 3205
3200 GOTO 3175
3205 A1=A
3210 A=A+D
3215 GOTO 3175
3220 R2=A
3225 IF P=2    THEN 3070
3230 IF R2<R1 THEN 3240
3235 GOTO          3248
3240 R3=R2
3245 R2=R1
3247 R1=R3
3248 IF R1=0.0 AND R2>2.0  THEN 3320
3250 IF R1<=2.0 AND R2>2.0 THEN 3270
3255 IF R1<2.0 AND R2<=2.0 THEN 3280
3260 PRINT
3265 PRINT
3270 PRINT"THE RATE OF RETURN FOR THE GIVEN CASH FLOW STREAM          ROR=";R1
3272 PRINT
3273 PRINT
3275 GOTO 3395
3280 PRINT
3285 PRINT
3290 PRINT"TWO DIFFERENT RATES OF RETURN FOR THE GIVEN CASH FLOW STREAM"
3295 PRINT"ARE CALCULATED"
3300 PRINT
3305 PRINT"                                        1-ROR=";R1
3310 PRINT"                                        2-ROR=";R2
3312 PRINT
3315 GOTO 3395
3320 PRINT
3335 PRINT
3340 PRINT"SORRY ,NO RATE OF RETURN IS CALCULATED"
3345 PRINT
3350 PRINT"THERE ARE TWO POSSIBLITIES"
3355 PRINT
3360 PRINT"1-RATE OF RETURN DOES NOT EXIST , BECUASE OF THE LARGE NEGATIVE"
3365 PRINT"  AMOUNT FOR YEAR ZERO ."
3370 PRINT
3375 PRINT"2-THE RATE OF RETURN IS EITHER EQUAL TO 0 % OR MORE THAN 200 % ."
3380 PRINT
3385 PRINT"PLEASE TRY ANOTHER CASH FLOW STREAM ."
3390 PRINT
3395 GOSUB 1600
3400 GOTO 3030
3405 RETURN
```

```
4995 REM
4996 REM
4997 REM                    (SUBROUTINE              AE)
4998 REM
4999 REM
5000 PRINT"ANNUAL EQUIVALENT CASH FLOW STREAM"
5005 PRINT
5010 PRINT"TO FIND AE , GIVEN CASH FLOW STREAM  Fj: j=0,N (N LESS THAN OR-"
5015 PRINT"EQUAL TO 50) ; AND i ."
5020 PRINT
5025 GOSUB 1500
5027 PRINT
5030 PRINT"ENTER THE VALUE FOR i, WHICH IS THE ANNUAL INTEREST RATE ."
5035 PRINT"EXAMPLE ;"
5040 PRINT"FOR i=26% , ENTER    0.26  ."
5045 PRINT
5050 PRINT
5055 PRINT"      i=?"
5060 PRINT
5065 INPUT A
5070 PRINT
5075 GOSUB 1400
5080 H=B*((A*((1+A)**N))/(((1+A)**N)-1.0))
5085 PRINT
5090 PRINT
5095 PRINT"              CASH FLOW                ANNUAL E C F"
5097 PRINT
5098 PRINT
5100 FOR J=1 TO N+1
5105 L=J-1
5110 IF L=0.0 THEN 5125
5115 H1=H
5120 GOTO 5130
5125 H1=0.0
5130 PRINT"YEAR   [ ";L;" ]";TAB(16);X(J);TAB(45);H1
5135 NEXT J
5140 PRINT
5142 PRINT"THE INTEREST RATE IS ,              i=";A
5143 PRINT
5145 PRINT"IF YOU WANT TO TRY ANOTHER INTEREST RATE ,"
5150 PRINT"ENTER  YES ,OTHERWISE  NO ."
5155 PRINT
5160 INPUT E$
5165 IF E$="YES" THEN 5045
5166 IF E$="YES" OR E$="NO" THEN 5170
5167 PRINT"IDENTIFIER IS NOT RECOGNISED.PLEASE TRY AGAIN."
5168 PRINT
5169 GOTO 5143
5170 GOSUB 1600
5175 GOTO 5045
5180 RETURN




5995 REM
5996 REM
5997 REM                    (SUBROUTINE          GRAPH)
5998 REM
5999 REM
6000 DIM Y(51),Q(21),R(21)
6005 PRINT"GRAPH      (i AGAINST NPW)"
6010 PRINT
6015 PRINT"THIS GRAPH CAN BE PLOTTED FOR ONE OR TWO CASH FLOW STREAMS,"
6020 PRINT"ON THE SCREEN ."
6025 PRINT
6030 PRINT"IF YOU WANT THE GRAPH TO BE PLOTTED FOR ONE CASH FLOW STREAM,"
6035 PRINT"ENTER  ONE ,FOR TWO CASH FLOW STREAMS, ENTER   TWO ."
6040 PRINT
```

```
6045 PRINT
6050 INPUT T$
6055 PRINT
6060 GOSUB 1500
6065 IF T$="ONE" THEN 6125
6066 IF T$="TWO" THEN 6070
6067 PRINT"IDENTIFIER IS NOT RECOGNISED.PLEASE TRY AGAIN."
6068 PRINT"ENTER     ( ONE ) OR ( TWO )."
6069 GOTO 6050
6070 PRINT"ENTRY OF CASH FLOW NO.2 ."
6075 PRINT
6080 PRINT
6085 PRINT"     N=?     (N <= 50)"
6090 INPUT N1
6091 IF N1<0 OR N1>50 THEN 6093
6092 GOTO 6095
6093 PRINT"INPUT DATA ERROR.PLEASE TRY AGAIN ( 0 < N <= 50 ) ."
6094 GOTO 6075
6095 FOR I=1 TO N1+1
6100 K=I-1
6105 PRINT"ENTER THE AMOUNT FOR YEAR    [ ";K;" ] ."
6110 INPUT Y(I)
6115 NEXT I
6120 GOTO 6325




6125 REM
6130 REM
6135 REM                    (GRAPH FOR ONE CASH FLOW STREAM)
6140 REM
6145 REM
6150 GOSUB 1300
6155 A=0.0
6160 FOR L=1 TO 21
6165 GOSUB 1400
6170 Q(L)=B
6175 A=A+0.05
6180 NEXT L
6185 M1=ABS(Q(1))
6190 FOR L=2 TO 21
6195 IF M1>ABS(Q(L)) THEN 6205
6200 M1=ABS(Q(L))
6205 NEXT L
6210 D2=M1/30.0
6212 GOSUB 9000
6215 PRINT"                              ((GRAPH))"
6220 PRINT"          -30 -25 -20 -15 -10 -5  0   5   10  15  20  25  30
6225 PRINT"i\PW    |----|----|----|----|----|----|----|----|----|----|----|
6230 A=0.0
6235 FOR I=1 TO 21
6240 P1=ABS(Q(I))/D2
6245 IF P1-INT(P1)<=0.5 THEN 6260
6250 U1=INT(P1)+1
6255 GOTO 6265
6260 U1=INT(P1)
6265 IF Q(I)<=0.0      THEN 6280
6270 PRINT A;TAB(40+U1);"*"
6275 GOTO 6285
6280 PRINT A;TAB(10+(30-U1));"*"
6285 A=A+0.05
6290 NEXT I
6300 INPUT V$
6305 PRINT"TO FIND THE APPROXIMATE VALUE OF PW ,FIND THE SCALE FROM THE PW"
6310 PRINT"AXIS AND MULTIPLY IT BY ,              D=";D2
6315 PRINT
6320 GOTO 6745
```

```
6325 REM
6330 REM
6335 REM                    (GRAPH FOR TWO CASH FLOW STREAMS)
6340 REM
6345 REM
6350 GOSUB 1300
6355 PRINT"                         CASH FLOW     NO-2"
6360 FOR J=1 TO N1+1
6365 L=J-1
6370 PRINT"YEAR    [ ";L;" ]";TAB(44);Y(J)
6375 NEXT J
6380 PRINT"TO CONTINUE          ENTER  O.K  ."
6385 INPUT V$
6390 A=0.0
6395 FOR L=1 TO 21
6400 GOSUB 1400
6405 Q(L)=B
6410 A=A+0.05
6415 NEXT L
6420 A=0.0
6425 FOR L=1 TO 21
6430 R(L)=0.0
6435 FOR K=1 TO N1+1
6440 R(L)=R(L)+(Y(K)/((1+A)**(K-1)))
6445 NEXT K
6450 A=A+0.05
6455 NEXT L
6460 M2=ABS(Q(1))
6465 FOR L=2 TO 21
6470 IF M2>ABS(Q(L)) THEN 6480
6475 M2=ABS(Q(L))
6480 NEXT L
6485 FOR K=1 TO 21
6490 IF M2>ABS(R(K)) THEN 6500
6495 M2=ABS(R(K))
6500 NEXT K
6505 D3=M2/30.0
6507 GOSUB 9500
6510 PRINT"                                    ((GRAPH))"
6515 PRINT"        -30  -25  -20  -15  -10  -5   0    5   10   15   20   25   30"
6520 PRINT"i\PW    |----|----|----|----|----|----|----|----|----|----|----|----|"
6525 A=0.0
6530 FOR J=1 TO 21
6535 W1=ABS(Q(J))/D3
6540 W2=ABS(R(J))/D3
6545 IF W1-INT(W1)<=0.5 THEN 6560
6550 O1=INT(W1)+1
6555 GOTO 6565
6560 O1=INT(W1)
6565 IF W2-INT(W2)<=0.5 THEN 6580
6570 O2=INT(W2)+1
6575 GOTO 6585
6580 O2=INT(W2)
6585 IF Q(J)<=0.0 AND R(J)<=0.0 THEN 6605
6590 IF Q(J)< 0.0 AND R(J)> 0.0 THEN 6645
6595 IF Q(J)> 0.0 AND R(J)< 0.0 THEN 6655
6600 IF Q(J)=>0.0 AND R(J)=>0.0 THEN 6665
6605 IF O1>O2                   THEN 6625
6610 IF O1<O2                   THEN 6635
6615 PRINT A;TAB(10+(30-O1));"0"
6620 GOTO 6700
6625 PRINT A;TAB(10+(30-O1));"*";TAB(10+(30-O2));"X"
6630 GOTO 6700
6635 PRINT A;TAB(10+(30-O2));"X";TAB(10+(30-O1));"*"
6640 GOTO 6700
6645 PRINT A;TAB(10+(30-O1));"*";TAB(40+O2);"X"
6650 GOTO 6700
6655 PRINT A;TAB(10+(30-O2));"X";TAB(40+O1);"*"
6660 GOTO 6700
```

```
6665 IF O1>O2 THEN 6685
6670 IF O1<O2 THEN 6695
6675 PRINT A;TAB(40+O1);"O"
6680 GOTO 6700
6685 PRINT A;TAB(40+O2);"X";TAB(40+O1);"*"
6690 GOTO 6700
6695 PRINT A;TAB(40+O1);"*";TAB(40+O2);"X"
6700 A=A+0.05
6705 NEXT J
6710 INPUT V$
6715 PRINT"(*) CASH FLOW STREAM NO-1, (X) CASH FLOW STREAM NO-2 AND"
6720 PRINT"(O) BOTH CASH FLOW STREAMS ."
6725 PRINT
6730 PRINT"TO FIND THE APPROXIMATE VALUE OF PW ,FIND THE SCALE FROM THE PW"
6735 PRINT"AXIS AND MULTIPLY IT BY ,              D=";D3
6740 PRINT
6745 PRINT
6750 PRINT"IF YOU WANT THIS PROGRAM TO PLOT ANOTHER GRAPH FOR DIFFERENT CASH"
6755 PRINT"FLOW STREAMS , ENTER  NEW ."
6760 PRINT"TO USE THE OTHER AVAILABLE INFORMATION , ENTER  START ."
6765 PRINT"IF NO MORE CALCULATIONS ARE REQUIRED , ENTER  END ."
6770 PRINT
6775 PRINT
6780 INPUT D$
6785 IF D$="START" THEN 1000
6790 IF D$="NEW"   THEN 6000
6795 IF D$="END"   THEN 1180
6796 IF D$="START" OR D$="NEW" OR D$="END" THEN 6800
6797 PRINT"IDENTIFIER IS NOT RECOGNISED.PLEASE TRY AGAIN."
6798 PRINT
6799 GOTO 6740
6800 RETURN


9000 REM
9005 REM
9010 REM                      (SUBROUTINE TO ROUND THE SCALE)
9015 REM
9020 REM
9025 X1=1
9030 X2=2
9035 X3=5
9040 IF D2<=X3 THEN 9080
9045 X1=X1*10
9050 IF D2<=X1 THEN 9090
9055 X2=X2*10
9060 IF D2<=X2 THEN 9100
9065 X3=X3*10
9075 GOTO          9040
9080 D2=X3
9085 GOTO          9105
9090 D2=X1
9095 GOTO          9105
9100 D2=X2
9105 RETURN
9500 X1=1
9505 X2=2
9510 X3=5
9515 IF D3<=X3 THEN 9550
9520 X1=X1*10
9525 IF D3<=X1 THEN 9560
9530 X2=X2*10
9535 IF D3<=X2 THEN 9570
9540 X3=X3*10
9545 GOTO          9515
9550 D3=X3
9555 GOTO          9575
9560 D3=X1
9565 GOTO          9575
9570 D3=X2
9575 RETURN
```

A. 3.4 Discounted Cash Flow Specimen Computer Output

THIS PROGRAM PRODUCES FOUR DIFFERENT PIECES OF INFORMATION ABOUT
ANY CASH FLOW STREAM FOR UP TO 50 YEARS .

THIS INFORMATION IS LISTED BELOW .

1- NET PRESENT WORTH .   (NPW)

2- RATE OF RETURN .   (ROR)

3- ANNUAL EQUIVALENT CASH FLOW .   (AE)

4- GRAPH ,i AGAINST NPW .   (GR)
   NOTE: WHEN GRAPH IS PLOTTED ,TO CONTINUE THE PROGRAM ,
   ENTER O.K .

IF YOU WANT TO RUN THIS PROGRAM , SELECT YOUR OPTION AND ENTER
ONE OF THE IDENTIFIERS , WHICH ARE SHOWN BETWEEN THE BRACKETS
ABOVE .
IF NO MORE CALCULATIONS ARE REQUIRED ,ENTER   END .

!NPW
NET PRESENT WORTH

TO FIND PW , GIVEN CASH FLOW STREAM Fj: j=0,N (N LESS THAN OR-
EQUAL TO 50) ; AND i .

ENTRY OF CASH FLOW STREAM

IF CASH FLOW STREAM IS ALREADY ENTERED AND YOU WANT IT TO BE USED
AGAIN , ENTER OLD , OTHERWISE ENTER NEW .

!NEW
ENTER THE VALUE FOR N ,WHICH IS THE NUMBER OF YEARS .
(DURATION OF CASH FLOW STREAM)
EXAMPLE;
CASH FLOW,   YEAR 0   YEAR 1   YEAR 2   YEAR 3
               -500   300   400   600
THE VALUE OF N IS EQUAL TO 3 ,THEREFORE ENTER   3 .

       N=?   (N <= 50)

!10
ENTER THE AMOUNT FOR YEAR   [0] .
!-8000
ENTER THE AMOUNT FOR YEAR   [1] .
!3500
ENTER THE AMOUNT FOR YEAR   [2] .
!2600
ENTER THE AMOUNT FOR YEAR   [3] .
!2100
ENTER THE AMOUNT FOR YEAR   [4] .
!2000
ENTER THE AMOUNT FOR YEAR   [5] .
!1500
ENTER THE AMOUNT FOR YEAR   [6] .
!1000
ENTER THE AMOUNT FOR YEAR   [7] .
!600
ENTER THE AMOUNT FOR YEAR   [8] .
!600
ENTER THE AMOUNT FOR YEAR   [9] .
!600
ENTER THE AMOUNT FOR YEAR   [10] .
!600

ENTER THE VALUE FOR i, WHICH IS THE ANNUAL INTEREST RATE .
EXAMPLE ;
FOR i=26% , ENTER   0.26 .

       i=?

!0.15

```
                              CASH FLOW
YEAR    [ 0  ]                                    -8000
YEAR    [ 1  ]                                     3500
YEAR    [ 2  ]                                     2600
YEAR    [ 3  ]                                     2100
YEAR    [ 4  ]                                     2000
YEAR    [ 5  ]                                     1500
YEAR    [ 6  ]                                     1000
YEAR    [ 7  ]                                      600
YEAR    [ 8  ]                                      600
YEAR    [ 9  ]                                      600
YEAR    [ 10 ]                                      600
```

THE INTEREST RATE $i=.15$

THE NET PRESENT WORTH FOR THE GIVEN CASH FLOW STREAM   PW=1452.406633152

IF YOU WANT TO TRY ANOTHER INTEREST RATE ,
ENTER YES , OTHERWISE ENTER NO .

!YES

    $i=?$

!0.25

THE INTEREST RATE $i=.25$

THE NET PRESENT WORTH FOR THE GIVEN CASH FLOW STREAM   PW=-516.48843776

IF YOU WANT TO TRY ANOTHER INTEREST RATE ,
ENTER YES , OTHERWISE ENTER NO .

!NO

IF YOU WANT TO TRY ANOTHER CASH FLOW STREAM , ENTER NEW .
TO USE THE OTHER AVAILABLE INFORMATION , ENTER START .
IF NO MORE CALCULATIONS ARE REQUIRED , ENTER END .

!START
THIS PROGRAM PRODUCES FOUR DIFFERENT PIECES OF INFORMATION ABOUT
ANY CASH FLOW STREAM FOR UP TO 50 YEARS .

THIS INFORMATION IS LISTED BELOW .

1- NET PRESENT WORTH .   (NPW)

2- RATE OF RETURN .   (ROR)

3- ANNUAL EQUIVALENT CASH FLOW .   (AE)

4- GRAPH ,i AGAINST NPW .   (GR)
   NOTE: WHEN GRAPH IS PLOTTED ,TO CONTINUE THE PROGRAM ,
   ENTER O.K .

IF YOU WANT TO RUN THIS PROGRAM , SELECT YOUR OPTION AND ENTER
ONE OF THE IDENTIFIERS , WHICH ARE SHOWN BETWEEN THE BRACKETS
ABOVE .
IF NO MORE CALCULATIONS ARE REQUIRED ,ENTER   END .

```
!ROR
RATE OF RETURN


TO FIND ROR , GIVEN CASH FLOW STREAM   Fj: j=0,N (N LESS THAN OR-
EQUAL TO 50) .

ENTRY OF CASH FLOW STREAM


IF CASH FLOW STREAM IS ALREADY ENTERED AND YOU WANT IT TO BE USED
AGAIN , ENTER  OLD , OTHERWISE ENTER  NEW .


!NEW
ENTER THE VALUE FOR N ,WHICH IS THE NUMBER OF YEARS .
( DURATION OF CASH FLOW STREAM )
EXAMPLE;
CASH FLOW,      YEAR 0       YEAR 1       YEAR 2       YEAR 3
                -500          300          400          600
THE VALUE OF N IS EQUAL TO 3 ,THEREFORE ENTER  3 .


       N=?      (N <= 50)

!10
ENTER THE AMOUNT FOR YEAR      [ 0 ] .
!-3600
ENTER THE AMOUNT FOR YEAR      [ 1 ] .
!500
ENTER THE AMOUNT FOR YEAR      [ 2 ] .
!600
ENTER THE AMOUNT FOR YEAR      [ 3 ] .
!700
ENTER THE AMOUNT FOR YEAR      [ 4 ] .
!800
ENTER THE AMOUNT FOR YEAR      [ 5 ] .
!900
ENTER THE AMOUNT FOR YEAR      [ 6 ] .
!1000
ENTER THE AMOUNT FOR YEAR      [ 7 ] .
!900
ENTER THE AMOUNT FOR YEAR      [ 8 ] .
!800
ENTER THE AMOUNT FOR YEAR      [ 9 ] .
!700
ENTER THE AMOUNT FOR YEAR      [ 10 ] .
!600




                        CASH FLOW
YEAR   [ 0 ]                            -3600
YEAR   [ 1 ]                             500
YEAR   [ 2 ]                             600
YEAR   [ 3 ]                             700
YEAR   [ 4 ]                             800
YEAR   [ 5 ]                             900
YEAR   [ 6 ]                            1000
YEAR   [ 7 ]                             900
YEAR   [ 8 ]                             800
YEAR   [ 9 ]                             700
YEAR   [ 10 ]                            600


THE RATE OF RETURN FOR THE GIVEN CASH FLOW STREAM        ROR=.151953125


IF YOU WANT TO TRY ANOTHER CASH FLOW STREAM , ENTER  NEW .
TO USE THE OTHER AVAILABLE INFORMATION , ENTER  START .
IF NO MORE CALCULATIONS ARE REQUIRED , ENTER  END .
```

```
!NEW
ENTER THE VALUE FOR N ,WHICH IS THE NUMBER OF YEARS .
( DURATION OF CASH FLOW STREAM )
EXAMPLE;
CASH FLOW,        YEAR 0       YEAR 1       YEAR 2       YEAR 3
                  -500          300          400          600
THE VALUE OF N IS EQUAL TO 3 ,THEREFORE ENTER   3 .


     N=?     (N <= 50)


!4
ENTER THE AMOUNT FOR YEAR        [ 0 ] .
!-10000
ENTER THE AMOUNT FOR YEAR        [ 1 ] .
!50000
ENTER THE AMOUNT FOR YEAR        [ 2 ] .
!-93500
ENTER THE AMOUNT FOR YEAR        [ 3 ] .
!77500
ENTER THE AMOUNT FOR YEAR        [ 4 ] .
!-24024
                         CASH FLOW
YEAR     [ 0 ]                           -10000
YEAR     [ 1 ]                            50000
YEAR     [ 2 ]                           -93500
YEAR     [ 3 ]                            77500
YEAR     [ 4 ]                           -24024




TWO DIFFERENT RATES OF RETURN FOR THE GIVEN CASH FLOW STREAM
ARE CALCULATED


                              1-ROR=.099609375
                              2-ROR=.2


IF YOU WANT TO TRY ANOTHER CASH FLOW STREAM , ENTER  NEW .
TO USE THE OTHER AVAILABLE INFORMATION , ENTER   START .
IF NO MORE CALCULATIONS ARE REQUIRED , ENTER   END .
```

```
!NEW
ENTER THE VALUE FOR N ,WHICH IS THE NUMBER OF YEARS .
( DURATION OF CASH FLOW STREAM )
EXAMPLE;
CASH FLOW,        YEAR 0       YEAR 1       YEAR 2       YEAR 3
                  -500          300          400          600
THE VALUE OF N IS EQUAL TO 3 ,THEREFORE ENTER   3 .


     N=?     (N <= 50)


!3
ENTER THE AMOUNT FOR YEAR        [ 0 ] .
!-1000
ENTER THE AMOUNT FOR YEAR        [ 1 ] .
!3600
ENTER THE AMOUNT FOR YEAR        [ 2 ] .
!4320
ENTER THE AMOUNT FOR YEAR        [ 3 ] .
!2700
                         CASH FLOW
YEAR     [ 0 ]                           -1000
YEAR     [ 1 ]                            3600
YEAR     [ 2 ]                            4320
YEAR     [ 3 ]                            2700
```

```
SORRY ,NO RATE OF RETURN IS CALCULATED

THERE ARE TWO POSSIBLITIES

1-RATE OF RETURN DOES NOT EXIST , BECUASE OF THE LARGE NEGATIVE
  AMOUNT FOR YEAR ZERO .

2-THE RATE OF RETURN IS EITHER EQUAL TO 0 % OR MORE THAN 200 % .

PLEASE TRY ANOTHER CASH FLOW STREAM .

IF YOU WANT TO TRY ANOTHER CASH FLOW STREAM , ENTER  NEW .
TO USE THE OTHER AVAILABLE INFORMATION , ENTER  START .
IF NO MORE CALCULATIONS ARE REQUIRED , ENTER  END .




!NEW
ENTER THE VALUE FOR N ,WHICH IS THE NUMBER OF YEARS .
( DURATION OF CASH FLOW STREAM )
EXAMPLE;
CASH FLOW,      YEAR 0      YEAR 1      YEAR 2      YEAR 3
                -500         300         400         600
THE VALUE OF N IS EQUAL TO 3 ,THEREFORE ENTER  3 .

     N=?     (N <= 50)

!4
ENTER THE AMOUNT FOR YEAR      [ 0 ] .
!-40000
ENTER THE AMOUNT FOR YEAR      [ 1 ] .
!10000
ENTER THE AMOUNT FOR YEAR      [ 2 ] .
!10000
ENTER THE AMOUNT FOR YEAR      [ 3 ] .
!10000
ENTER THE AMOUNT FOR YEAR      [ 4 ] .
!10000
                        CASH FLOW
YEAR    [ 0 ]                        -40000
YEAR    [ 1 ]                         10000
YEAR    [ 2 ]                         10000
YEAR    [ 3 ]                         10000
YEAR    [ 4 ]                         10000




SORRY ,NO RATE OF RETURN IS CALCULATED

THERE ARE TWO POSSIBLITIES

1-RATE OF RETURN DOES NOT EXIST , BECUASE OF THE LARGE NEGATIVE
  AMOUNT FOR YEAR ZERO .

2-THE RATE OF RETURN IS EITHER EQUAL TO 0 % OR MORE THAN 200 % .

PLEASE TRY ANOTHER CASH FLOW STREAM .

IF YOU WANT TO TRY ANOTHER CASH FLOW STREAM , ENTER  NEW .
TO USE THE OTHER AVAILABLE INFORMATION , ENTER  START .
IF NO MORE CALCULATIONS ARE REQUIRED , ENTER  END .
```

!START
THIS PROGRAM PRODUCES FOUR DIFFERENT PIECES OF INFORMATION ABOUT
ANY CASH FLOW STREAM FOR UP TO 50 YEARS .

THIS INFORMATION IS LISTED BELOW .

1- NET PRESENT WORTH .   (NPW)

2- RATE OF RETURN .   (ROR)

3- ANNUAL EQUIVALENT CASH FLOW .   (AE)

4- GRAPH ,i AGAINST NPW .   (GR)
   NOTE: WHEN GRAPH IS PLOTTED ,TO CONTINUE THE PROGRAM ,
   ENTER O.K .

IF YOU WANT TO RUN THIS PROGRAM , SELECT YOUR OPTION AND ENTER
ONE OF THE IDENTIFIERS , WHICH ARE SHOWN BETWEEN THE BRACKETS
ABOVE .
IF NO MORE CALCULATIONS ARE REQUIRED ,ENTER   END .

!AE
ANNUAL EQUIVALENT CASH FLOW STREAM

TO FIND AE , GIVEN CASH FLOW STREAM Fj: j=0,N (N LESS THAN OR-
EQUAL TO 50) ; AND i .

ENTRY OF CASH FLOW STREAM

IF CASH FLOW STREAM IS ALREADY ENTERED AND YOU WANT IT TO BE USED
AGAIN , ENTER OLD , OTHERWISE ENTER NEW .

!OLD

ENTER THE VALUE FOR i, WHICH IS THE ANNUAL INTEREST RATE .
EXAMPLE ;
FOR i=26% , ENTER   0.26 .

     i=?

!0.15

                CASH FLOW   ANNUAL E C F

YEAR [0]   -40000   0
YEAR [1]   10000   -4010.614063634
YEAR [2]   10000   -4010.614063634
YEAR [3]   10000   -4010.614063634
YEAR [4]   10000   -4010.614063634

THE INTEREST RATE IS ,   i=.15

IF YOU WANT TO TRY ANOTHER INTEREST RATE ,
ENTER YES ,OTHERWISE NO .

!NO
IF YOU WANT TO TRY ANOTHER CASH FLOW STREAM , ENTER NEW .
TO USE THE OTHER AVAILABLE INFORMATION , ENTER START .
IF NO MORE CALCULATIONS ARE REQUIRED , ENTER END .

```
!NEW
ENTER THE VALUE FOR N ,WHICH IS THE NUMBER OF YEARS .
( DURATION OF CASH FLOW STREAM )
EXAMPLE;
CASH FLOW,        YEAR 0       YEAR 1       YEAR 2       YEAR 3
                   -500         300          400          600
THE VALUE OF N IS EQUAL TO 3 ,THEREFORE ENTER  3 .

      N=?      (N <= 50)

!10
ENTER THE AMOUNT FOR YEAR      [ 0 ] .
!-30000
ENTER THE AMOUNT FOR YEAR      [ 1 ] .
!5600
ENTER THE AMOUNT FOR YEAR      [ 2 ] .
!8400
ENTER THE AMOUNT FOR YEAR      [ 3 ] .
!14000
ENTER THE AMOUNT FOR YEAR      [ 4 ] .
!27000
ENTER THE AMOUNT FOR YEAR      [ 5 ] .
!14700
ENTER THE AMOUNT FOR YEAR      [ 6 ] .
!7500
ENTER THE AMOUNT FOR YEAR      [ 7 ] .
!4900
ENTER THE AMOUNT FOR YEAR      [ 8 ] .
!2600
ENTER THE AMOUNT FOR YEAR      [ 9 ] .
!1800
ENTER THE AMOUNT FOR YEAR      [ 10 ] .
!1000


      i=?

!0.20




                  CASH FLOW                    ANNUAL E C F


YEAR  [ 0 ]      -30000                 0
YEAR  [ 1 ]       5600                  2987.391371743
YEAR  [ 2 ]       8400                  2987.391371743
YEAR  [ 3 ]       14000                 2987.391371743
YEAR  [ 4 ]       27000                 2987.391371743
YEAR  [ 5 ]       14700                 2987.391371743
YEAR  [ 6 ]       7500                  2987.391371743
YEAR  [ 7 ]       4900                  2987.391371743
YEAR  [ 8 ]       2600                  2987.391371743
YEAR  [ 9 ]       1800                  2987.391371743
YEAR  [ 10 ]      1000                  2987.391371743

THE INTEREST RATE IS ,                 i=.2

IF YOU WANT TO TRY ANOTHER INTEREST RATE ,
ENTER  YES ,OTHERWISE  NO .

!YES


      i=?

!0.15
```

```
                CASH FLOW              ANNUAL E C F

YEAR  [ 0 ]    -30000                  0
YEAR  [ 1 ]     5600                   3958.258792614
YEAR  [ 2 ]     8400                   3958.258792614
YEAR  [ 3 ]    14000                   3958.258792614
YEAR  [ 4 ]    27000                   3958.258792614
YEAR  [ 5 ]    14700                   3958.258792614
YEAR  [ 6 ]     7500                   3958.258792614
YEAR  [ 7 ]     4900                   3958.258792614
YEAR  [ 8 ]     2600                   3958.258792614
YEAR  [ 9 ]     1800                   3958.258792614
YEAR  [ 10 ]    1000                   3958.258792614

THE INTEREST RATE IS ,                    i=.15

IF YOU WANT TO TRY ANOTHER INTEREST RATE ,
ENTER  YES ,OTHERWISE  NO .

!NO
IF YOU WANT TO TRY ANOTHER CASH FLOW STREAM , ENTER  NEW .
TO USE THE OTHER AVAILABLE INFORMATION , ENTER  START .
IF NO MORE CALCULATIONS ARE REQUIRED , ENTER  END .




!START
THIS PROGRAM PRODUCES FOUR DIFFERENT PIECES OF INFORMATION ABOUT
ANY CASH FLOW STREAM FOR UP TO 50 YEARS .

THIS INFORMATION IS LISTED BELOW .

1- NET PRESENT WORTH .                ( NPW )

2- RATE OF RETURN .                   ( ROR )

3- ANNUAL EQUIVALENT CASH FLOW .      ( AE )

4- GRAPH ,i AGAINST  NPW .            ( GR )
   NOTE: WHEN GRAPH IS PLOTTED ,TO CONTINUE THE PROGRAM ,
   ENTER  O.K  .

IF YOU WANT TO RUN THIS PROGRAM , SELECT YOUR OPTION AND ENTER
ONE OF THE IDENTIFIERS , WHICH ARE SHOWN BETWEEN THE BRACKETS
ABOVE .
IF NO MORE CALCULATIONS ARE REQUIRED ,ENTER   END .
```

```
!GR
GRAPH       (i AGAINST NPW)

THIS GRAPH CAN BE PLOTTED FOR ONE OR TWO CASH FLOW STREAMS,
ON THE SCREEN .

IF YOU WANT THE GRAPH TO BE PLOTTED FOR ONE CASH FLOW STREAM,
ENTER  ONE ,FOR TWO CASH FLOW STREAMS, ENTER  TWO .


!ONE

ENTRY OF CASH FLOW STREAM


IF CASH FLOW STREAM IS ALREADY ENTERED AND YOU WANT IT TO BE USED
AGAIN , ENTER  OLD , OTHERWISE ENTER  NEW .


!NEW
ENTER THE VALUE FOR N ,WHICH IS THE NUMBER OF YEARS .
( DURATION OF CASH FLOW STREAM )
EXAMPLE;
CASH FLOW,      YEAR 0      YEAR 1       YEAR 2       YEAR 3
                -500        300          400          600
THE VALUE OF N IS EQUAL TO 3 ,THEREFORE ENTER   3 .

     N=?     (N <= 50)

!10
ENTER THE AMOUNT FOR YEAR     [ 0 ] .
!-68000
ENTER THE AMOUNT FOR YEAR     [ 1 ] .
!20000
ENTER THE AMOUNT FOR YEAR     [ 2 ] .
!20000
ENTER THE AMOUNT FOR YEAR     [ 3 ] .
!14000
ENTER THE AMOUNT FOR YEAR     [ 4 ] .
!14000
ENTER THE AMOUNT FOR YEAR     [ 5 ] .
!14000
ENTER THE AMOUNT FOR YEAR     [ 6 ] .
!9000
ENTER THE AMOUNT FOR YEAR     [ 7 ] .
!9000
ENTER THE AMOUNT FOR YEAR     [ 8 ] .
!9000
ENTER THE AMOUNT FOR YEAR     [ 9 ] .
!9000
ENTER THE AMOUNT FOR YEAR     [ 10 ] .
!9000




                        CASH FLOW
YEAR    [ 0 ]                        -68000
YEAR    [ 1 ]                         20000
YEAR    [ 2 ]                         20000
YEAR    [ 3 ]                         14000
YEAR    [ 4 ]                         14000
YEAR    [ 5 ]                         14000
YEAR    [ 6 ]                          9000
YEAR    [ 7 ]                          9000
YEAR    [ 8 ]                          9000
YEAR    [ 9 ]                          9000
YEAR    [ 10 ]                         9000
```

```
                                    ((GRAPH))
               -30  -25  -20  -15  -10  -5    0    5    10   15   20   25   30
    i\PW       |----|----|----|----|----|----|----|----|----|----|----|----|
    0                                                                        *
    .05                                                           *
    .1                                                  *
    .15                                           *
    .2                                      *
    .25                                *
    .3                             *
    .35                         *
    .4                        *
    .45                    *
    .5                  *
    .55              *
    .6             *
    .65          *
    .7           *
    .75         *
    .8        *
    .85       *
    .9      *
    .95     *
    1      *
    !0.K
```

TO FIND THE APPROXIMATE VALUE OF PW ,FIND THE SCALE FROM THE PW
AXIS AND MULTIPLY IT BY ,   D=2000

IF YOU WANT THIS PROGRAM TO PLOT ANOTHER GRAPH FOR DIFFERENT CASH
FLOW STREAMS , ENTER NEW .
TO USE THE OTHER AVAILABLE INFORMATION , ENTER   START .
IF NO MORE CALCULATIONS ARE REQUIRED , ENTER END .

!NEW
GRAPH   (i AGAINST NPW)

THIS GRAPH CAN BE PLOTTED FOR ONE OR TWO CASH FLOW STREAMS,
ON THE SCREEN .

IF YOU WANT THE GRAPH TO BE PLOTTED FOR ONE CASH FLOW STREAM,
ENTER ONE ,FOR TWO CASH FLOW STREAMS, ENTER   TWO .

!ONE

ENTRY OF CASH FLOW STREAM

IF CASH FLOW STREAM IS ALREADY ENTERED AND YOU WANT IT TO BE USED
AGAIN , ENTER OLD , OTHERWISE ENTER NEW .

!NEW
ENTER THE VALUE FOR N ,WHICH IS THE NUMBER OF YEARS .
(DURATION OF CASH FLOW STREAM)
EXAMPLE;
CASH FLOW,   YEAR 0   YEAR 1   YEAR 2   YEAR 3
                 -500   300   400   600
THE VALUE OF N IS EQUAL TO 3 ,THEREFORE ENTER   3 .

     N=?   (N <= 50)

!2
ENTER THE AMOUNT FOR YEAR   [0] .
!-1000
ENTER THE AMOUNT FOR YEAR   [1] .
!2500
ENTER THE AMOUNT FOR YEAR   [2] .
!-1540

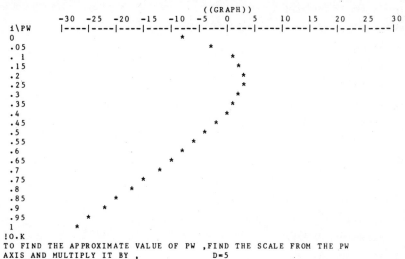

```
                        CASH FLOW
YEAR    [ 0 ]                              -1000
YEAR    [ 1 ]                               2500
YEAR    [ 2 ]                              -1540


                                   ((GRAPH))
            -30  -25  -20  -15  -10  -5    0    5    10   15   20   25   30
  i\PW      |----|----|----|----|----|----|----|----|----|----|----|----|
  0                                         *
  .05                                  *
  . 1                                    *
  .15                                     *
  .2                                       *
  .25                                      *
  .3                                      *
  .35                                     *
  .4                                    *
  .45                                 *
  .5                                *
  .55                             *
  .6                            *
  .65                        *
  .7                       *
  .75                     *
  .8                    *
  .85                 *
  .9               *
  .95            *
  1           *
  !O.K
TO FIND THE APPROXIMATE VALUE OF PW ,FIND THE SCALE FROM THE PW
AXIS AND MULTIPLY IT BY ,             D=5
```

IF YOU WANT THIS PROGRAM TO PLOT ANOTHER GRAPH FOR DIFFERENT CASH
FLOW STREAMS , ENTER NEW .
TO USE THE OTHER AVAILABLE INFORMATION , ENTER START .
IF NO MORE CALCULATIONS ARE REQUIRED , ENTER END .

!NEW
GRAPH   (i AGAINST NPW)

THIS GRAPH CAN BE PLOTTED FOR ONE OR TWO CASH FLOW STREAMS,
ON THE SCREEN .

IF YOU WANT THE GRAPH TO BE PLOTTED FOR ONE CASH FLOW STREAM,
ENTER ONE ,FOR TWO CASH FLOW STREAMS, ENTER TWO .

!TWO

ENTRY OF CASH FLOW STREAM

IF CASH FLOW STREAM IS ALREADY ENTERED AND YOU WANT IT TO BE USED
AGAIN , ENTER OLD , OTHERWISE ENTER NEW .

!NEW
ENTER THE VALUE FOR N ,WHICH IS THE NUMBER OF YEARS .
(DURATION OF CASH FLOW STREAM)
EXAMPLE;
CASH FLOW,   YEAR 0   YEAR 1   YEAR 2   YEAR 3
                 -500   300   400   600
THE VALUE OF N IS EQUAL TO 3 ,THEREFORE ENTER 3 .

     N=?   (N <= 50)

!10

```
ENTER THE AMOUNT FOR YEAR      [ 0 ] .
!-1800
ENTER THE AMOUNT FOR YEAR      [ 1 ] .
!500
ENTER THE AMOUNT FOR YEAR      [ 2 ] .
!300
ENTER THE AMOUNT FOR YEAR      [ 3 ] .
!300
ENTER THE AMOUNT FOR YEAR      [ 4 ] .
!200
ENTER THE AMOUNT FOR YEAR      [ 5 ] .
!200
ENTER THE AMOUNT FOR YEAR      [ 6 ] .
!200
ENTER THE AMOUNT FOR YEAR      [ 7 ] .
!200
ENTER THE AMOUNT FOR YEAR      [ 8 ] .
!100
ENTER THE AMOUNT FOR YEAR      [ 9 ] .
!100
ENTER THE AMOUNT.FOR YEAR      [ 10 ] .
!100
ENTRY OF CASH FLOW NO.2 .


     N=?      (N <= 50)
!10
ENTER THE AMOUNT FOR YEAR      [ 0 ] .
!-2500
ENTER THE AMOUNT FOR YEAR      [ 1 ] .
!500
ENTER THE AMOUNT FOR YEAR      [ 2 ] .
!500
ENTER THE AMOUNT FOR YEAR      [ 3 ] .
!500
ENTER THE AMOUNT FOR YEAR      [ 4 ] .
!500
ENTER THE AMOUNT FOR YEAR      [ 5 ] .
!500
ENTER THE AMOUNT FOR YEAR      [ 6 ] .
!500
ENTER THE AMOUNT FOR YEAR      [ 7 ] .
!500
ENTER THE AMOUNT FOR YEAR      [ 8 ] .
!500
ENTER THE AMOUNT FOR YEAR      [ 9 ] .
!500
ENTER THE AMOUNT FOR YEAR      [ 10 ] .
!500
```

```
                    CASH FLOW
YEAR    [ 0 ]                        -1800
YEAR    [ 1 ]                         500
YEAR    [ 2 ]                         300
YEAR    [ 3 ]                         300
YEAR    [ 4 ]                         200
YEAR    [ 5 ]                         200
YEAR    [ 6 ]                         200
YEAR    [ 7 ]                         200
YEAR    [ 8 ]                         100
YEAR    [ 9 ]                         100
YEAR    [ 10 ]                        100


                    CASH FLOW    NO-2
YEAR    [ 0 ]                        -2500
YEAR    [ 1 ]                         500
YEAR    [ 2 ]                         500
YEAR    [ 3 ]                         500
YEAR    [ 4 ]                         500
YEAR    [ 5 ]                         500
YEAR    [ 6 ]                         500
YEAR    [ 7 ]                         500
YEAR    [ 8 ]                         500
YEAR    [ 9 ]                         500
YEAR    [ 10 ]                        500
TO CONTINUE            ENTER  O.K  .
```

```
!O.K
                                   ((GRAPH))
            -30  -25  -20  -15  -10  -5   0    5   10   15   20   25   30
  i\PW      |----|----|----|----|----|----|----|----|----|----|----|----|
0                                             *                        X
.05                                      *              X
.1                                    *        *
.15                                *     X
.2                               *   X
.25                             *X
.3                           X*
.35                          X*
.4                         X  *
.45                       X   *
.5                       X    *
.55                      X    *
.6                    X       *
.65                   X       *
.7                  X         *
.75                 X         *
.8                X           *
.85               X           *
.9                X           *
.95            X              *
1              X              *
!O.K
(*) CASH FLOW STREAM NO-1, (X) CASH FLOW STREAM NO-2 AND
(0) BOTH CASH FLOW STREAMS .

TO FIND THE APPROXIMATE VALUE OF PW ,FIND THE SCALE FROM THE PW
AXIS AND MULTIPLY IT BY ,            D=100


IF YOU WANT THIS PROGRAM TO PLOT ANOTHER GRAPH FOR DIFFERENT CASH
FLOW STREAMS , ENTER  NEW .
TO USE THE OTHER AVAILABLE INFORMATION , ENTER   START .
IF NO MORE CALCULATIONS ARE REQUIRED , ENTER   END .




!NEW
GRAPH        (i AGAINST NPW)

THIS GRAPH CAN BE PLOTTED FOR ONE OR TWO CASH FLOW STREAMS,
ON THE SCREEN .

IF YOU WANT THE GRAPH TO BE PLOTTED FOR ONE CASH FLOW STREAM,
ENTER  ONE ,FOR TWO CASH FLOW STREAMS, ENTER  TWO .

!TWO

ENTRY OF CASH FLOW STREAM


IF CASH FLOW STREAM IS ALREADY ENTERED AND YOU WANT IT TO BE USED
AGAIN , ENTER  OLD , OTHERWISE ENTER  NEW .


!NEW
ENTER THE VALUE FOR N ,WHICH IS THE NUMBER OF YEARS .
( DURATION OF CASH FLOW STREAM )
EXAMPLE;
CASH FLOW,      YEAR 0       YEAR 1       YEAR 2       YEAR 3
                -500          300          400          600
THE VALUE OF N IS EQUAL TO 3 ,THEREFORE ENTER  3 .

     N=?      (N <= 50)
```

```
!15
ENTER THE AMOUNT FOR YEAR      [ 0  ] .
!-50000
ENTER THE AMOUNT FOR YEAR      [ 1  ] .
!6000
ENTER THE AMOUNT FOR YEAR      [ 2  ] .
!6000
ENTER THE AMOUNT FOR YEAR      [ 3  ] .
!6000
ENTER THE AMOUNT FOR YEAR      [ 4  ] .
!6000
ENTER THE AMOUNT FOR YEAR      [ 5  ] .
!6000
ENTER THE AMOUNT FOR YEAR      [ 6  ] .
!8000
ENTER THE AMOUNT FOR YEAR      [ 7  ] .
!8000
ENTER THE AMOUNT FOR YEAR      [ 8  ] .
!8000
ENTER THE AMOUNT FOR YEAR      [ 9  ] .
!8000
ENTER THE AMOUNT FOR YEAR      [ 10 ] .
!8000
ENTER THE AMOUNT FOR YEAR      [ 11 ] .
!5000
ENTER THE AMOUNT FOR YEAR      [ 12 ] .
!5000
ENTER THE AMOUNT FOR YEAR      [ 13 ] .
!5000
ENTER THE AMOUNT FOR YEAR      [ 14 ] .
!5000
ENTER THE AMOUNT FOR YEAR      [ 15 ] .
!5000




ENTRY OF CASH FLOW NO.2 .


     N=?      (N <= 50)
!10
ENTER THE AMOUNT FOR YEAR      [ 0  ] .
!-80000
ENTER THE AMOUNT FOR YEAR      [ 1  ] .
!12000
ENTER THE AMOUNT FOR YEAR      [ 2  ] .
!12000
ENTER THE AMOUNT FOR YEAR      [ 3  ] .
!12000
ENTER THE AMOUNT FOR YEAR      [ 4  ] .
!12000
ENTER THE AMOUNT FOR YEAR      [ 5  ] .
!12000
ENTER THE AMOUNT FOR YEAR      [ 6  ] .
!12000
ENTER THE AMOUNT FOR YEAR      [ 7  ] .
!12000
ENTER THE AMOUNT FOR YEAR      [ 8  ] .
!12000
ENTER THE AMOUNT FOR YEAR      [ 9  ] .
!12000
ENTER THE AMOUNT FOR YEAR      [ 10 ] .
!12000
```

```
                              CASH FLOW
YEAR    [  0  ]                                 -50000
YEAR    [  1  ]                                  6000
YEAR    [  2  ]                                  6000
YEAR    [  3  ]                                  6000
YEAR    [  4  ]                                  6000
YEAR    [  5  ]                                  6000
YEAR    [  6  ]                                  8000
YEAR    [  7  ]                                  8000
YEAR    [  8  ]                                  8000
YEAR    [  9  ]                                  8000
YEAR    [ 10  ]                                  8000
YEAR    [ 11  ]                                  5000
YEAR    [ 12  ]                                  5000
YEAR    [ 13  ]                                  5000
YEAR    [ 14  ]                                  5000
YEAR    [ 15  ]                                  5000


                              CASH FLOW      NO-2
YEAR    [  0  ]                                 -80000
YEAR    [  1  ]                                  12000
YEAR    [  2  ]                                  12000
YEAR    [  3  ]                                  12000
YEAR    [  4  ]                                  12000
YEAR    [  5  ]                                  12000
YEAR    [  6  ]                                  12000
YEAR    [  7  ]                                  12000
YEAR    [  8  ]                                  12000
YEAR    [  9  ]                                  12000
YEAR    [ 10  ]                                  12000
TO CONTINUE              ENTER   O.K  .


!O.K
```

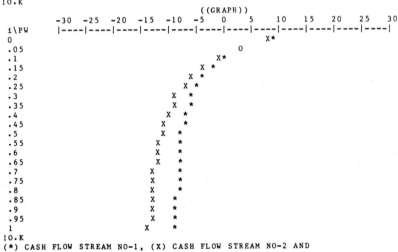

```
                                    ((GRAPH))
        -30  -25  -20  -15  -10  -5   0    5    10   15   20   25   30
 i\PW   |----|----|----|----|----|----|----|----|----|----|----|----|
 0                                          X*
 .05                                     O
 .1                                    X*
 .15                                  X *
 .2                              X  *
 .25                             X *
 .3                          X      *
 .35                         X      *
 .4                          X    *
 .45                        X      *
 .5                         X    *
 .55                      X      *
 .6                       X      *
 .65                      X      *
 .7                    X        *
 .75                   X        *
 .8                    X        *
 .85                   X     *
 .9                    X     *
 .95                   X     *
 1                    X      *
```

```
!O.K
(*) CASH FLOW STREAM NO-1, (X) CASH FLOW STREAM NO-2 AND
(O) BOTH CASH FLOW STREAMS .

TO FIND THE APPROXIMATE VALUE OF PW ,FIND THE SCALE FROM THE PW
AXIS AND MULTIPLY IT BY ,            D=5000


IF YOU WANT THIS PROGRAM TO PLOT ANOTHER GRAPH FOR DIFFERENT CASH
FLOW STREAMS , ENTER  NEW .
TO USE THE OTHER AVAILABLE INFORMATION , ENTER  START .
IF NO MORE CALCULATIONS ARE REQUIRED , ENTER  END .


!END
```

APPENDIX 4 — Design Specification Pro-Forma and Commentary

(Thanks are due to the "Asset Management Group
of the Institute of Physical Distribution
Management" for their permission to publish
this pro-forma and commentary.)

DESIGN SPECIFICATION PRO-FORMA

1   **Identifying Number**

2   **Issue Number**

3   **Function** (In basic terms, what function is the article to perform
     when we have designed it?) _____

     _____

     _____

     _____

4   **Application** (Of what system is this requirement a part?)

     _____

     _____

     _____

5   **Origin** (By what means, when and by whom was the requirement
     first made known? Usually we give here a reference to a letter,
     visit, telephone conversation or other discussion.)

     _____

     _____

6   **Customer's Specification** (If the customer has already written a
     specification, its identifying number should be quoted; if the
     customer has not written a specification we should say so)

     _____

     _____

7   **General Related Specifications** (If we are required to work within
     the framework of existing general specifications, standards or
     definitions, or if existing documents are likely to be useful, their
     numbers should be quoted.)

     _____

     _____

8   **Safety** (Are any special safety precautions to be taken?)

_____

_____

9   **Environment**

    9.1   Ambient temperatures _____

_____

    9.2   Ambient pressures _____

_____

    9.3   Vibration _____

_____

    9.4   Acceleration _____

_____

    9.5   Contaminants _____

_____

    9.6   Climate _____

_____

    9.7   Installation limitations _____

_____

    9.8   Affect on other parts of the parent system (eg compass safe
        distance, radio interference). _____

_____

    9.9   Other environmental factors _____

_____

10   **Number-Off and Delivery Programme**

_____

_____

_____

11   **Price** (Note that this may require a complex statement if prices
reduce from prototypes through increasing batch sizes.)

_____

_____

_____

12 Functional Requirements

12.1 Performance and acceptable tolerances. (This will generally be a complex statement of the permissible range of many variables to be obtained in the presence of stated ranges of other variables.)

12.2 Life

12.3 Unacceptable modes of failure

12.4 Reliability

12.5 Servicing restrictions

12.6 Other functional requirements

13 Any Other Relevant Information

13.1 Limitations of manufacturing facilities

13.2 Special procedural requirements

13.3 Other relevant information

14 Action Required (Preparation of proposal, preparation of detail drawings, manufacture of prototypes or manufacture of full production quality.)

COMMENTARY

If we look at this pro forma we can see how its use forces the designer to consider the customer's total cost of ownership of the product to be designed.

1 and 2   Identifying Number and Issue Number

In any later discussion of the product it will be necessary to know what the designer set out to do, and because it is likely that the specification will change several times it is necessary to identify it so that there is no ambiguity. Perhaps, most important of all, the customer and the manufacturer will at some stage agree on a selling price and the design specification number and issue will be quoted in the contract as a definition of what the customer is buying. As we shall see, this implies that the contract does not merely commit the manufacturer to supply the product for a stated, first selling price but also commits him to ensuring that the customer's subsequent cost of ownership is limited.

The use of an issue number also makes us realise that what we design may have to be modified (raising the issue number of the specification may be an essential part of the modification). A modification will involve cost: the cost of new drawing; the cost of re-testing; the cost of replacing the parts needing modification; the cost to the customer of using a part which needs modification to bring it to the necessary level of performance or reliability; and the cost of lost time while changes are made.

3   Function

Although this is usually a simple, qualitative statement of what the product is intended to do for the customer, this function must be seen by the customer to have a money value. The customer must, in fact, think that the function performed by the product will be worth the cost of owning it.

The driver must believe that the convenience of a car is worth paying for even though the price he pays in the showroom is only about 20% of what he will ultimately pay for ownership. The Ministry of Defence believes that the national security provided by a tank or military aeroplane is worth paying for, even though the total cost of keeping the tank or aeroplane at readiness will be several times that of the initial purchase price.

4   Application

Nearly always, the product to be designed will be a component or sub-component of a larger system. The valve we are designing may be part of an engine which is part of an aeroplane, which in turn is part of a transport system. The product cannot be considered outside the system of which it is part and it may be that an optimum system will be achieved when a component, considered in isolation, is sub-optimum. Excessive fuel consumption may mean that the lightest aircraft cabin environment control system does not lead to the lightest aeroplane.

More significant, however, is the fact that failure of the product that we are designing may mean failure of the system of which it is a part. The cost of repairing the engine may have to include the cost of grounding the aeroplane — the cost of a hundred unhappy passengers, the cost of keeping the aeroplane on the apron of a foreign aerodrome for 24 hours and, most of all, the cost of keeping expensive capital equipment tied up while the aeroplane is earning no revenue.

5   Origin

We need to know who first made known the customer's requirement so that we may set up paths for discussing the design. We must make sure that those discussions bring in the views of service engineers, the maintenance staff and the operators for it is probable that use, service and repair will cost the customer more than the first purchase of the product.

6   The Customer's Specification

A customer who knows his business will ensure that the specification calls up a minimum acceptable life, a minimum acceptable reliability and even a minimum acceptable maintainability because short life, low reliability or expensive maintenance would increase the customer's cost of ownership much more than a high purchase price. If the customer is not already aware of these features, the manufacturer will not lose by drawing his attention to them.

Usually, the customer will not merely request minimum levels of life, reliability and maintainability but will require tests to demonstrate that these levels will be met.

7   General Related Specifications

Some customers (particularly the government) require that we meet not only the requirements of the design specification but also general requirements that are published separately. Among these general requirements may be that operating, servicing and maintenance manuals be supplied with the equipment. Sometimes the form that such manuals are to take is prescribed and certainly a knowledge of the maintenance and servicing organisation (of say the army or the RAF) is expected.

The designer should, of course, design the operating, servicing and maintenance procedures and tools (which may include special test equipment) when he designs the product but it is useful to be reminded that to do so may be a part of the contract between the customer and the supplier.

8   Safety

Designing for safety is necessary if only because, subconsciously perhaps, we put a high money value to human life or human well being. The customer will certainly be required to make payments if anyone is killed or injured by the product, while the law (or the insurance companies) will insist that certain precautions are taken to avoid damage to life. Such precautions as safety valves, system duplication, designing against hazards, designing guards or insurance premiums all add to the customer's cost of ownership and minimising these costs is a function of the designer.

9 Environment

The designer must design the product to work in given environmental conditions and the environment will affect the life and the reliability of the product. It may sometimes be desirable to insulate the product from the environment (by say, antivibration mountings, heat shields, artificial atmospheres) if the cost of the extra complication may be traded off against longer life. The designer must also be on his guard against the temptation to design to too formidable an environment so that the cost of the design is increased by meeting conditions (and proving integrity in those conditions) which will occur so rarely that the failures they cause will add little to the cost of ownership.

10 Number-Off and Delivery Programme

The number-off affects the design because it affects the method, and hence unit cost, of manufacture. The number-off also affects the operating, servicing and maintenance procedures that must be used by the customer.

When will the customer be justified in investing in special tools, central servicing depots or specialised training for maintenance staff? How will the customer (and the supplier) devise a spares holding policy? Will the designer consider the spares holding policy in his design of subassemblies?

The delivery programme adds costs for the customer if it cannot be met because it delays the time when the product will be earning money. In any case, time has a money value because the cost of capital forces us to discount future cash flows to lower present values. £100 received today may be better than £115 received in a year's time.

11 Price

A customer will know that the cost of owning a product will generally be many times the cost of its first purchase price. By insisting that minimum values of life, maintainability, reliability, etc, are specified and agreed in any contract the customer is ensuring that he is budgeting for the cost of ownership after purchasing the product.

12 Functional Requirements

12.1 As with the environment, the designer must guard against specifying an unnecessarily restricting performance which could complicate the design, reduce reliability and add operating costs. He should also specify the performance which optimises the parent system.

12.2 Life of a product is one of the most significant factors in calculating the cost of ownership. It is, of course, a probabilistic property of the product and so we may be involved in expensive endurance testing in extremes of environment to demonstrate life expectation with stated confidence (usually life will be drawn from a Weibull distribution). Sometimes life can be forecast only with the aid of extensive reliability records of earlier products.

Life must, however, be considered from two viewpoints: component life and model life. If the customer has to choose between two different designs which are functionally suitable and similar in purchase price and running costs, then the one with the longer component life will give the lower total cost of ownership. The manufacturer and customer will also consider the model life. This is the period between the first conception of the product and the time at which the use of the product is finally discontinued. It is quite common for this period to be 30 years and cover many developments of the basic product.

Aircraft engines designed in the 1940s are still in everyday use although powers, lives and reliabilities have been increased many times. Military and civil aircraft designed in the 1940s are still in service, although their running costs have been decreased with service and development. A model which has been in service for a long time has benefited by the development of the procedures and policies for servicing, maintaining and operating so that it becomes obsolete only because a new model has made a significant advance in cost reduction or has made the function of the original model redundant.

12.3 Unacceptable modes of failure are really those modes of failure to which the customer has attributed virtually infinite costs.

12.4 Reliability is, of course, directly related to both maintenance and service. The balance between the cost of unscheduled repair and scheduled servicing is determined from reliability and directly related to the cost of ownership. Designing for a specified reliability implies reliability testing and the collection of reliability data from the field.

12.5 Servicing restrictions clearly affect the cost of ownership. Repairs in the field will be quite different in cost and effectiveness from repairs undertaken in the supplier's factory. Repairs with semi-skilled workers will be different from those expected from specialist mechanics. The design of the servicing procedure is an important part of the design of the product.

13   Any Other Relevant Information

13.1 Manufacturing facilities include testing and proving facilities so the factors which affect the cost of ownership may not be determinable if these facilities are limited.

13.2 Special procedural requirements may be directly concerned with maintenance procedures, with the hierarchy of servicing establishments, with spares provisioning, etc, all of which directly affect the cost of ownership.

Index